Praise for Joe Caruso

"*The Power of Losing Control* is a wonderful reference guide for those in search of a better life! I strongly recommend this book to all who wish to benefit from Joe's insight and wisdom."

> —David Brandon, Chairman and Chief Executive Officer,
> Domino's Pizza

"Changing one's perspective can be the key to enhancing personal and corporate performance. This book provides the tools that will help you enrich your personal life and unlock new opportunities when guiding the growth of companies in this fast-paced and ever-changing business climate."

> —Paul M. Bisaro, President and Chief Operating Officer,
> Barr Laboratories, Inc.

"The simplicity of what Joe teaches makes it seem almost magical. I have never seen such dramatic, long-lasting results achieved in such a short time. Had I not experienced it myself, I would have thought it impossible."

> —Bennett Derman, President, The GTS Companies, Inc.,
> Los Angeles, California

"As a former Vice President of Human Resources for a major automotive supplier, training and culture changes were a big part of my job. I've studied Joe Caruso and his techniques. I've interviewed and worked with his clients. And I've personally employed his methods and concepts. When it comes to culture change, I'm convinced there's no better guy in the country than Joe Caruso. His concept about the 'power of losing control' absolutely establishes the basis for individual and organizational transformation. I believe Joe Caruso is on the brink of leading corporate America through a shift in approach that hasn't been seen since *7 Habits* crossed-over to become the training bible."

> —Marilyn Opdyke, President of The Opdyke Group

"As a mother of a blended family with seven children as well as a dynamic career in an Internet start-up firm, I understand what it means to feel out of control. Joe Caruso has given me the most practical advice on how to understand, accept, and manage myself. I'll never forget, 'I have power in it, but no control over it.' Great stuff that just works...."

> —Christine Willig, Vice President of Product Development,
> Thinkronize, Cincinnati, Ohio

"Joe, I've seen you speak a number of times at Board of Directors' meetings, to rooms full of CEOs, and to large public audiences. Your message is universal, and your talent is undeniable. I want you to know that when *The Power of Losing Control* becomes a book, you're going to have a huge corporate market due to the number of CEOs who will make it required reading for all their employees. And I'll be one of the first in line."
　　—George Gorno, Chairman and CEO, Gorno Ford; Member, YPO

"Joe has the unique ability to cut through the minutiae to the key issues, bring agreement amongst the executives involved, and then help them implement solutions that take the whole organization to another level. His understanding of human behavior and how to make organizations function harmoniously is unparalleled."
　　—Rick Vlasic, CEO, OE Learning; Member, YPO

"I've never seen such an impact from a one-day program. I didn't think people could change the way they have. What's even more impressive is that the change is lasting."
　　—Jonathan Holtzman, CEO, The Village Green Companies;
　　Member, YPO

"The biggest challenge in helping an organization make a transition is getting the top people to transition themselves. I've watched Joe Caruso get high-powered, successful, smart, and self-assured people to listen and even change their minds. This makes him a CEO's greatest tool."
　　—Alex Burkulas, CEO, Cygnus Systems

"I met you in 1996 when you were a speaker for Columbia Sussex Annual Meetings. I walked away from that meeting so empowered by what I had learned about myself. In 1997 our hotel went from the bottom of our company to the top in Guest Service scores. We received several awards and recognition for our efforts. I have grown so much as an individual, both personally and professionally. Thank you for helping me so much."
　　—Glena Zimmerman, Director of Sales, Holiday Inn, Dayton, Ohio

"The only problem with Joe Caruso and Caruso Leadership Institute is being able to effectively respond to all of the business they helped us generate!"
　　—Doug Cryderman, CEO, Douglas Electric, Southgate, Michigan

"I went from being an average salesperson to the top salesperson in my company nationally thanks to Joe Caruso and his incredibly effective approach to sales." —Peter Winchester, Winegardner & Hammons, Cincinnati, Ohio

The Power of Losing Control

Finding Strength, Meaning, and Happiness in an Out-of-Control World

Joe Caruso

GOTHAM BOOKS

GOTHAM BOOKS
Published by Penguin Group (USA) Inc.
375 Hudson Street, New York, New York 10014, U.S.A.
Penguin Books Ltd, Registered Offices: 80 Strand, London WC2R 0RL, England
Penguin Books Australia Ltd, 250 Camberwell Road, Camberwell, Victoria 3124, Australia
Penguin Books Canada Ltd, 10 Alcorn Avenue, Toronto, Ontario, Canada M4V 3B2
Penguin Books (NZ) Ltd, Cnr Rosedale and Airborne Roads,
Albany, Auckland 1310, New Zealand

Published by Gotham Books, a division of Penguin Group (USA) Inc.
Previously published as a Gotham Books hardcover edition.

First Gotham Books trade paperback printing, February 2004
10   9   8   7   6   5   4   3   2   1

THE LIBRARY OF CONGRESS HAS CATALOGED THE
GOTHAM BOOKS HARDCOVER EDITION AS FOLLOWS:
Caruso, Joe.
The power of losing control : finding strength, meaning, and happiness
in an out-of-control world / by Joe Caruso.
p.   cm.
ISBN 1-592-04003-5 (hc.)
1-592-40048-5 (pb.)
1. Control (Psychology)   2. Choice (Psychology)   3. Mind and body. I. Title.
BF611.C34 2003
158.1—dc21   2002041632

Printed in the United States of America
Set in Apollo MT
Designed by Sabrina Bowers

To my friend, my love, my wife, Carol. Honey, you have taught me more about love than I ever thought I could learn.

And to my friend, my teacher, my father, Mickey Caruso, who continues to inspire and teach me every day.

Contents

Acknowledgments

For every name that follows there are at least a dozen more I would have liked to include, but if I did, I'd be the first writer in history whose acknowledgment page became an acknowledgment chapter. I'd especially like to thank the following:

Ruth Caruso, for the love she gave and the lessons she taught.

Christine Willig, for being a living saint and loving friend and for your undying, selfless support of me and my work.

Lauren Marino and Bill Shinker for being a lady and a gentleman of the highest order. It's been an honor and a pleasure creating this book for you. I don't believe any writer could ever ask for a better editor/publisher team.

Mark Roy, Lisa Johnson, Jean Anne Rose, Brooke Capps, and all the rest of the dream team at Gotham Books.

Judy Kern, for your skill at the art of midwifery.

Natasha Kern, for believing in me and helping find the perfect publisher for this book.

Alex Burkulas, for being the best example of a best friend through it all.

Bill Vlasic, for breaking my story and literally making me front-page news.

Rick Vlasic, for your friendship and for doing so much to help me help others.

Dr. Todd Davison, for lending his expertise, giving his love, and sharing his mind.

Gus Vonderheide, for always, always being there, no matter where "there" is.

Mike, Dave, and Rob, for your unfailing love and support. I'm proud to be your brother.

My clients and friends who've readily and generously offered their support and love through the years it took to write this book.

Introduction

Like the bumper sticker says, change happens. Things *will happen*—both good things and bad things—and we really have no control over either. People defy our plans and let us down. Circumstances bring us to our knees. Planes fly into buildings. And it all happens without our permission.

We live in a world we can't control. We have voice mail, e-mail, PDAs, Franklin Planners, personal computers, cell phones, and every timesaving, life-organizing device imaginable—yet we've never felt so out of control and out of time. We're stressed out, scared to death of life, closing in on death, and trying to "find ourselves" in the meantime. It seems the more we try to control all the elements in our lives, the more out of control life becomes.

The chances of turning fifty years old without ever being confronted by an "out-of-control experience" are slim to none. Issues such as a forced job change, the loss of a loved one, a sudden serious illness, a teenager on the brink, a bad marriage, or simply the realization and recognition of the physical problems that come with aging can leave us feeling out of control. And while all this is happening, our relative sense of time gives us the feeling that each year is passing more quickly than the last. So our desire for peace, purpose, and meaning becomes ever more urgent. *The Power of Losing Control* confronts this human paradox by explaining how to stop wasting our precious and finite energy on what we can't control. Once we learn to bring all of that misdirected energy to what we *can* control, and learn to respond to both the good and the bad in a way that serves us, the meaning of our lives is enhanced and we find greater power, peace, and success in our lives.

The fact is that stress and anxiety are control-related issues. The degree of stress or worry we feel can be directly related to how strongly we feel that if we can't control something or someone, something "bad" will happen either to us or to someone we love.

I began studying this subject in earnest in 1978. My motivation was highly personal and very compelling. I was facing a life-threatening illness and had a very limited amount of the strength and energy I would need to fight for my life. For the first time in my life I didn't have the luxury of wasting energy. But in order not to waste it, I first needed to become highly aware of what I could affect, what I could control, and what I couldn't afford to worry about because it was out of my power to control it.

I began reading and studying what the most noted psychologists, philosophers, mystics, and masters had to say about how our psychology drives our behavior. I became fascinated by the realization that our fears and fantasies never even have to come true in order to impact us in life-changing ways. The more I studied, learned, and personally experimented, the more fascinated I became by how we think, feel, and act, and how and why those thoughts, feelings, and actions affect our actual experiences.

When we understand that our essence as humans is grounded in our personally created myths or stories (as Madeleine L'Engle says, "Stories help us claim our meaning"), and that our myths drive our behavior, we begin to perceive the power of congruency and transition. As humans, we cannot behave over time, or with any great consistency, in a manner that is incongruent with our personal myth. Just as all businesses have a culture that is driven by their corporate myths, all individuals are micro-cultures driven by their personal myths. In this way, myth, while not necessarily true, is actually greater than truth, because it determines thoughts, feelings, and behaviors.

Understanding this helped me realize how to transform the way I thought and felt in my own life in a way that may have saved my life. As a result of more than twenty years of personal study, I'm now considered a leading expert on the subject of helping people change the way they think, feel, and behave. I'm called upon as a speaker at association and sales meetings, at conferences, and at conventions. I also consult with CEOs and senior-level managers about how to improve the ways their companies and their employees function. My clients include American Express, Ford Motor Company, and the American Academy of Motion Picture Arts and Sciences. What I say to them, however, is as applicable to private life as it is to any corporate culture.

What I speak about is both personal and universal, or, as a client once put it to me, "There are many people out there who claim to be experts on one thing or another they've never personally experienced. And there are also plenty of people who've survived many challenges, but have never figured out how to use their experiences to find a better meaning for themselves—let alone how to communicate that understanding to others. You, however, are like an expert on the subject of the *Titanic* who's also a survivor of the shipwreck."

When I'm called upon to meet with corporate executives and staff, I may not know anything about their specific business, and I certainly wouldn't consider myself qualified to tell them how to run it. What I can do, however, is to help them see and think about *themselves* differently within the framework or context of their business.

One basic truth I've learned is that none of us can stand in another person's shoes or view the world through another person's eyes. We all see our world reflected in ourselves, and ourselves as a reflection of our world. And so, by shifting the perspective from which we view the world, we'll also be seeing ourselves differently. My role is to facilitate that change in perspective. I help people to see differently, which in turn allows them to respond differently to what they see.

I've learned that most people believe learning and growth come from looking at something new and finding the familiar in it, but it's the opposite that's actually true. When we see the familiar world differently, we will behave differently in it because it simply isn't possible to respond in a way that isn't congruent with what we see and still remain sane. If you've tried to change your behavior without first changing your perspective, you've probably met some form of failure. While we're all unique and individual, we are all human, and as humans we are all subject to the ways our thoughts and emotions affect our behaviors. When we're unaware of why we're feeling, thinking, or acting in ways that don't serve us, we're driven by a need to validate and justify our thoughts, feelings, and actions, rather than change them. The better we understand *why* we think, feel, and act the way we do, the better we can use that knowledge to our advantage by making those processes work for us rather than against us.

I rarely speak at events that are open to the public, and so, although I do write a column for a local newspaper and I am heard on local radio each morning, the executives and CEOs of the companies that hire me have, until now, effectively determined and limited the number of people who are able to hear what I have to say. For the first time, with this book, I am able to share what I've learned with a much wider audience and act as a kind of personal consultant to teach every reader.

I don't know if what I've written will be motivating for you, because I don't know what motivates you. But I do know that what you'll find in these pages is information and advice that's been tested in real-life circumstances and that has helped me personally, as well as my clients, to find power in a world that's beyond our control.

In this book I'll be sharing some stories from my own life and from my professional experience as I explain how we can learn to rewrite the myths that shape our lives. If I could summarize in a nutshell the wisdom I've gained from my life's study and my work, it's simply this: We live in an out-of-control world, and there's nothing we can do to change that fact. But the success and happiness we all seek isn't out of our control. And the key to finding it lies in our ability to know how to accept what we can't control and bring all of our energy to what we can. This is when our energy turns to power. It's *The Power of Losing Control.*

The Power of Losing Control

Chapter 1

You Have Power in It, but No Control over It

The happiness which we receive from ourselves is greater than that which we obtain from our surroundings. . . . The world in which a man lives shapes itself chiefly by the way in which he looks at it.
—Arthur Schopenhauer,
The World as Will and Ideas

If you'd asked me to describe myself in 1978, I'd probably have told you I was a pretty regular—if somewhat shorter than average—guy. I'd grown up in a working-class family with three brothers, a dog of unknown origin who looked more like a Westie than anything else, a mother who wouldn't let us eat in the living room, and a father who worked six days a week at Ford Motor Company and was the smartest guy I knew. I'd gone through the usual adolescent angst and come out the other side no worse for the wear than anyone else.

I was, in what turned out to be the most horrible and yet the most transforming year of my life, a sophomore at Central Michigan University, living away from home for the first time, and feeling pretty good about myself. I had a girlfriend, a 3.4 grade point average, and a seat in the honors wind ensemble playing clarinet. And then, in October, my world turned upside down.

For about three months I'd been walking around with a painfully swollen left testicle, which was, as you might imagine, for an eighteen-year-old male, both an embarrassment and a source of some concern. When I finally consulted a doctor, however, he didn't seem too worried and simply prescribed a course of antibiotics. When those didn't cure me, he decided I must have a cyst and scheduled me for surgery to have it removed. I remember thinking, at the time, that the surgery was really going to cut into my social life and put me behind in my class work. But again, my doctor didn't express any real concern, and so, even though this was my first surgery, I was mostly preoccupied with thinking about the size of the scar it might leave.

■ ■ ■

When I opened my eyes for the first time after the operation, I was still groggy from the anesthetic. I remember seeing both my parents standing at the foot of my bed, and then I dozed off again. When I woke up the second time, they were still there, and I could tell by the look in their eyes that something must be very wrong.

"Can you hear me?" my dad asked, patting my hand.

"Sure," I said, making a feeble attempt at humor. "They didn't operate on my ears."

And then he gave me the news that would change my life forever. "They had to remove your left testicle," he said, struggling valiantly to control his emotions. "You had a tumor that turned out to be malignant."

I don't think I really processed what he was saying right away. I know that I never associated the word *malignant* with cancer. The idea that I might have cancer never crossed my mind, even when the doctors at the local community hospital where I'd had my surgery told me they were transferring me to the University of Michigan hospital for further tests. But the seven doctors lined up against the wall of my room just days after my transfer would clarify the situation soon enough.

One of them, who introduced himself as the oncologist, stepped forward and announced that I had a four-inch tumor in my abdomen, two tumors in my right lung, and one in my left lung, and that the cancer had already spread to my lymph nodes. They weren't sure whether it had also reached my brain. He also informed me, in no uncertain terms, that my cancer was incurable and that I would die within a year.

The wave of nausea that came over me as I listened to those words was just a prelude to the total physical debilitation I'd be living with for the next two years, but at the moment, I couldn't know that. What I did know was that the idea of dying at the age of eighteen was completely unfathomable to me. *I can't be dying*, I wanted to scream at them. *I feel perfectly healthy!* Nevertheless, the doctor didn't mince words. In 1978, testicular cancer was a death sentence. The cure rate for my type of cancer at such an advanced stage was absolute zero. I can joke about it now, but at that time there were no cancer-survivors groups for the simple reason that there wouldn't have been anyone to attend the meetings.

The only course of treatment the oncologist and his team had to offer me sounded worse than no treatment at all—participation in a national study involving an experimental protocol that included both chemotherapy and surgery. At that time, chemotherapy was in its infancy; the doctors had very little knowledge of what it would or wouldn't do, and even less ability to control it. They told me I'd be receiving five chemotherapy treatments in the course of a week. They'd then wait three weeks and give me the next round of treatments. There would be four rounds of chemo in all, over a period of four months. It could, I was told, destroy my lungs, my liver, my kidneys, and my hearing. The doctors in charge of the study projected that no more than 3 percent of patients would survive as long as four months, but if by chance I made it through the chemo, they'd then remove what remained of my tumors in a series of three surgeries that would take place over six weeks. If I survived all of that, they'd consider the experiment a success, and then they'd just sit back and observe me, waiting to see what happened. I'd be volunteering to act as a guinea pig, and yet the doctors, despite their bleak prognosis, clearly wanted me to say yes.

My two choices appeared to be to die more slowly, in pain, or to die sooner, in pain and bald from the chemo. It seemed like an insane choice. And how could they be asking me to choose how I wanted to die? I didn't want to die at all. I wasn't *supposed* to die before I'd even had a chance to live! I was angry, terrified, and definitely in shock, but when they explained that by agreeing to participate in their experiment I might be providing them with the information they'd need to be able to cure some other person sometime in the future, I didn't think I had the right to deny them that chance. And, while I myself had no hope of survival, I couldn't just lie back and allow my parents to watch me die without at least trying whatever treatment was available.

■ ■ ■

Being diagnosed with incurable cancer would probably be at the top of just about everyone's list of worst fears, but whatever particular fears are on your list, they're no doubt as terrifying to you as my cancer was to me. We live in a world where any one of our most feared events or experiences can strike without warning at any moment, causing us to spin completely out of control, and the stress of living with that reality on a daily basis is too much for any of us to bear. As a result, we respond by creating an elaborate set of constructs and behaviors that give us the *illusion* of control. I, for example, had been pretty sure that my own life was completely under control. As I've said, I was doing well in school, I had a girlfriend, and it had certainly never occurred to me in my wildest dreams that my health would betray me in such a life-shattering way. I was still very young, however, and I hadn't yet had much firsthand experience with the many ways our illusions of control can be put to the test. But the longer we live, the more we come to understand how fragile our control can be, the more fearful we become of losing that control, and the more we begin to clutch and grab for whatever little control we've convinced ourselves we have. The problem, of course, is that there's no such thing as being a little bit in control. If we're not in complete control of something—whatever it is—then we really have no control over it at all. And how many things can any of us claim to control in that way?

Think about someone or something you *believe* you can control—your spouse, your child, your health, your income, your dog, or whatever makes sense to you. Can you control whatever it is you've chosen absolutely, forever, in every conceivable circumstance? I truly doubt it. Your spouse might run off to Tahiti with the secretary or boss, your child might throw a tantrum in the supermarket or decide to drop out of college against your wishes and go to work on a dude ranch, your dog might get run over, your company might lay you off, and your health—no matter how well you "take care of yourself"—might fail you as mine did. But I'm sure you really knew that all along, which means that whatever you thought you were controlling, you must also have understood on some level that it could go out of control at any minute, when you least expected it, without your wishing it, and, as a result of that understanding, you've been constantly expending your energies in an ultimately futile effort to ensure that that didn't happen. And you've probably been thinking that *if only* you had *more* control, every other aspect of your life would be better.

My own youthful illusions of control were destroyed the moment those doctors handed me their diagnosis, and with virtually no hope of survival, I grasped at the one thing about my situation I felt I *could* still control—I began to plan my own funeral. I told my parents I didn't want everyone sitting around bawling. I wanted them to have a party where people could eat and drink and listen to some of the music *I* liked, which, at the time, was by Elvis Costello, the Beatles, and Sinatra, and also the big band sound. I don't think I actually planned the menu. My mind wasn't really on the details. I just thought that if I let my parents know I had come to terms with my death and was "okay" with it, they would be, too. And the only way I knew to make them understand that I was comfortable with my fate was to talk about my death, which meant talking about my funeral. Crazy as that now sounds, even to me, it seemed at the time to be perfectly logical, and I really thought I was doing something kind and loving for them. In retrospect, of course, I can see that not only was I being the ultimate control freak—who else, after all, would even try to dictate what other people did *after his death?*—but also that my "loving gift" was actually causing them tremendous pain. Although they never said so to me, my planning was just tearing my parents up inside, and after a while they poured out the heartache they were feeling to one of my nurses.

■ ■ ■

I'd been going through several days of testing before the doctors could begin my chemotherapy treatments and had just returned to my room after a chest X ray when Jeannie, my oncology nurse, asked if we could talk.

I'd have been happy to talk to Jeannie anytime. She was the "cool" nurse, a five-foot-tall bundle of energy who was always smiling and always had time for everyone. I couldn't imagine how she remained so upbeat when she must have known that nearly every one of her patients would die. On this occasion, however, she wasn't smiling, and her voice sounded both serious and urgent.

"What are you doing talking to your parents about your funeral arrangements as if you were going to die right away?" she asked.

She'd never spoken to me like that before, and I must have been a bit startled. "Because the doctors told me I would," I responded defensively. "They said my cancer was fast-growing and incurable, and that my chances of surviving the therapy were about three percent."

"You're partially right about that," she admitted, her tone softening a bit, "but I want you to listen to me. Right now, your cancer *is* fast-growing and it *is* incurable, but what your doctors told you is that they believe three percent of those in the program *will live* through the treatment."

"That's exactly what I said," I answered stonily.

"No, it isn't!" she insisted. "Think about it. What if *you* just happened to be among that three percent? What would your chances of surviving the chemotherapy treatments and the surgeries be then?"

"I guess one hundred percent," I admitted reluctantly, still a bit confused by her logic.

"Right," she congratulated me, as if I'd just given a correct answer in class. "And if you survive the treatment, you might be in remission for a while, isn't that so?"

"Well, I guess so. But they also told me that no one with my cancer has ever gone into remission. And, in any case, it would still be incurable. I'd still be going to die." How was she going to get around that one, I wondered, eager to hear anything she had to say that might commute my life sentence. But Jeannie didn't seem the least bit challenged.

"Joe, let me ask you a question," she went on after taking a deep breath. "Why did you decide to take part in this program?"

"Well, the doctors told me it might help them to learn something that could lead to their finding a cure for my kind of cancer."

I could see her eyes light up. "So," she said softly. "You do think that someday *someone* is going to be the first person ever cured of this cancer?"

"Well, yes, I guess so. Someone would have to be the first."

"Then why couldn't that someone be you?" she asked, her blue eyes staring right at me.

I was silent for a moment, before venturing tentatively, "Are you telling me I could live? That the first person to be cured could be me?" The idea that someone might actually be offering me a ray of hope was almost more than I could comprehend.

"I can't tell you that, Joe," she admitted. "But I can tell you that if you've already decided it *won't* be you, it definitely won't. If you've already decided you're going to die, there's nothing anyone can do to help you." And, without waiting for a reply, she left the room.

■ ■ ■

Twenty-five years ago, the idea that the mind could influence the body was still something of a new thought. Norman Cousins's seminal book *Anatomy of an Illness*, which discussed how powerful a weapon the mind can be in the war against disease, would not be published until the following year. Deepak Chopra would not come on the scene for quite some time. Although some hospital personnel—usually not the doctors—might discuss basic visualization techniques, "the mind-body connection" and "spirituality" were terms generally confined to religious institutions and the counterculture. Cancer patients were looked upon as the walking dead, and any form of cancer was more likely to be whispered about behind closed doors than discussed in any kind of open forum.

Nevertheless, Jeannie's words made sense to me. If I were already planning to die, I probably would. But what was I *supposed* to be thinking about, if not my impending death? The answer, obviously, was life, but living was something I hadn't even considered since my diagnosis. How would I go about doing that? Clearly, I wasn't going to be visiting Disney World or surfing the big waves off Waikiki any time soon, since the ordeal I still had ahead of me precluded those options, or any others remotely like them.

If you've just realized in the most urgent way possible that you're going to die, you need an equally urgent reason to concentrate on living—or at least I did. I needed a reason to fight for my life. I began to think about what life is all about, what the purpose of living is—more specifically, what is the purpose of *my* life? It seemed to me, the more I thought about it, that life must be about physical, spiritual, mental, and emotional growth—because what we all do, consciously and unconsciously from the moment we're born until the moment we die, is to grow. One of the surest ways to grow, mentally, emotionally, and spiritually, is by achieving greater understanding. At that point I knew I couldn't control the physical growth of my body—the cancer and the chemicals they'd soon be pouring into me had denied me that ability. But I could still control my mental and emotional growth, and, if I weren't going to live long enough to accumulate the wisdom and understanding that usually comes with age, the only way I could think of to grow and understand was to study the thinking of those who had, and to find out what they had come to understand about life and living. At least then, if by some chance I did survive, I would have gained something positive to take with me for the rest of my life.

Although I certainly hadn't read Aldous Huxley when I began my studies, I later found in his introduction to *The Perennial Philosophy* the strongest possible validation there could be for what I was going to be doing: "If one is not oneself a sage or saint," Huxley wrote,

> the best thing one can do, in the field of metaphysics [the study of the essential nature of reality], is to study the words of those who were, and who, because they had modified their merely human mode of being, were capable of a more than merely human kind and amount of knowledge.

In other words, the surest way to attain wisdom, if one isn't already wise oneself, is to read—and try to assimilate and apply—the teachings of those who have. And that's what I set out to do.

■ ■ ■

While I understood on some level, even then, that the conversation I'd had with Jeannie that day contributed to saving my life, I now see that what she did for me was both simple and at the same time profound. She didn't just *tell* me that planning my funeral was wrong. She didn't try to argue me out of what I was doing. And she certainly didn't give me false hope. Instead she expressed her thoughts in a way that allowed me to connect with what she was saying and find a new way of defining myself with relation to my disease. In other words, through that one conversation she was able to provide me with the tools I needed to gain a different perspective on my circumstances in the world and see that there was a different course of action available to me.

In effect, she helped me to shift the context within which I was viewing my illness. According to the *Random House College Dictionary*, the word *context* means "the parts of a written or spoken statement that precede or follow a specific word or passage, usually influencing its meaning or effect," or "the set of circumstances or facts that surround a particular event, situation, etc." In other words, the context is *the general that gives meaning to the specific*. If we see a particular word or phrase, or witness a particular event, we can't really know that we've understood its specific meaning until we've read it or viewed it in *context*. If we see a man running down the street, for example, we can't really understand the meaning of his action until we become aware of its context. He might be running from a mugger, or because he just snatched someone's purse, or because he saw someone being hit by a car and is running to get help.

The importance of context was brought home to me in a way that actually made me laugh one evening when I was traveling on business and having dinner alone in one of those revolving restaurants that seem to be so popular with certain hotels. As I glanced up from studying the menu, a couple got off the elevator and was led to a table close to mine. I noticed them particularly because the distinguished-looking gentleman was wearing an ascot, and I thought to myself how unusual that was these days. Shortly afterward, another guy, this one in a brightly colored Hawaiian shirt, emerged from the same elevator and, spotting the first couple, yelled clear across the dining room, loud enough for everyone to hear, "So, how'd you like that bitch this afternoon?" I couldn't quite believe my ears, and I was also embarrassed for the ascotted gentleman and his companion. I turned away, not wanting to be caught staring, and looked out the window. Just at that moment the revolving restaurant presented me with a view of the convention center across the street from the hotel and of the large sign welcoming visitors to the event being held there—an international dog show. Obviously, in that context, the word *bitch* took on a different meaning.

Understanding the power of context in any specific circumstance is one of the most profoundly important aspects of all human experience. My specific circumstance on the day I had that talk with Jeannie was my cancer, a condition over which I had absolutely no control. Our conversation didn't change that, but it did allow me to understand that I had the power to shift the context within which I viewed that condition, which would, in turn, change the meaning it had for me. Before our conversation, I was devoting my energies to maintaining some illusion of control—and I say illusion because, clearly, no matter how carefully I planned for my own funeral, I'd have no way to be sure that, after my death, those plans were actually carried out. And, in any case, how could it possibly benefit me to try to control something I wouldn't even be around to witness?

After that conversation, however, I somehow understood that the only control I actually had lay in the way I chose to respond to my situation. I had the power to decide what I would think about and how I would think about it—that is, the power to decide what I would do with my life for whatever time I had left.

■ ■ ■

Shifting your context isn't something that can be accomplished simply through the power of positive thinking or reciting affirmations. It requires that you arrive at a radically new way of understanding your situation, a way you can believe in and that meets your specific needs, because only when the new way works better for you than the old way will you truly commit to it. When that happens, you will be experiencing a true epiphany that can actually change the entire course of your life, as it did mine.

My decision to study life rather than plan for my death provided the positive context I needed in that moment, in my specific set of circumstances. To further define and clarify the reasons for what I'd decided to do, I developed what people now might call a "mission statement," even though the term hadn't even been coined at the time, and I probably wouldn't have known what it meant, in any case. My personal mission statement was (and still is) to devote my life to learning all I could about life and to developing myself to the best of my abilities to help other people, in and beyond my lifetime—and (I added three years later) to enjoy it.

Luckily, as it turned out, I'd been primed even before my illness to appreciate the wisdom that could be achieved by studying the wisdom of others. For my Introduction to Philosophy course at college, I was blessed to be taught by one of the most inspiring and challenging teachers I've ever encountered, a man whose brilliance inspired me to try to learn how to think better myself. The way I'd decided to do that was by studying those who were universally acknowledged to be the great thinkers of the past, and to that end I'd already begun to read Will Durant's *The Story of Philosophy*. Now I recommitted myself to reading and studying five hours a day, five days a week, for whatever time there was left for me.

■ ■ ■

My commitment notwithstanding, this new context within which I was approaching my illness would soon be put to the most difficult test I'd ever had to take.

My chemotherapy treatments were to be given intravenously in the evening, and after the first one I was given medication to help me sleep. I awakened in the middle of the night, still groggy, freezing cold, horribly nauseated, and startled by a persistent banging sound. In my confused condition, it took me a moment or two to figure out that the banging was coming from the headboard of my bed. I was shivering so violently that my body was actually causing the metal headboard to bang against the wall.

I stumbled toward the bathroom, dragging my IV pole and feeling as if I were about to explode from both ends. This wasn't a nightmare; it was really happening. I couldn't believe it was possible to go from feeling relatively healthy one day to being sicker than I'd ever imagined anyone could be. And I knew it wasn't just going to be a matter of getting through this night. The doctors had already told me that I'd feel worse with each successive dose of chemotherapy, and at that moment, I was too sick to summon up the energy to imagine any end to the torture, which would, to a greater or lesser degree, continue for the next two years.

I spent the first week of each of the next four months in the hospital receiving my nightly chemotherapy. And at the end of that week I went home to "recover." My recovery consisted of two weeks of intestinal torture followed by a week of trying to eat whatever I could in order to regain enough strength to return to the hospital for the next round of chemo. By the end of the first four months, there was not a hair left on my body, I was so thin I couldn't even sit in a chair without a pillow, and the nerves in my fingers were so inflamed I couldn't turn a doorknob—but I was alive. And since I was alive, the doctors still needed to remove what was left of my tumors. After the first surgery, they told me I'd be ready for the second at the point where I had enough strength to walk the length of my parents' driveway and back, so you can imagine how weak I must have been. By the end I was totally debilitated and covered in raw surgical scars, and I still had a second round of "maintenance" chemo to go through. In fact, it would be two and a half years before the doctors told me, on one of my by-then-routine follow-up visits, that the odds of my cancer's recurring were somewhat better than the odds that I'd be hit by lightning. And even then, they never said I was cured; I've been in "remission" now for more than twenty years.

■ ■ ■

Despite all of that, I somehow managed to cling to the one truth I'd taken away from my conversation with Jeannie. I *could* still direct whatever energy I had toward choosing how I would live whatever life I had left. While I might not have any control *over* my situation, I could still have power *in* it by choosing how I would respond to whatever was happening to me.

My choices were twofold—to continue to live as normally as I could as much of the time as I could, and not to abandon the commitment I'd made to my studies and my context. The first part wasn't so easy in the beginning, while I was living with the horribly sickening and debilitating effects of first the chemotherapy and then the surgeries, but as I began to feel better over the course of the next two years, I did my best, between visits to the hospital for periodic blood tests, X rays, and ultrasounds, to follow my father's always sage advice to be as "normal" as I could, because, as he told me, "You need to stay as close to normal as possible. Adjust your behavior to the part that's well, not the part that's sick. If you can get up and get dressed, do it. And if you can't do it every day, that's okay, too." In fact, it wasn't too difficult to do what he suggested, because, by that time, cancer had become "normal" to me and I could no longer imagine life without it.

But if the physical effects of my treatments meant that living life as usual wasn't really an option for me, being so sick also meant that I couldn't be tempted away from my books by the offer of a game of hoops with my brothers or a jog around the park. During those short periods when I wasn't either throwing up or moaning in pain, there wasn't much I could do *but* read. As it was, the value of reading had been imbued in me by my parents from the time I was a small child. I still remember the day when my mother asked me to carry something out to the car for my aunt Wanda, who'd been visiting with Mom in the kitchen. As I opened the rear door to put in whatever it was (and *that* I can't remember), I saw three paperback books on the backseat. And I remember teasing my aunt because they were all romance novels. But I also recall her response: "I read everything. You can learn something even from a bad book." To this day, I think of reading as studying, and I never sit down with a book without a pencil and pad next to me.

Like most working-class families of the time, we didn't have many books in the house, but my father did have a shelf of about twenty volumes, including *Peace of Mind* by Rabbi Joshua Loth Liebman and *The Will to Live* by Arnold A. Hutschnecker, a medical doctor ahead of his time who, in 1951, was already writing about the dynamic interaction between body and mind. I started reading those books by the time I was about eleven and still have them with me today. So now, with my so-called mission statement firmly in mind, I determined to finish *The Story of Philosophy* and then move on to the writings of some of the philosophers Durant had written about. Working my way through Plato, Kant, and Schopenhauer wasn't easy, and I certainly wasn't speed-reading. There were days when I was so sick I couldn't concentrate for more than five minutes at a time. But I never abandoned my commitment.

During those years, and over the years since, I've read not only the philosophers I started out with, but also the writings of Ken Wilber and Joseph Campbell, and *As a Man Thinketh* by James Allen. I've read psychology ranging from Viktor Frankl's *Man's Search for Meaning* to Carl Jung's *Modern Man in Search of a Soul*. I've read books on spirituality that took me from Huxley's *The Perennial Philosophy* to Thomas Merton's *No Man Is an Island*, Thomas Cleary's *Essential Confucius* and, more recently, Karen Armstrong's *Buddha*. And I've looked at the human experience from the point of view of scientists like Albert Einstein, Stephen Hawking, and Werner Heisenberg. The more I read, the more I realized that all these wise people shared the same desire—to find some truth greater than themselves with which they could connect and thus elevate the meaning of their lives. To do this is everyone's greatest wish.

■ ■ ■

And so, by following my plan, I not only found in my readings information I could use for elevating the meaning of my own life, but I also discovered the source of my power in a situation that was completely beyond my control. Finding power in a situation where you feel you've lost all control is a paradox—an apparently self-contradictory statement or situation, or two opposite truths that, rather than canceling each other out, actually lead to a greater truth. The great poet John Donne used the power of paradox often to point to a truth that could be expressed no other way, as in these lines from his "Holy Sonnet 140" in which he addresses God:

> Take me to you, imprison me, for I,
> Except You enthrall me, never shall be free,
> Nor ever chaste, except you ravish me.

A simpler example might be the statement "less is more." Or, to put it in modern parlance, a paradox simply expresses a truth that's "counterintuitive." To think about how two apparently contradictory statements or thoughts can lead to a higher truth, just visualize a triangle. The bottom two angles of the triangle lie at either end of the bottom line. Label them "power" and "losing control," respectively. If you follow those two angles (or concepts) up the sides of the triangle to the point where they come together at the top, they ultimately connect. It was Aristotle who said, "The knowledge of opposites is one," meaning that by considering two apparently contradictory truths we can arrive at a higher or more meaningful kind of truth.

In this case, power and loss of control, considered separately, do seem like contradictory concepts. But if you look at the triangle, you can see that the more you are able to accept what you can't control (moving up the right side of the triangle), the more previously wasted energy you will have to bring to those things you can (moving up the left side), until the two come together at the top to create greater power and peace for yourself, or, a higher meaning for your life.

I define "higher meaning" as understanding ourselves and the world around us in a way that makes it easier to create the happiness we seek. It's a kind of understanding that allows us to define the events, circumstances, and outcomes in our lives in a way that makes us feel powerful rather than victimized and helpless. The idea of losing control might at first seem very frightening because, after all, you've spent your entire life establishing an elaborate construct for the very purpose of feeling in control. You might think that if you gave that up, your whole world would come crashing down around your ears. But if your control is only an illusion created to ward off your fears, wouldn't you simply be giving up a mistaken idea rather than control itself?

WHAT CAN YOU CONTROL?

Draw a vertical line down the center of a piece of paper, creating two columns. At the top of the left-hand column write the words "Can Control." At the top of the right-hand column write the words "Can't Control." Now consider the things in your life that you think you can control, such as your spouse, your child, your friends, your coworkers, your parents, even your health, and list them in the left-hand column. Look at that list again. Can you actually, totally control the way they think, what they do, how they behave? Can you actually control your health? Can you give yourself a heart attack at the count of three? Can you make yourself stop breathing? While you might be able to hold your breath, you can't make yourself stop breathing. Can you stop your heart from beating? If you're truly being candid with yourself, you will determine that all the things I've asked you to consider actually belong in the right-hand column under "Can't Control." ■

Consider the enormous amounts of energy you waste in the average day, week, and year trying to maintain your illusion of control. Couldn't you have used that energy more positively in other ways?

I learned, in a terrible and sudden way, how futile it is to waste that precious energy in the moment my cancer was diagnosed. But you don't have to wait to be diagnosed with a terminal illness to give up your illusion of control. You can begin right now by reexamining your life within a more powerful and edifying context.

In his book *The Perennial Philosophy*, Aldous Huxley says, "A true saint finds the crisis in every moment." We tend to think of the word *crisis* as denoting something negative, but its actual definition, according to *The Random House College Dictionary* (revised edition) is "a stage in a sequence of events at which the trend of all future events is determined; a turning point." If we think of crisis in that context, it becomes clear that what Huxley is saying is that, in every moment of our lives, there is the opportunity for true transition, for improving all our outcomes in the future. I think of this concept quite often and was reminded of its truth once again just the other day. I was having lunch with a gentleman named Steve, who had heard me speak five years before. During lunch, he told me that, while he couldn't remember everything I'd said (I'd have been shocked if he could), the one thing that struck him in a way he'd never forget was that, at eighteen years old, I'd had a life experience that gave me a sense of my own mortality. He was thirty-eight at the time, and until that day, he said, he'd never really considered that his own life had a timeline and that it would end. He'd just sort of thought that, in some way, he'd be around for most of forever. Considering the "now" of his life in the context of his inevitable death, he said, had led him to a more profound understanding of what it means to be alive and to the realization that he could approach his life each day in a way that would bring him greater happiness.

■ ■ ■

I'm sure that right now, if you wanted to, you could come up with a number of outcomes, people, or events in your life that you feel a need to control. I suggest, however, that much of that sense of need is driven by fear—the fear that if you don't control these things something bad will happen to you. Just for fun, try to stop thinking about those things and consider something different—that within the context of your own life, time is relative, and each passing year will be shorter than the last. Time itself is immutable. A minute in 1895 consisted of sixty seconds and that year consisted of 365 days, just as this year will (considering that neither falls in a leap year). Your *version* of time, however, the version that is your life, is unavoidably relative to your perception of it. When you were five years old, one year was an entire fifth of your life. When you were ten, one year was an entire tenth of your life. So the passing of a year seemed to you a relatively long time. But today, one year is a much smaller percentage of your life. That's why each year seems to go by more quickly for us as we get older. However old you are as you're reading this, consider that this will be the longest year of your life, for the rest of your life. And each successive year will appear to pass more quickly than the last.

You can decide to use this context to depress you or to empower you. Steve used it to reconsider how and what he decided to focus his energies on each day as he chose between his fears and his goals. It helped him to let go of things he couldn't control and begin to bring all his energy to what he could control . . . himself. Not in the future, not in the past, but in the now. Instead of using his energy to grab frantically at control, which is like trying to grab a fistful of water, Steve shifted the context within which he viewed his life. And, by doing that, he was able to begin harnessing the power of losing control for himself—without having to face a life-threatening disease as I did.

■ ■ ■

If you were asked to choose between control and happiness, is there any doubt in your mind what that choice would be? I don't think so. But what you have to realize is that these two concepts are by their very nature mutually exclusive. Nearly everything you do to maintain control—or the illusion of control—is driven by your fear of the unknown, of not being prepared for every possible contingency. And it stands to reason that anything you do out of fear simply cannot lead to happiness. If, however, you are willing to shift your context so that fear is no longer motivating your behavior, you can *choose* a different motivation. You can know, with a deep certainty, that whatever life throws your way, you can choose how to respond to it—you can have *power* in that situation. You can choose happiness. You can choose love.

One example of the relationships among control, fear, and love—and one you, too, might relate to—springs from my mother's attempt to control the behavior of four exuberant, rambunctious sons. One cardinal rule in our house was that the living room was off-limits to all of us except on those rare, carefully monitored occasions when we had special "company." The living room housed the "good" furniture, including the stereo, the glass coffee table, and the couch we weren't allowed to lie on. In effect, my mother had complete control of the living room; it was always neat, organized, and perfectly clean. It was always "visitor ready." But as I look back on my life, I realize that not much living actually went on in that room. The living happened in the kitchen, where friends and family usually congregated to be fed both emotionally and physically. It's not that the kitchen wasn't neat—in fact, it was very orderly—it's just that my mother didn't feel the need to control either the room or the behavior of everyone in the room. As a result, that's where we found our nourishment and love.

My mother's need to control the living room stemmed from her fear that one of us boys would spill something, break something, or otherwise defile its pristine perfection; and while there's nothing wrong with a parent's wanting to keep one room in the house free of the havoc children can wreak, I'm simply using this example to illustrate that when we try to control things out of fear, we might lose out on living in the process.

■ ■ ■

I can't say that I understood all of this intellectually with a sudden flash of insight at the time of my conversation with Jeannie, or even for years afterward, but what I did understand on some gut level was that it would serve me better to devote whatever time I was allotted to living the best life I could than it would to lie down and just prepare to die. And I did understand that how I chose to use that time was about the only power I had in the situation, although sometimes I didn't even have that. Sometimes my emotions or thoughts were in themselves beyond my control. But even then I still had the power to continue engaging in the *process* of *trying* to better understand, accept, and manage myself. I could take myself in hand as if I were walking a little puppy on a leash, and each time I started to zig or zag or wander off course, I could gently pull myself back and ask myself whether what I was thinking or feeling or doing was really the most useful or positive thing I could think or feel or do in that situation, in that moment. And the more I practiced doing that, the better I got at it. I'm still doing it, because, as I've already said, growth is a process that begins at birth and continues for the rest of our lives. And, over the years, I've been fortunate enough to have found a way to share what I've learned with others in order to help them achieve the kind of peace, love, and happiness I've found for myself.

■ ■ ■

During a talk I gave recently to members of the Young Presidents' Organization in Washington, D.C., I spoke about my cancer and explained how shifting my context and acknowledging my lack of control had allowed me to get through the most trying experience of my life. During the question-and-answer period afterward, a gentleman in the back of the room raised his hand and asked me pointblank whether I now considered my illness a blessing or a curse. His question caught me off-guard because, strange as it may seem, no one had ever asked it before. So I took a few minutes, during which I fought my urge to give the easy answer that I knew would impress my audience and assembled the most thoughtful and honest response I could give, which was that, in fact, it had been both. While it was certainly the most difficult and worst time of my life, I said, it had also created the impetus for me to commit to the studies that had led to my life's work, and so, in that sense, it was also my greatest gift.

At the end of the program, I was signing some books when I noticed that the man who'd asked the question seemed to be waiting to speak with me. Finally, when we were the only two people still in the room, he approached. I could see that he was tense, barely in control of his emotions, and his voice trembled as he looked me in the eye and said, "My cancer . . ."

As he paused to regain his composure, a million thoughts raced through my mind. He'd been diagnosed with incurable cancer, but for him there was no experimental protocol, no miracle cure . . . and then I told myself to stop making up his story for him and just wait to hear what he had to say.

"My cancer," he said again, "was my son's physical disability. Today you taught me that it's also my gift." We both had tears in our eyes as he gave me a quick one armed hug and left the room.

Somehow, I'd found the words that had allowed him to reexamine the context of his life, and I was humbled to think that even though I had absolutely no control either over him or over his son's condition, I'd somehow had the *power* to influence him through what I'd said as well as through my living example. In that moment I'd made a powerful connection and perhaps changed a life. No sense of control could have brought me that kind of happiness.

■ ■ ■

At this point I want to make perfectly clear what exactly it is you can look forward to if you're willing to give up your illusions and discover the power of losing control. There's an old song titled, "I Never Promised You a Rose Garden." Well, you could say life is like that song. For all its joys, it is also full of challenges you can't simply opt out of accepting. The German philosopher Georg Wilhelm Friedrich Hegel said, "Struggle is the law of growth." And, at the risk of appearing presumptuous, I'd like to add to that statement three of my own:

- Sometimes pain is a choice.

- The nature of the struggle is up to us.

- We don't have to let fear control us.

Have you ever been lying in bed, perfectly comfortable, thinking to yourself that you never want to move? And then your hip or your leg begins to bother you and you know you have to move. The act of moving or rolling over is going to cause you some temporary discomfort, but in the end, you'll have arrived at a state of *greater* comfort. That's the way life is—in order to reach a higher level of comfort we have to go through some discomfort. But I'm suggesting that sometimes we put ourselves in more discomfort than we need to because we've chosen to engage in a struggle that isn't necessary, or that it isn't possible to win (such as the struggle to control that which we can't), and I further suggest that we do that out of fear.

■ ■ ■

How many times have you seen a mother distraught because her child was caught smoking or drinking? How often has a college student been reduced to tears because his professor gave him a lower grade than he thought he deserved? How many employees begin to lose their self-esteem the minute they lose their jobs or get passed over for the promotions they expected?

These types of things happen all the time. And for people who live with illusions of control, they can have devastating effects. The mother who thinks she can control her son or daughter will experience great emotional distress when reality proves otherwise. The student who thinks his hard work will "control" the grade his professor assigns him will be crushed when reality proves him wrong. And the employee who feels that her loyalty and hard work will control her employer's treatment of her will have trouble recovering from the realization that her employer is not subject to her control.

I'm not saying that these folks should not try as hard as they can to effect the best outcomes for themselves. I'm merely saying that if they believe their efforts can control those outcomes, they are living with an illusion that will only serve to make them vulnerable to severe emotional distress.

The power of losing control is about learning how to let go of trying to control the uncontrollable outcomes and circumstances in our lives. To do anything else is a blueprint for living a life that is driven by stress, fear, and disappointment. I'm not suggesting that we shouldn't do everything we can to make our dreams and desires come true. But letting go of the illusion that we have complete control over our outcomes will free us from our fears, allow us to bring more of ourselves to the work we need to do, and enable us to find happiness and power no matter what life brings our way.

In the following chapters I provide you with specific tools and strategies for learning to move past your fears and give up your unnecessary struggle for control. When you do that, you'll be able to move through your challenges more quickly, with less pain, and instead of being a victim of your fears, you'll be able to reclaim your power in any situation. That is the true promise of *The Power of Losing Control*.

Chapter 2

We Are the Stories We Tell Ourselves We Are

> *We do not see things as they are.*
> *We see them as we are.*
> —The Talmud

Indulge me for a moment and visualize this scenario:

You're holding a newborn baby girl, and as you gaze into her unfocused blue eyes you can only marvel at the unlimited exciting experiences and opportunities life has in store for her. The possibilities for this new life, you think to yourself, are virtually endless.

And then imagine that, by some miracle, you suddenly *knew* everything she would experience in her entire life, and, by some further miracle, you had the ability to whisper in her ear all that you knew, and she would hear and remember it.

Would you tell her? I'd be willing to bet that you wouldn't.

On the one hand, by telling her, you'd certainly be saving her all the needless fears and anxieties each of us has about our unknown future. But, on the other hand, you'd be robbing her of all the excitement and anticipation that go along with the limitless possibilities her life has to offer. And I would also suggest that you'd be robbing her of her true purpose for being, which is—as it is for all of us—to define her own meaning through the way she responds to the events and experiences in her life.

The Importance of Storytelling

A story is, in fact, a context. It's the "broader picture," the landscape that gives meaning to everything within it. A story creates the connections, associations, and relationships that allow us to make sense of what would otherwise be meaningless raw data, and it is our ability to make those connections that keeps us sane. Connections create understanding, and without understanding, we are unable to navigate in the world. When we lose those connections, as happens when we suffer various forms of dementia, we lose our meaning and we literally lose ourselves.

That little baby you were holding a few moments ago was already attempting to create her own stories and make the connections that would gradually begin to define the world for her, and, at the same time, define who she was in that world. We all do it every day, from the moment of our birth. We make a connection between "mother" and "feeding." We connect "feeding" with "satisfaction." And so on, endlessly. As we mature and develop, we make more and better connections, which increases both our understanding and our ability to function.

We are both the authors and the protagonists of our own stories, and our stories are always projections of ourselves. That's not only a fact; it's also key to understanding the power of losing control, because if we write our own stories, it stands to reason that we can also rewrite them, which means changing the context within which we view both ourselves and the world we live in. If we can change that context in a way that serves us better, we'll be making better connections, and, by doing that, we'll be elevating our own meaning. That's what I did all those many years ago when Jeannie gave me the gift of allowing me to change the context within which I viewed my own illness.

I did not, I hasten to add, directly change my *perception* of my illness. Perception is, for each and every one of us, reality. What we perceive to be true is, in and of necessity, the truth. And my truth was that I would die. Jeannie didn't change that, nor did she attempt to do so. The fact is that, at the time of my diagnosis, testicular cancer, particularly in a stage as advanced as mine, was a death sentence, and it would have been irresponsible of her to try to persuade me otherwise—in addition to which I wouldn't have believed her. But she did help me shift my *perspective* on the situation. She allowed me to understand that, since I wasn't dead yet, it would be pointless—in fact self-defeating—to concentrate on my death and that it would be much more productive to concentrate on, and make the most of, what remained of my life.

Your Biography Is Not Your Story

The events in your life that make up your biography are just the facts or raw data from which you "create" your stories. It's the way you "see" or interpret that biographical data that creates the context of the story itself. And since your ability to interpret that data is limited by the perspective from which you view it—that is, from your own mind and through your own eyes—the stories you create may not always be congruent with objective fact. Imagine, for example, that you're looking at a close-up photograph of a white-pillared colonial mansion, a gracious plantation home straight out of *Gone With the Wind*. Now imagine that you're shown another photograph of that same home with a ten-year-old child standing next to it. The so-called mansion is tiny in relation to the child, and you realize it's actually a doll's house. Those two photos taken together explain both context and perspective. By seeing the house in context with the child, you've changed your perspective, which automatically changes your reality. You'll never again be able to think of that house as a mansion; seen from that new perspective, it will always and forever remain a doll's house.

But most of us don't have the opportunity to change our perspective quite so easily. In fact, we're more likely to cling tenaciously to whatever story we've already created to help us make sense of the world. Have you ever reminisced with a sibling or a childhood friend and been amazed by how differently you recalled the same events? Or perhaps you thought some experience you'd shared had been important, exciting, certainly memorable, while your sibling or friend had no recollection of it at all? That's because each of you was creating your own stories, from your own unique perspective, and your story was coloring, perhaps even distorting, those remembered events. Perhaps you've heard of the psychological phenomenon known as "blocking," which describes our amazing capacity to "forget" experiences that, for whatever reason, we simply prefer not to remember. An extreme example of this would be blocking the memory of traumatic abuse or an accident or act of violence that was too painful for you to recall. But the same process occurs—unconsciously, of course—on a daily basis, as we struggle to make the events in our lives "fit" the stories we've created.

Yes, that's what we all do—every day. Think about it. Our stories create the connections that allow us to make sense of the world around us. And so, if our world didn't conform to our story, we'd have no way of making sense of it. From our own limited point of view, we make up stories that give sense to our world and define our place within it; we then act upon the "reality" we've created, and, by doing that, we *make* the world conform to our view of it. In other words, we use our stories to determine our future, even though we don't necessarily realize that that's what we're doing.

I recently worked with a forty-three-year-old gentleman named Jim who had problems in his relationships with women, both at work and in his personal life. He believed that women couldn't be trusted and if he didn't "manage" them properly, they'd manipulate him in some way. (This has apparently been a common problem for some men throughout history. The ancient historian Livy tells us that when the free women of Rome marched into the forum in 195 B.C. to demand the repeal of the Oppian Law of 215 B.C., which forbade women to use gold ornaments, varicolored dresses, or chariots, Cato predicted the ruin of Rome if the law was repealed. "From the moment that they become your equals they will be your masters," he cried out.)

As we talked, Jim told me that his mother was one of the most manipulative people he'd ever met, and he talked about the terrible pain and stress she'd created for him, his brothers, and his father throughout her lifetime. It quickly became clear that Jim was taking a collection of past experiences with one woman in his past and projecting them onto all the other women in his present. His story about his mother became a story about all women. And his response to this self-constructed reality was to not trust any female. One can only imagine how this approach had negatively affected his relationships with women. What is clear, however, is that his story—based on his past—was contributing to the determination of his future.

I had to work with Jim for quite a while before he figured out that there is no manipulation gene exclusive to the female gender, and that no one (male or female) can manipulate you if you don't allow it.

■ ■ ■

Here's another example of how we use our stories from the past to validate our present thoughts and behaviors, and how the world will line up to coincide with whatever it is we believe to be true. A forty-year-old divorcée whose husband had left her for a woman half her (and his) age might, for example, have told herself that "All men are jerks." That's her story from events that occurred in her past, but it will also determine her future. She will either unconsciously make sure she continues to meet men who validate her view of the males of our species or she'll allow her preconceived story to color her view of any man she meets. Either way, for her, all men will continue to be jerks, which just about eliminates the possibility of her finding happiness with a new man.

But that same woman could just as easily have created a different story based on the same events. She might have had enough positive experiences with other men to decide that her husband, the jerk, was an exception rather than the rule, and that perspective would have allowed her to form new relationships validating its reality for her.

THIS IS YOUR LIFE

Imagine that your life was being featured on *Biography* and that all the facts, events, and time sequences were accurate. Imagine further that I saw the program and became so fascinated with your life that I watched it a hundred times, until I felt as if I really knew you. What if I ran into you on the street and told you I felt I really knew you? Would you think I could know you simply by knowing the events of your life? If your answer is no, you've understood all along what I've been talking about in this chapter; the real story of who you are isn't about what happens to you as much as it is about how you interpret and define what happens to you.

The word *biography* comes from two Greek words, *bios*, or "life," and *grapho*, which means "to write." Try writing two versions of your biography. In the first version, stick with just the facts or events as they happened. Express them as dispassionately as you can, perhaps even reducing them to a list. Leave out how they made you feel or how you reacted to them.

In the second version of your biography, make a list of how a hero or heroine might respond to some of the more difficult events from your first biography. Their responses have nothing to do with your reality, but they should be reasonable and viable responses. Does this help you to understand that the events in your life and your responses to them and feelings about them are actually two separate things? Can you select one or two events from the first biography and reframe your definitions of them in a way that would make you feel better about them? Maybe, for example, you were once fired from a job and became very depressed because you felt you had somehow failed or because your self-definition had been so attached to your work. Could you, instead of losing your self-esteem or your sense of self, have taken the opportunity to review your options and moved on to a better career choice? Could you have turned an apparent setback into an opportunity for true transition? ■

Our stories can have positive or negative effects on our lives. If they're serving us well, validating our sense of self, and contributing to our happiness, then there's no reason to change them. For many of us, however, that's simply not the case, and when negative stories become so much a part of our unconscious being that they drive our behavior (and we don't even understand what it is that's making us repeat our mistakes and preventing us from finding the happiness we seek), they take on a meaning that's more powerful than truth. They take on the power of myth.

How Stories Become Myths

In ancient times, civilizations created myths to explain phenomena they couldn't understand in any other way, including how the world began, the origins of men and animals, and the basis for certain forms of human activity. From the story of Atlas, who was said to support the Heavens on his shoulders, to the tale of Prometheus, who was credited with lighting a torch with fire from the sun and giving it as a gift to man, myths were the means by which ancient peoples interpreted the natural world and the societies in which they lived.

The Egyptians, for example, saw the scarab (dung beetle) emerge from the ground rolling a ball of dung before it. They saw its mysterious appearance as an indication of spontaneous self-creation and associated its activity with the movement of the sun across the sky each day. As a result, the scarab became part of their mythology as a symbol of immortality and resurrection. In other words, they noticed a phenomenon they couldn't explain and made up a story that provided a way for them to understand it, because, as I've said, that need for understanding is a fundamental component of the human condition.

Now, of course, we have modern, "scientific" ways of explaining these phenomena, and, as a result, the word *myth* has come to signify a story that is "less than true." But for those who believe them, myths are actually stories of a higher order; they are greater and more powerful than truth. And so it is with the stories we tell ourselves we are. If it's "our story," it can take on the power of myth and become the force that literally drives our thoughts, feelings, and behaviors. I call these most powerful of stories our "driving myths." If it's someone else's story, however, it is often, to the rest of us, less than true. That's why two people may experience the very same event and yet interpret it so differently. It's why siblings or friends can have such different views of their shared past.

I was the second oldest of four brothers who were all very close in age. In those days there was a very popular commercial for a car rental company that said something like, "We're number two, so we try harder." I somehow accepted that tag line as a universal truth about being number two and connected it with my position in the family. (I'm sure there were a number of other things that validated my number-two story, but for some reason it's the commercial that stands out in my memory.) The fact that I was second oldest began to mean that I needed to try harder than my older brother, Mike, in order to achieve the same levels of success. Whether it was in school, in sports, or making friends, my number-two myth put me at an immediate disadvantage that drove a very determined approach to life. It wasn't until later that I realized that the only objective "truth" about my myth was that I was, in fact, the second oldest of four brothers. Everything else was my own creation. As I learned to examine my driving myths, I was able to see how the story I'd made up about being number two had impacted my life.

■ ■ ■

Mythology was the basis upon which ancient religions were built, and thinking in terms of religious belief is a good way to explain why myths have so much power for those who believe them and yet can be viewed as mere fiction by those who don't.

Let's assume that a Christian and a Muslim agree to study each other's religions and read each other's holy books and then come together to discuss them.

"Well," the Muslim might say. "It's a good book, your Bible. It has some wonderful stories in it. In fact, it's full of stories, and they convey powerful messages."

"So, you liked it, then?" asks the Christian, delighted by his friend's response.

"Oh, yes," answers the Muslim. "But you Christians forget that they're just stories. You take them too literally. A virgin birth, all those miracles—those things couldn't really have happened."

"Well, I can see the value in the stories of your religion, too," replies the Christian. "And I'd like to make a point similar to yours. How could your people really believed that Mohammed journeyed from Mekkah to Jerusalem in one night on the back of a white horse-like animal? I mean, really—you take those stories too literally."

I'm sure you get the picture: Religious or otherwise, if the story is yours, it's the truth; if it's not, it's a myth. Or, as Robert Walter, Director of the Joseph Campbell Foundation has said, "We are, in essence, who we tell ourselves we are." Once you accept that, you will understand that your driving myths are, for all intents and purposes, the foundation for the meaning you give to your existence, for better or for worse.

How Myths Function in Everyday Life

Myths exist on every level, from those a culture shares collectively to those that determine family dynamics to the ones that drive our individual lives. Among the myths of American culture are:

- The pioneer spirit created our society.
- We can all go from rags to riches.
- The son of a ditchdigger can grow up to be president.
- You can succeed at anything, as long as you work hard enough.

I'm sure if you think about it, you can add a few more of your own.

And think about your own family. When you get together for birthdays or holidays, do you find yourselves retelling and laughing about the same stories? Do you have a "black sheep" uncle? A profligate cousin? A "smart" sibling? A grandfather who "coulda made a million if he'd only—"? Do you talk about "the Smith sense of humor" or "the Jones green thumb"? We all do it, and what we're really doing as we retell these stories is comparable to a tribe's sitting around a campfire and retelling the myths that are the foundation of its culture.

And the same, of course, is true of our personal myths. The more we repeat them to ourselves, the more powerful they become; the more powerful they become, the more they determine our behavior; the more we behave *as if* those stories were true (like the man who believed all women were manipulative), the more they will become self-fulfilling prophecies.

■ ■ ■

Here are a few general concepts that might form the basis for your personal driving myths:

- Life is hard.

- A job well done is its own reward.

- Nice guys finish last.

- The grass is always greener on the other side.

- The rich are different from you and me.

If you subscribed to the myth that life has to be hard, chances are you'd do your best to make sure your experience conformed to that belief. You might consistently put yourself in difficult situations in order to prove yourself right, or you might make any experience more difficult than it had to be just to see yourself as the hero or heroine of your own struggle.

If you believe that a job well done is its own reward, you just might be preventing yourself from receiving a more tangible and satisfying form of reward or recognition for the good job you've done. Do you think nice guys finish last? Do you consider yourself a "nice guy"? Surely you can see where that myth would lead. Or how about "the grass is always greener"? There's simply no way that view of the world could possibly lead to happiness, no matter how much you accomplished. And finally, the last one: If you truly believe the rich are different from you and *me*, aren't you de facto precluding the possibility that you might ever be rich? If *you* were rich, you wouldn't be you, would you? Or at least that's the story you've been telling yourself.

WHAT IS YOUR STORY?

See if you can begin to uncover some of your own driving myths by examining your story. Pretend you have a pen pal in another state or province whom you really want to tell about yourself. You want your pen pal to get to know the real you. What would you tell this person? Perhaps you'd start with a physical description and then go on to describe your likes and dislikes. Let's call these your "whats." Now see if you can describe the whys behind some of your whats. In other words, write about why you look the way you do in terms of how you wear your hair or the kinds of clothes you wear. Then go on to explain *why* you like the things you like and *why* you dislike the things you dislike. Tell your pen pal what your life was like growing up and what your family was like. Write about everything that is important to you and why.

This can actually be a lot of fun. When you've finished, read what you wrote. As you read, see if you can identify any of your driving myths coming through in your story.

If you'd like to take this exercise a step further, log onto the World Wide Web and see how many personal home pages you can find. Read them carefully and see if you can guess what each person's driving myths are based on the information he or she chose to publish on the Web site. If "we are the stories we tell ourselves we are," what do you think their stories are? ■

If our personal driving myths are preventing us from achieving true happiness and becoming the best we can be, why do we seem to cling to them with such tenacity? There might actually be more than one reason. The first is that we need very much to be *right*. Our myths are so powerful that we'll do almost anything to prove them true, even though what we're doing may not be in our best interests. The reasons for that are basically the same as the reasons we make up our stories in the first place—they give us the illusion that we have some control over the world we inhabit. If we decide that the world works in a certain way, and we then behave in a way that ensures that the world will respond as we assumed it would, we can actually tell ourselves that we're in control of our world. But, of course, that sense of control is all built on the illusion we created in the first place—our own driving myth.

The second reason we might be unable to give up unproductive or self-destructive driving myths is that they've become so firmly embedded in our subconscious that we're not even aware of what those myths are. That was sadly true of someone I met following one of my speaking engagements.

I was in the lobby of the hotel where the conference was taking place, killing time before I had to leave for the airport, when a gentleman approached and asked if I could help him with what he characterized as a "major challenge" in his life. We sat down at a table in the corner of the bar area, and he launched into his story.

"I've hardly told this to anyone," he said, "but before we begin, you need to know that I'm an abused child."

"You're what?" I interrupted, purposely raising my voice.

"I—I'm an abused child," he repeated, stuttering in his embarrassment.

"How old are you?" I asked.

"I'm forty-five," he said, apparently a bit puzzled by the question.

"And how old were you the last time you were abused?" I asked, the edge still in my voice.

"I—I guess I was about seven."

"Well, then," I persisted, "why would you come and ask me to help you and then begin by telling me a lie?" The gentleman looked totally confused at that point, so I went on. "You're a forty-five-year-old business executive who hasn't been abused in more than thirty-five years, and yet you just told me you're an abused child. That's what I'd call a lie."

"I thought I said I *was*," he mused, almost as if he were trying to recall his own words.

"No. In fact, you stated *twice*, quite emphatically, that you *are* an abused child. If you really want my help, and not just my sympathy, it's time you stopped lying to both of us."

My approach may have been a bit harsh, but I knew our time together was limited, and since he had approached me, I believed that, having observed me during the conference, this gentleman now felt safe with me.

After a few moments of silence, he began to rock back and forth ever so slightly. I've seen the same reaction in others who suddenly see the world as inconsistent with their own driving myth. When he finally looked up, the expression on his face was remarkably warm and peaceful.

"Thank you," he said. "Thank you so much. I just knew you'd be able to help me."

"You're quite welcome," I told him honestly. "But I didn't really do anything. You did it."

In fact, all I'd done for this gentleman was to give him the opportunity and the ability to "see" what had been obvious to me—but was clearly not obvious to him. I'd allowed him to change the perspective from which he viewed a "fact" of his past, put it into a new context, and so change the way he responded to that fact. By doing that, I was creating an opportunity for him to *change* his behavior, which would automatically change his perception or reality. I couldn't change his history any more than he could, and I certainly didn't want to dismiss the importance of the role his abuse had played in his life. Had I tried to do either of those things, he wouldn't have wanted or been able to "hear" what I was saying any more than I'd have been able to listen to Jeannie if she'd tried to diminish the importance of my illness or its impact on my life.

But once he became aware of how his distorted perspective was limiting his ability to respond productively to his present circumstances, he opened the possibility of rewriting the story of his *future* to ensure a happier outcome.

You Can Rewrite Your Own Story

I'm sure most of us have asked ourselves at one time or another why we keep making the same mistakes, why we keep attracting the wrong people and situations into our lives, why we don't just *get* it after all this time. But I would urge you *not* to spend your time and energy pursing the answers to those questions, because doing so would not be the best or most effective way to change your present beliefs or behavior.

Your current driving myths were created in the past; they are the results of your past experiences and your responses to those experiences. You can't change either what happened in the past or the way you responded to what happened in the past—in other words, *you cannot rewrite your biography*, but you *can* if you *choose* to, change the way you respond to circumstances in the present, which will inevitably change the course of your life in the future. That's what I mean by shifting your context. Rather than asking yourself what underlying myths had been driving your behavior in the past, it would be more useful to simply ask yourself if a particular thought, emotion, or behavior is serving you in the present, and—if the answer is no—to seek a context that would allow you to change those unproductive emotions, thoughts, and behaviors for new ones that could bring greater meaning to your life. If you can do that—and in the following chapters I provide you with the tools you'll need—your myths will naturally change. It's all part of a process, and as you'll see, it's the process itself that you need to concentrate on, because the results will occur of their own accord.

One of the most dramatic shifts in context I've ever heard of—and one that without doubt changed the course of modern history—is the story of how Mahatma Gandhi came to realize his power in the fight for the freedom and equality of his people.

After graduating from law school in England, Gandhi returned to India to begin his career as a barrister. In the English system of law, there are two categories of attorney: solicitors, who handle cases out of court, and barristers, who go to court or, as the English say, plead before the bar. At his first court appearance, Gandhi was so terrified that, when it came time for him to speak, he was literally struck mute and couldn't utter a single sound. With everyone in the courtroom watching and then laughing at him, he panicked, handed his legal briefs to a colleague, and fled. That was the beginning and the end of his career before the bar. As a result of his humiliation, he gave up any thought of a public career. His driving myth—whether or not he was consciously aware of it—told him he simply wasn't equipped for public life, and he sought more low-profile work as a solicitor, which wouldn't require his speaking in a public forum.

Not long after, Gandhi traveled to South Africa on behalf of a client who had provided him with a first-class train ticket. But in

South Africa, people of color weren't allowed to ride in the first-class carriage. Gandhi was told he'd have to move to the third-class compartment, and, when he refused, he was tossed off at the next station in the middle of the night with no overcoat and no luggage.

For what was left of the night Gandhi sat contemplating the humiliating injustices the people of India and South Africa had to live with under colonial rule, and because of that one experience, the timid former barrister who couldn't imagine himself following a public career experienced a profound shift in context that would impact the history of the world. He went from seeing himself as a powerless individual to believing that one person could make a difference if truth were on his side and he were willing to fight for what was right, and, furthermore, he came to see himself as having the power to be that individual. Notice that he didn't, in that moment, change either the facts of the world as it was or his situation within that world. He did, however, recognize that it would be possible for him to change the way he responded to that world. He gave up any illusion of his ability to control the world and at the same time gained his power in it.

His is one of the greatest types of driving myth ever conceived because it served not only his own needs but also the needs of his fellow men. But it's important to understand that he didn't try to examine the myth that had caused him to give up his budding public career, nor did he consciously make a decision to change the myth itself. Rather he had an experience that allowed him to change the perspective from which he viewed not only the world but his place within that world, as well, and as a result, his thoughts and behaviors naturally changed, which, in turn, changed his perception or driving myth or reality—whichever you choose to call it.

REWRITE YOUR OWN MYTH

Imagine that you are a commodity. Interested parties could actually purchase stock in you if they chose to do so. One of the ways they would decide your value is by reading your annual report. Like most annual reports, yours would report your earnings and your bottom line. And like most annual reports, yours would tell your story—your humble beginnings, your history, and your plans for your future. Of course, all of this would have to be described in a way that would entice potential investors.

Write the story of your life in the context of an annual report about you. Be responsible and report the hard facts as they are. But be sure to put yourself in the best possible light in terms of your intelligence, your will, your personality, your potential, and most of all your history. Be diligent about keeping your report as true and as positive as you possibly can, remembering that no annual report reveals all the problems and challenges the company faces.

When you're done, read through your report and see if you can make it even more attractive without saying anything that isn't actually true.

Now, consider how you might think, behave, and define things in your life in a way that would be consistent with your annual report. After all . . . it is true. ■

Remember that our stories are the contexts we use to make the connections that give meaning to our lives. If we can create better contexts, we'll be writing better stories that will allow us to make better connections and so elevate our meanings.

Congestion on the Highway— The Power of Other People's Driving Myths

If, as I've been saying all along, our driving myths—the stories we tell ourselves that drive our behavior—are, of necessity, unique to us and the result of our own perspectives, it stands to reason that all the people around us also have myths of their own, which may or may not conform to ours. And since each of us believes our own myth to be the "truth," we are always, consciously or unconsciously, trying to validate those myths by persuading others to accept them, as well.

Gandhi's ability to influence others to accept his driving myth as part of their own changed the course of millions of lives. His ability to shift the contexts of others was a unique gift that sprang from understanding the importance of leading by example. He lived his beliefs; what he said was absolutely congruent with what he did, and because of that, his behavior gave tremendous power to his words.

■ ■ ■

It's also possible for someone with a negative driving myth to believe in it so deeply, live it so compellingly, and espouse it so eloquently that he or she can influence others to adopt it, as well.

Each of us is probably confronted with someone else's negative driving myth on a daily basis, and whether we're aware of it or not, we're constantly making decisions that could conceivably shift our context for better or worse. A story my father told me long ago provides a perfect example of how negatively another person's driving myth can affect our context if he or she believes it, lives it, and presents it compellingly enough to override our own.

As a young man, Dad lived in a suburb just outside of Detroit. Like most people who lived in southeastern Michigan in those days, he worked in an auto factory. Each morning he and a young German fellow were picked up and driven to work by one of their colleagues. The driver was a deeply dissatisfied person who looked upon and defined everything in his world as a problem created specifically to inconvenience and frustrate him. He hated his job (which he considered pointless and stupid), his managers were all jerks, life "sucked," and so on.

The German kid's attitude was diametrically opposed to that of the driver. He couldn't wait to get to work each day; he liked everyone; he was happy all the time. The driver, of course, couldn't tolerate any of that because it totally invalidated his own driving myth. And because each of us so desperately needs to be "right" about our own version of the truth, he was constantly haranguing the kid, trying to shift the young man's context. But the kid really did like his job, he really was happy, and he wasn't having any of it.

The driver, however, was relentless; he simply wouldn't give up. Finally, one day, after the kid had once more reiterated how much he liked his job and how lucky he was to have it, the driver asked him, "Do you realize what you do?"

"I make cars," the kid replied.

"No, you don't," the driver responded with total conviction. "You're not making cars. You've *never* made a car. All you do is move pieces of metal from one place to another. You take a piece from here and put it over there. And then you do it again. You do it over and over, all day long. That's all you do. You're not making cars; you're moving pieces of metal."

The kid didn't say a word, but my dad told me that, from that moment on, he was absolutely changed. His context, the meaning he had given his job, and, therefore, his own sense of identity, were completely shattered. Until that moment, he'd seen himself as a part of and contributing to something greater than himself, and doing that had allowed him to elevate his own meaning. But the driver had offered him a new and compelling context that, in that moment, made sense to him. It was a bad context, but its undeniable logic had convinced him nevertheless. And, without considering whether it served him, he accepted it, and his life changed for the worse.

■ ■ ■

The CEO of a small company once called on me to work with his management team. The problem, as he defined it, was that he couldn't find people to hire who "knew what they were doing." He was in a very specialized business, manufacturing products for automotive suppliers. His father had started the business, and my client had been running it for about fifteen years. In that time he'd changed plant managers about a dozen times. Every time I met with him, he'd regale me with stories about the industry, his family, and how unique his business was, and tell me that "a person either knows things or he doesn't." It didn't take long to figure out that the source of the problem wasn't a lack of good potential employees. The problem was my client's myth. He had what I call the "Immaculate Perception" myth, which is not uncommon among CEOs of small family businesses. The essence of this myth is that the owner believes that because of his life experience, family background, or entrepreneurial skills (or all three), he has somehow been injected with a divine understanding that is now exclusive to him. When asked how he knows what he knows about his business, his answer is usually, "You get a feel for these things," or "It's obvious." When I try to talk with these people about how we might be able to help their managers learn what they need to know, the typical response is, "The problem is that they don't know, and if they don't know, you can't teach them."

In this case, the CEO's negative myth was not only hurting him and his business, but dooming his managers, as well.

THE POWER OF
OTHER PEOPLE'S DRIVING MYTHS

History is full of examples of great leaders from many walks of life whose personal driving myths have positively and negatively affected large numbers of people. Confucius's philosophy helped shape the thoughts and habits of an entire culture. Hitler's vision of the perfect Aryan nation led his people to war. Jesus Christ's belief in his own personal story was the force behind the rise of Christianity as a major religion. And many people who may not be so well known have touched others in significant ways because of the conviction with which they communicated their own personal myths.

Sit down with a piece of paper and a pencil, and write down the names of all the leaders you can think of who have, through the powerful influence of their personal driving myths, helped to change the lives of others for better or worse. They may be politicians or philosophers, writers, managers of companies, or third-grade teachers. You may have known them personally or simply read about them. Can you see how their driving myths served as positive contexts that they could apply to the various challenges they faced in their lives? ■

The Power to Help Others Change Their Myths

It's important to remember, whether we're discussing Gandhi or the driver of that car pool, that neither of those people actually had *control* over anyone else. All they could really control was their own behavior, which was, of necessity, driven by their personal myths. But the degree to which these men believed the truth of their own myths, and the fact that their own behavior so compellingly demonstrated the truth of their beliefs, gave them the power to influence others.

The worst thing we can do—ever—is to destroy another person's healthy and meaningful context. Mark Twain, one of the greatest American writers of all time, was an atheist and a notorious cynic. When he married, his wife was a devout Christian with a deep and abiding faith in God. That faith elevated her meaning by providing her with a connection to a higher power. But, as Twain regretfully admitted in his autobiography, which was written after her death, the force of his own relentless cynicism and atheism shattered her faith and, in some profound way, broke her spirit. I wasn't there, of course, but from my own experience I would suggest that it was not simply Twain's own beliefs but also his ongoing *example*, as well as his unparalleled ability to compellingly *express* those beliefs that caused his wife's tragic loss of faith in her own myth and context.

But, at the other end of the spectrum, the very best thing we can do for another person is to help him or her find a better context—one that will allow him or her to rewrite his or her story and so elevate the meaning of his or her life. It was Henry Ford who said, "Whether you believe you can or you believe you can't, you're right." In other words, because we each have such a profound need to be right, we will make whatever we believe come to pass in one way or another.

The only power we have over others comes from our ability to let them see for themselves that they have the power, in their own situation, to change the context within which they see themselves and respond to their world. We do that by making connections with them that allow them to shift their perspective and so elevate their own meaning. And if we are able to do that, we will also be giving our own lives greater meaning. Without seeking to do so directly, we ultimately elevate our own meaning by helping others to elevate theirs.

Before we can connect with and help anyone else, however, we must first learn to understand, accept, and manage ourselves. Since, as I hope I've made clear by now, we have no control over anyone or anything beyond ourselves, it stands to reason that we must first figure out if the stories we're telling ourselves are serving us well, or if they're preventing us from achieving the positive outcomes that have always seemed somehow beyond our grasp. Only by shifting our own context and finding a perspective that will give greater meaning to our own lives can we find the power in our own situation that allows us to make the meaningful connections with others that will ultimately elevate both our own lives and theirs.

■ ■ ■

In the following chapter, I attempt to help you to understand and appreciate the fact that your lack of control over anyone or anything beyond yourself is not a limitation but a gift, because it means that no one else and no external situation can claim control over you. If you accept that, you'll see that you have absolute power in your own life as well as the responsibility to make the choices and connections that will elevate the meaning of your life. It really is all up to you.

Chapter 3

"We're All in This Together . . . Alone"*

> We can understand one another; but each
> of us is able to interpret himself to himself
> alone.
>
> —Herman Hesse

If perception is reality, and if each of us perceives the world through our own unique set of senses, it follows logically that no two people's realities will be exactly the same. Hence, each one of us is essentially alone in his or her world. And yet we spend our entire lives trying to make connections and form relationships with other people. Indeed, making those connections and forming those relationships are among the most rewarding aspects of anyone's life, and we'll be talking more about how to make better, more meaningful connections in the following chapter. But that doesn't change the essential fact that we are the sole inhabitants of our primary world—ourselves.

We're born alone, we die alone, and we live our lives in denial of those two facts. I made that discovery during my cancer treatment. I was blessed to have the constant comfort and support of my family and friends, but I knew there was no way they could fully understand

*Lily Tomlin

what I was going through and that I was, despite their sympathy and caring, alone in my experience. I realized then that no matter how often any one of us says, "I know how you feel" or "I feel exactly the same way," the fact is that we can *never* really know how anyone else feels and that our feelings are never exactly the same as anyone else's.

The Futility of Denial

The idea that we are each truly alone is scary, and because of that we spend most of our lives in denial. Most commonly, we deny our fear and seek to banish our aloneness in one or more of three ways, by stating metaphorically and through our actions any of the following:

- I don't need you.

- I need to experience me through you.

- I need you to validate me by having you experience me.

People who say "I don't need you" are, in effect, shouting down their fear by whistling in the dark. They don't want your help, they'll never ask for your help, and if you attempt to offer help, they'll tell you you're interfering. But their protests are never issued calmly or quietly, and the vehemence of their expression belies the truth of their words.

I have a lovely friend who went through a rather difficult divorce more than ten years ago. Although she is certainly a very capable woman, it was her husband who looked after all of their money matters, including the earning of it. As a result of the circumstances surrounding her divorce, my friend became very bitter about men in general and adamant to the extreme that it was now no one's responsibility but her own to provide for herself and her two children. Fortunately, she was able to earn enough money to maintain her previous lifestyle and, after a while, even to do some things she'd not been able to do before. I saw her often, and we always talked about how well she was doing. She was proud of her ability to make money and of her children's recent accomplishments. But it was never very long before the conversation shifted to how stupid most people (especially men) are, how most needy people (especially men) are, and that she herself didn't need anybody. That part of the conversation was never pleasant and always focused on her most recent trials, travails, and challenges. Each time we parted company, I was left with very mixed feelings—happy, certainly, that my friend was independent and financially stable, but also sad that she seemed so defiantly, self-righteously unhappy.

■ ■ ■

At the opposite end of the spectrum from my friend who was so determined never to "need" anyone again are those who are attempting to live vicariously by experiencing themselves through others. Their insecurity makes them needy; they require another person, such as a child, a spouse, or a friend, to complete them. They've written their own story but live with the constant need to have it validated by others. And while they may think they're being loving and caring, they are invariably placing an impossibly heavy burden on the one they claim to love.

That has been the unfortunate experience of Ed, a forty-four-year-old man whose sixty-five-year-old mother has called him no fewer than three times a day, every day, for more than twenty years. During that time, Ed has also visited his mother almost every day. In fact, Ed cannot go anywhere or do anything without his mother being the first to know. Ed is now engaged to be married and, although his mother likes his fiancée just fine, she also thinks the bride-to-be has a lot to learn about life and especially about Ed. Every day Ed and his mother talk about his relationship with his fiancée and about their wedding plans, and every day the conversation deteriorates into an argument. Because he wants to appease his mother, Ed usually gives in and lets her have her way. He then faces his fiancée and pleads with her to understand. Ed's mother is in denial of her essential aloneness, and her denial is now having a negative effect on her relationship with her son, the person she loves the most.

■ ■ ■

Finally, there are those who attempt to deny their aloneness by demanding that others see the world exactly as they do, which—as I've already said—is simply not possible. We've all met these people. They're the bossy ones who're always telling us what we've *got* to do or what we've *got* to understand. If they can make us see things from their point of view (which we can't do, since we can't stand in their shoes, look through their eyes, or process with their brain), they believe, they'll no longer be alone.

When we were growing up, my brothers and I used to joke about our uncle Norm, a nice enough man with many fine qualities who, nonetheless, had a very particular way of communicating. Even as little kids, we knew how every conversation with Uncle Norm would go. Perhaps he'd see some tomatoes from our garden sitting on the counter. Uncle Norm would then puff on his ever-present cigar and say, "Last year I grew some tomatoes that were the size of cantaloupes. You see, what you gotta do is . . ." And then he'd go on to tell us how to grow tomatoes. Or perhaps he'd see a postcard someone had sent while on vacation. In that case, we'd be sure to hear about where we should go on vacation, what to do when we got there, and perhaps even what and how to pack. Actually, Uncle Norm was happiest when we were at his house, eating his food, cooked the way he liked it, and letting him know how good it was. He desperately needed the constant validation that resulted from knowing others shared his view of the world.

HOW OFTEN DO YOU SEEK VALIDATION?

Take some time to think about all the interactions you've had with various people during the past several days. Whatever was the subject of your conversation—movies, food, work, vacation, the weather—consider how much of what you said reflected your own thoughts and feelings rather than those of the person with whom you were interacting. The next time you have a conversation with that individual, try asking questions that will draw out his or her thoughts and feelings. Pretend you're a talk show host asking your guest about issues or events in his or her life that will interest your audience. If you pay close enough attention, you may begin to hear more than what he or she thinks or feels. In fact, if you listen carefully, you might just hear a revelation of his or her driving myths. ■

However much we deny it, and whatever compensatory behaviors we indulge in, our aloneness will, nevertheless, remain a fundamental aspect of our existence. Wouldn't the sane choice be, therefore, to accept it? Once we understand and accept that each of us is essentially alone in our world, it becomes easier and more logical to accept the fact that we cannot control anything or anyone other than ourselves. And, the greater our level of awareness, the less interest we'll have in trying to control things we can't.

I remember as a child having one of those toy steering wheels that attaches to the dashboard of a car. As I sat on the passenger side of the car, I actually believed I was doing the steering, and I was fascinated with that toy. But once I realized my control of the steering mechanism was only a fantasy, I quickly lost interest and stopped trying to steer. Once we realize a behavior isn't useful, if it doesn't serve any purpose, we're much more likely to be willing to give it up.

I'd like to suggest, however, that, having accepted your lack of control, you can look at it from a different perspective that will allow you to change the context within which you view your aloneness and to embrace it as a gift rather than fear it. Think of it this way: If we have no control over anyone or anything other than ourselves, it must be equally true that no other person or situation can have control over us. Our life is ours alone, and we can choose what we want to do with it. We can have power in it. That's a gift we ought to embrace—but it's also a responsibility.

The Gift of Responsibility

Both the gift and the responsibility of accepting our aloneness hark back to the fact that "we are the stories we tell ourselves we are." In other words, it is our responsibility, and ours alone, to discover and define our own meaning. That responsibility goes hand in hand with the gift of our autonomy and freedom of choice. If we create good stories for ourselves, and if our behaviors are governed by positive driving myths, our lives will be more fulfilling. If the stories we create do not serve us well, it is our responsibility to rewrite them. Before we can learn how to do that, however, we need to become highly aware of ourselves. We need to become conscious of when our thoughts, behaviors, and actions are being driven by our fears, our neediness, and our egos.

Clearly, then, it is also our responsibility to examine ourselves in order to determine whether our behaviors are serving us well and producing the outcomes we desire, and, if we determine that they are not, to change the context of our story. Luckily, you already have all the tools you need to do that. You've spent your entire life defining reality and reacting to your definitions, although chances are—if you still feel there's something missing or your life isn't as meaningful as you'd wish it to be—that it may be time for you to begin examining the *way* you form your definitions and create your stories. Up until now, you've been using the tools you have as well as you know how, but as your level of understanding increases, your behavior will change to meet that higher level of understanding.

When you first start a new job, chances are you won't do it as well as you will after you receive some training. Or let's say you enjoy fishing; chances are that if you know the correct bait, which lures, and the proper rod to use, you'll catch more fish than if you didn't know those things. In the same way, practicing being aware of your aloneness will diminish your desire to try to control things you can't.

PRACTICING ALONENESS

When you're feeling out of control—angry, anxious, fearful, whatever—
try taking the following four steps:

1. First change your context. Say to yourself, "I have no control over
   it, but I have power in it. This is reality."
2. Then ask, "Does this emotion, feeling, or behavior serve me?"
3. Then ask yourself, "So, where is my power? What is the best thing
   I can do that will make the greatest difference?"
4. Then do it.

Remember that the goal here isn't to be comfortable but rather to learn
how to better deal with the discomfort you're already feeling. The solution to getting rid of bad feelings isn't to ignore them or avoid them but
to think and do things that will reduce their negative effects on your life
and eventually make them go away. ■

Examining or considering ourselves is something we do every
day, in the course of our every interaction, because it's virtually impossible for us to consider our world *without* considering ourselves.
Since we experience the world from our own unique perspective,
with our own unique perceptions, we can *never* truly be completely
objective observers.

Ralph Waldo Emerson said, "We can't give our opinions about
anything without revealing a piece of ourselves." Think about it.
Even on the most mundane level, every one of our likes and dislikes
reflects some aspect of who we are. Let's say you and a friend go to
the movies together. Afterward, you exchange "reviews" of the film
you've just seen. Your friend says, "Oh, I didn't really like it. It was
too sad."

"But it was very moving," you say. "That's exactly why I did
like it."

You're each revealing something about your own unique reality,
something of who you are. And the same is true of any reaction that
reflects what we might call "personal taste" or "sensibility." How
you see the world reflects who you are, and who you are determines

how you see the world. Your world is *always* subjective because it is a direct reflection of your story.

Unfortunately, most of this self-reflection takes place unconsciously, which means that we may be allowing less than positive stories or contexts to prevent us from elevating the personal meaning we all seek. To change those contexts and stories, we need to consciously think first about what particular people, places, or things we find either attractive or repelling, and then to consider what it is about ourselves that has led us to those conclusions.

Timothy Miller, Ph.D., might have been discussing the importance of context when, in his book *How to Want What You Have*, he explained one of the tenets of cognitive psychotherapy, which, he said,

> holds that emotions and behaviors originate from thoughts, which in turn originate from beliefs. Thoughts are often repetitive and illogical, and beliefs are often incorrect. In short, the thoughts and beliefs that produce unhappy feelings and unwanted behaviors are essentially bad habits. Repetitive, harmful thoughts can be monitored, and they can often be altered the same way that other bad habits are altered. When habitual, harmful thoughts are altered, people feel better and behave more constructively.

A couple—we'll call them Mary and Bill—who happen to be friends of mine, recently asked me to help them with a problem that was creating difficulties in their relationship. Of course, I agreed to do whatever I could. Mary and Bill both defined the problem as Bill's impatience. Although Bill could always provide a good reason for becoming impatient, it seemed that his impatience always sparked an argument, and those arguments were becoming more and more frequent.

After listening to them for some time, I decided that what I needed to do was to help Bill find a better context within which to view those times when he felt self-righteously impatient.

"You know," I began, "this is a common challenge for a lot of people and has been for thousands of years." (That opening validated both Mary's assessment of where the problem lay and Bill's right to his impatience.) "In fact," I went on, "Your problem brings to mind a quote from an ancient philosopher named Lao-tzu. Back in 604 B.C. Lao-tzu said that, when we face difficult circumstances that try our patience, it's important that we teach ourselves to 'respond rather than react.'" I then went on to explain that in the context of Lao-tzu's definition, there is a key distinction between a response and a reaction. A reaction is instant, fully charged by emotion, and devoid of consciously directed thought, whereas a response is more measured because it is driven more by thought and consideration than by emotion. A reaction does not consider its own consequences, whereas a response is *determined* by considered consequences.

After that, we went on to discuss some of the situations that had caused Bill to become impatient, and I asked him to tell me whether he felt he'd reacted or responded in those situations. Once he agreed that he would define his words and actions as reactions, I asked him to explain what he would have said and done differently if he'd chosen to respond instead of reacting. Bill was able to find a way he might have responded in each of these situations, which indicated that he clearly understood the difference. But, he went on to point out, while it might be relatively easy in retrospect to talk about how one *could* have responded, it would be much more difficult for him to actually do that in the moment.

I asked Bill if he thought it would be impossible or merely difficult. "Well," he replied, "I'm sure it's not impossible." I then asked him if he thought the greater peace and comfort he'd feel, not to mention how it would improve his relationship with Mary, would be well worth any amount of effort, and he indicated that it would. I told him that I agreed with him but that I knew it would also require a strong will and a good mind, both of which, thankfully, were at his disposal. He nodded.

We agreed that with diligence and practice it would probably become easier for him to choose when he would do well to respond rather than react. I also made sure Bill knew that both Mary and I understood that he might still sometimes react when he should respond, and because we knew that he was sincerely doing the best he could as often as he could, we would forgive him.

"You know," said Bill, "This makes sense. It just might work.

But, Joe, I have one more question. What about when people are simply being so stupid that you just can't handle it?"

"Oh, yes." I replied. "I forgot to tell you. Old Lao-tzu had advice for those times also. In fact, I remind myself of these words quite often in my own life. He said, 'Respond intelligently even to the unintelligent.' "

■ ■ ■

Although, as I've said, we can never be truly objective about ourselves, we need to be as dispassionate and candid as possible as we examine the roots of our unproductive behaviors in order to access the power we all have within ourselves to find greater meaning in our lives. Each of us needs good contexts, meanings, and definitions in order to live a good life.

"Isn't That Interesting!"

When most of us begin to truly examine ourselves, if we discover something we're less than pleased with, we tend to do one of three things: We overlook it, we justify it, or we punish ourselves for it. The rational thing to do would be to change it, but most of us never get that far.

A woman named Cynthia, who works for a longtime client who happens to service the movie industry in Los Angeles, asked if she could talk with me one-on-one. When we sat down together, she began to tell me about the many challenges she was currently facing—"recovering" from a recent divorce, dealing with some minor health issues, and battling an ongoing weight problem that was the legacy of "all kinds of childhood issues." She summarized her story by saying that life is always a struggle but that all in all, things were good.

I told her it sounded as if she'd had a very interesting life, and she readily agreed. I then suggested that her life had all of the makings of a movie except for one. Being so familiar with the industry, that comment piqued her curiosity, as I knew it would, and she immediately wanted to know which element was missing. "Well," I said, "as a member of the audience watching your life story, I'm sure I'd be interested in the characters and caught up in the drama of it all. I'm sure I'd cry when you went through your more difficult times and cheer when you had your various victories. The part I'd miss, the part that I'd want to see and feel, is the part where you celebrate what you're passionate about, the part where you're doing what you love and actually having fun with it." She agreed that was an element that was, indeed, missing in her life.

I suggested that she'd been so busy paying attention to her troubles that she had none left to give to developing and nurturing her passions. I suggested that her childhood had ended a long time ago and that if we walked through the building, I could point out any number of people who were facing much greater and more debilitating health issues than she. I told her that she'd been doing a great job making every other part of her movie dramatic and interesting. Now it was time to bring her passion into the picture.

Cynthia agreed and promised to do just that. Some months later, on a subsequent visit to the company, I had the opportunity to ask her about her health and some of the other problems we'd discussed. She shrugged off my question and asked me to stop by her desk so that she could show me pictures of the beautiful flowers she was growing in her new flower gardens. It seems that Cynthia had decided to expend less energy rationalizing her woes and more energy developing her passion.

To some extent, we all need to rationalize and justify ourselves; it's what allows us to believe our emotions and actions are sane. But we should be conscious of when we're doing it, which is the first step toward accepting ourselves. I, for example, love fast food. I know it isn't good for me, but I rationalize and justify my behavior by telling myself (or you, if you asked me) that I don't have any other bad dietary habits, I don't eat it that often, and I eat enough "healthful" food to allow myself this minor indulgence. I'm sure you also have habits you know to be "bad" that you rationalize and justify in much the same way. No harm, no foul, I say, so long as you're *aware* that whatever you're doing isn't really good for you and it isn't doing any really great damage either to you or to others. It's when you tell yourself it *isn't* bad for you that you begin to run into trouble. Rationalization without realization is the problem.

But most of us resist examining ourselves too closely because we're afraid of what we might find. We're so invested in maintaining our self-respect that we don't ever want to expose what we consider our flaws or mistakes even to ourselves. As result of this fear, any attempts we do make at introspection become compensatory. We'll either ignore or choose not to see what we really should be looking at, or we'll go overboard in the other direction and be too judgmental of ourselves, playing the role of our own personal drill sergeant and forever punishing ourselves for any failure to live up to our own high standards.

If you've ever watched an international figure-skating competition, you know how important the execution of each jump and spin is to the skater's technical score. And you've seen more than one elite athlete brought down by his or her own nerves. But if you've watched the exhibition programs that always follow the competitions, you've also seen how much freer those same skaters are when they know there are no judges keeping score. I suggest that in order to explore yourself with as much objectivity and as little fear as possible, you dismiss the judge that resides in your psyche and think of what you're doing as an exhibition skate.

■ ■ ■

It was Ben Zander, director of the Boston Philharmonic and the prestigious World Youth Orchestra, who provided me with one of the best exercises I know for reducing self-censure and increasing objectivity. He told me that every year, when the students who've worked so hard to earn their place in the orchestra arrive for rehearsal, they're so terrified of making a mistake and perhaps being judged as less than worthy by either the director or their peers that they actually play too carefully. They're paying so much attention to getting the notes right that their playing lacks any feeling or passion.

Knowing that this is going to happen, he's come up with what has turned out to be a foolproof way to relax them and loosen them up. At the beginning of every season he issues an edict. He tells his students that he wants them to play with as much passion as they have. He acknowledges that in order to do that, they will be more likely to make mistakes. The maestro then instructs his orchestra members about what to do if and when they make a mistake. Anyone who makes a mistake is to immediately stop playing, throw up his or her hands, and say out loud, "Isn't that interesting!" With that, he picks up his baton and starts the piece again. Only this time, the students play their hearts out. Sure enough, it's only a matter of time before one of them hits a clunker and yells out, "Isn't that interesting!" And each exclamation is followed by two things—a bit of laughter and even more passionate music.

If you, too, throw up your hands and say "Isn't that interesting!" each time you discover some emotion or behavior you'd rather ignore, justify, or punish yourself for, I guarantee that it will help you begin to see and accept yourself more objectively. It might even make you smile. And it will give you the freedom and courage to look at more and more of your behaviors and emotions, which will in turn increase your understanding, lead to your making better connections, and ultimately improve and elevate the meaning of your life.

Remember Bill, who had a problem with patience? Understanding the meaning of the words *respond* and *react* provided him with a more useful context for choosing his own words and actions. But those words also served another purpose. They provided both Mary and Bill with a phrase they could use to remind themselves when they were in one of those moments where they could practice responding. In that way, the phrase served as their own private version of "Isn't that interesting!"

In order to *change* the way we think, act, or feel, we first have to give ourselves permission to think, act, or feel in a way that doesn't serve us. Further, we have to accept that it's okay and even intelligent of us to be able to recognize and acknowledge to ourselves when that is happening. We might even go so far as to call ourselves brilliant simply *because* we realize our thoughts, actions, or ideas are not serving us. We can't fix problems we don't see.

What Are You Afraid Of?

Gerald G. Jampolsky, in his book *Love Is Letting Go of Fear*, has this to say about these two most basic emotions:

We are always expressing either love of fear. Fear is really a call for help . . . a request for love. Fear and love can never be experienced at the same time. By choosing love more consistently than fear, we can change the nature and quality of our relationships.

When I asked Todd Davison, Chairman of the Department of Psychology at Columbia Hospital in Milwaukee, Wisconsin, to explain to me *how* we express our emotions through either love or fear, he said simply, "Joe, it's a biological fact."

The autonomic nervous system, which controls our body's involuntary physiological reactions to stimuli (such as our pupils' retracting in bright light), is divided into two parts: the sympathetic nervous system and the parasympathetic nervous system. When we're frightened or under extreme stress, the sympathetic nervous system sends out chemical "messages" that cause, among other physical reactions, our hearts to beat faster, our mouths to go dry, and our blood vessels to contract. These physiological reactions in turn affect our sensory perception, including our peripheral vision. You may have experienced these reactions as what is commonly called "fight or flight syndrome." When we're in this condition, it's physiologically impossible for us to be "seeing things clearly," and our actions or reactions are not "natural"—they're compensating for our fears. When the crisis is over, the parasympathetic nervous system sends out other chemical messages that return all systems to normal.

A client named Susan recently told me of a personal experience during which she became literally blinded by fear. She was visiting Disney World with her entire extended family when she suddenly realized that her five year-old daughter was missing from their group. Everyone panicked and began calling the child's name. Susan raced to the lost and found. By the time she got there her heart was pounding, her mouth was dry, and she was perspiring heavily. She ran up to the first Disney employee she saw and frantically screamed that her daughter was missing. She went on to describe what the little girl was wearing, and where and when she'd last seen her. She'd been pleading with the young worker for several minutes before he could finally get her to pay attention long enough to see that her daughter had been sitting right next to him all along.

Susan had actually been physically blinded by her fear. Her thoughts drove her sympathetic nervous system into a "fight or flight" mode that restricted her capacity to see. When she told me this story, she described her field of vision as being "like wearing blinders." She couldn't see anything except the guy she was screaming at.

When we're operating out of fear, we can count on our biology to respond in kind. Our sympathetic nervous system will create physiological changes that restrict blood flow to some areas of our bodies and provide more to others. While this reaction can give us increased strength and speed, it can also limit what we see and what we are capable of considering or thinking about.

■ ■ ■

Like fear, love comes in many guises: You can love your spouse, your children, your parents, your siblings, your friends, your pets, even yourself. You love each one in a different way, but there's always one common denominator—acceptance. To love others is to accept them. And, similarly, to love ourselves is to accept ourselves as we really are, which obviously also requires that we know our true selves.

If we don't feel that we're getting or giving love or acceptance at any given moment, from or to ourselves or anyone else, it's almost always because we're afraid. If we're angry or judgmental or experiencing any other negative emotion, the root cause of our feeling is fear.

When I first thought about it, I wondered whether I could really prove the truth of that statement, because if I could, it would be a tool I could use for managing myself. And so I decided to test it both on myself and on those I met in random circumstances, even on people I didn't know and hadn't spoken to. While I was in the throes of my little experiment, I overheard a woman in noisy argument with the clerk behind the check-in reservations counter at a hotel. She was clearly so angry about what she perceived to be some lack of service that she wasn't even listening to what the young man had to say. What could she have been afraid of? I asked myself. And the answer was immediately clear: She was afraid that she was in some way being taken advantage of.

And then there was the teenager stamping her foot and crying because her father had just told her she had to be home by midnight. Apparently she was afraid that her friends would think she was a baby and leave her out of their plans altogether.

Or think back again to my friend who was divorced and overly self-sufficient. She was clearly hurt and angry, but what was she afraid of? Probably that if she entered another relationship, she'd just be dumped again.

Try it yourself the next time you get somewhat annoyed or angry about something you're reading in this book. It's certainly not a failure on your part, but you can use it as an opportunity to stop and reflect, think about the exact point at which what you were reading made you angry, and ask yourself, "What is it he was telling me that made me afraid?" Just doing that will give you the power to change the context within which you were considering what you read and provide an opportunity for you to change the way you've chosen to respond to it.

THREE NEGATIVE THOUGHTS

Sometimes we're in a bad mood for no apparent reason, but sometimes things happen that can put us into a bad mood. Either way, the next time you're walking or riding down the street and make three observations in a row to which you attach a negative emotion—such as (1) someone cuts in front of you, and your first impulse is to do the same to him, (2) you see a GOING OUT OF BUSINESS sign on a storefront and immediately decide the economy is going down the tubes, and (3) it starts to rain, and you decide the bad weather will prevent you from getting home at the hour you'd planned—stop yourself, throw up your hands, and say out loud, "My, isn't that interesting? I'm in a bad mood. I wonder what I'm afraid of." Now, give yourself credit for recognizing your mood, and see if there were three positive conclusions you could have drawn from those same observations.

I have a friend named Barbara who never seems to be bothered by someone's cutting in front of her on the freeway. Once, when I was driving with her and somebody rudely and dangerously cut in front of her, I asked her if she ever got mad when that happened. "Well," she said, "I used to, but I don't anymore. I decided a long time ago that it didn't do me any good to have something that lasts for three seconds bother me for three hours."

"That's great," I said. "But how did you stop getting mad?"

"Oh, that's easy and actually kind of fun. You see, when someone cuts me off, I make up his story for him—or her, because sometimes it's actually a woman. And instead of giving him a bad story like, 'This is a jerk who doesn't know how to drive and has no respect for the safety of others,' the way I used to, I give him a good story. I tell myself that he must be on his way to the hospital where his wife is about to give birth to their new baby. I realized that whether it's a good story or a bad one, I'm writing it for him, so I might as well write one that makes me feel better rather than worse."

In the case of being cut off on the highway, it's not too hard to figure out that the fear driving our anger is probably the fear of being involved in an automobile accident. Barbara, however, recognized that her anger wouldn't help her to avoid that, and so she discovered a way to find her power in the situation by dealing with both her fear and her anger.

Doing this exercise will allow you to separate your perceptions from your conclusions and realize that your conclusions are actually *your choice*. That understanding will help you to shift your perspective and proceed with a more positive outlook. ■

If we're angry, then we need to look for the fear that's fueling the anger, because it's always easier to acknowledge fear than anger. Fear, after all, is not, in and of itself, necessarily bad. It can, in the proper circumstances, save our lives. Anger, on the other hand, is an emotion we've been taught we ought to control or suppress, so acknowledging our anger will generally make us feel worse about ourselves. What we need to understand, however, is that both anger and the underlying fear that fuels it are perpetuated by our desire to be right. When we feel afraid, we have no problem validating our fear, which, of course, makes us feel even more afraid. When we're angry, we can come up with great reasons for justifying that, too, because if we couldn't justify it to ourselves, we'd have to admit we were wrong. Once we begin to become more aware of how our desire to be right drives us, we can use even that awareness to our own advantage.

I did just that not too long ago when I was flying from Los Angeles to Miami for a speaking engagement. For various reasons, I had to change planes twice, and by the time I boarded my final flight I was hungry, cranky, and not in the mood to deal with the obviously angry eleven-year-old girl who was my seatmate. She was huffing and puffing, sighing and fidgeting, and clearly wanting me to acknowledge that she was *mad!* So when I turned to her and asked in my most sympathetic voice, "Having a bad day?" she immediately launched into a long-winded recitation of the many wrongs that had been done her in the course of her journey. I could see where this was leading and decided to cut it off at the pass. "Well, then," I said, "I can see you have a right to be mad. How long do you think you're going to stay angry?"

She thought for a minute and said, "Fifteen minutes."

"Good, then," I replied, opening my book, "I'll talk to you in fifteen minutes." I used her desire to be right to work to my advantage. You've chosen to be mad, I was saying, and if you're that smart and powerful, then you must also have the power to decide when you'll be "unmad." If she wanted to maintain her need to be right, she would also have to be "right" about when she'd stop being angry. I gave her a way to choose to stop being angry.

Fifteen minutes later, I set my book aside and said, "So, where are you from?" It was the beginning of a delightful conversation with one of the smartest, most endearing eleven-year-old girls I've ever met.

For the most part, however, justifying your anger simply means that you'll never truly know what created it, which means you won't know how to end it, either. We'll be talking a lot more about fear and how to let go of it in Chapter 5 but suffice it to say for now that the more objectively we're able to examine ourselves, the more we'll understand about ourselves, the better able we'll be to accept ourselves, and the better equipped we'll be to manage and change those behaviors and emotions that are preventing us from creating better meanings for ourselves.

And, of course, we must remember that the *only* aspect of our lives we're able to control and manage is ourselves.

You and Your Secondary World

If you are the sole inhabitant of your primary world, then everyone and everything outside yourself belongs to your secondary world— the world over which you have no control. To understand that concept, it might help you to think of yourself driving your car in traffic. How you interact with the other cars on the road is vital to your own well-being, but you have no direct control over any car other than your own. All you can do is to be certain that your own car is well maintained and that you drive it with as much care and awareness as possible. You have power in your ability to handle and maintain your own car but no control over anyone else's.

The problem with trying to find your own meaning or self-definition in terms of your relationships with elements of your secondary world—be they spouses, children, jobs, wealth, fame, or . . . you name it—is that you have no control over those relationships. They can change, deteriorate, or simply go up in smoke at any time, and if that happens, who will you be then?

■ ■ ■

Dr. Mihaly Csikszentmihalyi, a psychologist and the noted author of *Flow: The Psychology of Optimal Experience*, has said that one of the major constraints placed on people's ability to enjoy what they're doing is that they're always conscious and in fear of how they appear to others and what others might think of them, which is, to my mind, just another way of saying that they define themselves through their relationships with others.

I had the privilege of meeting with Dr. Csikszentmihalyi in his office at the University of Chicago, and I took advantage of the opportunity to ask him what he thought of my theory concerning the negative impact of defining oneself in terms of external circumstances that would inevitably change. Here's what he had to say in response:

When they ask me how I got interested in this kind of thing, I say it was really when I was a kid in World War Two. I was ten years old in Europe, and as the war ended, most of our family and acquaintances lost either their jobs or their family or their money and house, which burned or was bombed. I could see all these people falling apart, not having anything to draw on. Except, then, you find one or two people who seem to take it all in stride and do something about it . . . and essentially that's when I decided that there is something here that nobody's talking about. What's the difference between these types of people? Why do most people collapse when you take away the supports? The supports are the job, family, et cetera. And how come some of them keep staying up? This is a major part of my work also. It's a critical element of being able to find flow in life.

As Dr. Csikszentmihalyi confirmed to me in that discussion, it's critical to our mental and emotional well-being that we learn to accept the specifics of our lives that we can't control while at the same time finding our power in those things we can control. Or, as Plato put it more than three hundred years before the birth of Christ, "The man who makes everything for happiness depend on himself, and not upon other men, has adopted the very best plan for happiness."

And yet, if you refer to the title of this chapter, you'll see that it says, "We're all in this together . . . alone." How then, in our aloneness, do we form those connections that bring us together?

Making Connections in Your Secondary World

Our aloneness does not mean that we're all destined to be lonely. To the contrary, I don't for a minute deny that our associations and connections with the people and circumstances in our secondary world are very much part of the way most of us define ourselves. And, in fact, those connections and associations unequivocally serve to edify our meaning—but only so long as the core or foundation of our self-definition remains separate and apart from those connections.

To understand why this is so true, you've only to think about love and romance. If love is based on need, it must also stem from fear—the fear that the person we most need won't "need us back," or won't need us anymore, or won't need us at all, and will, therefore, leave us. And, as we've already discussed, any emotion driven by fear cannot at the same time be driven by love. In time, our fear will manifest itself as manipulation, jealousy, competition, or other emotions and behaviors that will destroy the relationship. And, just as important, if we define ourselves through others, we have, in fact, lost our own selfhood, because, as I've said, if we lose that relationship, we'll also have lost ourselves.

■ ■ ■

If, on the other hand, you truly know yourself, commit yourself to understanding and managing yourself, and find the power within yourself to achieve the goals that will enhance and elevate the meaning of your life, you will find that your ability to influence others through your example will be exponentially enhanced.

Let's reconsider for a moment the story of Gandhi, who, as I said in the previous chapter, was able to change the lives of millions of others for the better. There are two stories about this great leader that clearly demonstrate not only the source of his great power but also his awareness of that source. The first story involves a reporter who ran up to Gandhi's train just as it was pulling out of the station, breathlessly begging for some message he could take back to his people. Gandhi hurriedly scribbled a few words on a scrap of paper and handed it out the window to the reporter. On the paper he had written, "My life is my message."

Another episode in the great man's life demonstrates how the same ability to lead by example remains equally valid on a much more intimate scale. A mother brought her young son to Gandhi, saying, "Gandhi-ji, my son eats too much sugar, and it's bad for his teeth. Please tell him to stop."

Gandhi asked the woman to please return with her son in two weeks, and when she did, he looked the little boy in the eyes and said, "You shouldn't eat so much sugar. It's bad for your teeth."

The mother thanked him profusely and, as she and her son were leaving, asked, "But why didn't you simply tell him this two weeks ago?"

"Because," Gandhi replied, "two weeks ago I was still eating sugar."

Selfish or Selfless? The Power of Influence

Our culture is so aware of how "bad" it is to be selfish that many people will go so far as to mangle the English language just in order to avoid using the word *me* in a sentence for fear of even *appearing* to be selfish. And yet "selflessness" is really nothing more than a mythical ideal because true selflessness would require a total obliteration of the self.

With that conundrum in mind, let's take one final look at the life of Gandhi. If I asked, you'd probably agree that he was one of the most selfless human beings ever to walk the earth. And yet it's also possible to look upon his life and activities as totally selfish, because he did everything his way without ever considering anyone else's point of view. In fact, virtually everything any one of us does could be considered selfish because it's always the result of a decision we make for ourselves. What is it, then, that makes one person selfish and the other selfless? The difference lies in whether that action helps to elevate your own meaning *by serving something greater than yourself*.

Since your control stops with yourself, your only power lies in focusing on yourself and doing what you can to make yourself happy. And if that's true, I propose to you that the way to truly make yourself happy and at peace with yourself is to elevate the meaning of your life by acting in a way that serves some good greater than yourself. If your selfish behavior isn't doing that, it isn't serving you, and once you become aware of that, you have the power to change it.

Once more it comes down to the fact that we are all alone in our primary world. The better you understand that, the more able you will be to accept and manage yourself, to become happier and more confident.

And the more secure you are within yourself, the better able you will be to make meaningful connections with those in your secondary world and use your power of influence to help them enhance the meaning of their lives because you'll be leading by example.

■ ■ ■

In the following chapter, I'll be talking more specifically about how to make connections in your secondary world that will reward and elevate not only your own meaning but also that of those with whom you connect. For now, however, it's important to reiterate that the *only* power you have in that world is the power of influence.

The most successful negotiators know this only too well and use that knowledge to their advantage. They don't waste their energy trying to control the people on the other side of the table over whom they know they have no control. Instead, they use their energies in order to persuade, and they know that when they do get the other party to agree to some kind of compromise it's because they've been able to demonstrate that there's a different way to do things that will serve them better than the old way. Once people realize that what they're doing doesn't serve them—as I did when I discovered I wasn't really steering my father's car—they are more likely to begin to lose interest in it and become willing to consider the new way. But if those negotiators believed they could control the people with whom they were negotiating, they wouldn't see any need to pay attention to them, to listen to them, to make connections with them—and as a result, they'd be unable to reach a positive outcome.

Paradoxically, we make meaningful connections with other people by accepting the reality of our aloneness and finding power in our ability to understand, accept, and manage ourselves. This, in turn, can give us more power to influence others through our example and our words.

Chapter 4

Making Connections Count

> *The most important single ingredient in*
> *the formula of success is knowing how to*
> *get along with people.*
>
> —Theodore Roosevelt

The term "rules of engagement" is actually a military phrase that's used to delineate the circumstances under which troops can initiate or continue combat. In this chapter, I'll be using it in quite a different sense. Just as there are rules that guide the human experience in our primary world, there are those that apply any time we attempt to connect with anyone in our secondary world. I've found that there are four fundamental rules that are always at work, whether we're aware of them or not, and I call these four rules the Rules of Engagement.

We are all, as I hope I've already made clear, alone in our primary world. But it's in our secondary world that we operate every day of our lives, and it's only through making connections and forming relationships within that secondary world that we are able to elevate our meaning by enhancing the meaning of others. Ultimately, doing that is what will bring us happiness, and happiness, we've now learned, is our ultimate goal. But if we have no control over these people who, nevertheless, can be so important to our happiness and our meaning, what are we to do?

Know Your Gig

By this point you may be starting to see that the key to the happiness and success we seek is not how skilled or talented we are, but rather how well we can learn to understand, accept, and manage ourselves. Similarly, the first step toward making meaningful connections is to understand who you are within the context of your secondary world—in other words, to know your gig.

Gig is an expression taken from the world of music that's used as a synonym for *job*. To know your job is, in effect, to know your place in the world at any point in time and in every place over time. And, if you don't have a clear idea of what your job is in any given situation, there's no way you can do that job well. Here's a musical example to illustrate that musical definition:

■ ■ ■

I'd just come home from a business trip and stopped in a local Italian restaurant for dinner. There was a young woman at the piano who'd obviously been hired to provide background music for the restaurant's patrons. The only problem was that she didn't seem to be very good at it. She was all dressed up in a black velvet gown and certainly looked the part. But she was playing a Stevie Wonder tune that she didn't seem to know very well.

Because I thought I'd be able to help her out, I asked the waiter if she could come over for a moment during her break. When she did, I introduced myself and asked if she were a music student. "Why, yes," she said. "How did you know?" Well, I knew she was a student because it was clear that she wasn't a professional, but I wasn't about to tell her that. Instead, I asked where she went to school, and it turned out I knew her piano professor.

Because I was asking her questions and getting her to talk about herself rather than tooting my own horn, we'd already made a connection that allowed her to relax and feel comfortable with me. "Is this your first gig?" I asked, pretty sure that I already knew the answer to that one, as well. When she said it was, I asked how long she was supposed to play each night. Of course, it was the standard four hours of the dinner service, but the problem, I realized, was that this young woman knew only two hours' worth of tunes and was trying to fill in with songs she hadn't really mastered. She was relieved and grateful when I told her that she really had to know only enough songs to get through about an hour and a half because that's probably the longest time any one party of diners would be in the room.

I brought up the Stevie Wonder tune and said I'd noticed that she hesitated at a certain point. "I forgot the next chord," she admitted ruefully. "Well," I said sympathetically, "that can happen to anyone, but what you really need to do in that situation is vamp. Just keep playing, repeat the same chord if you have to, but don't stop. Your job is to provide background music, and that means no one's attention is really focused on what you're playing. As a 'recovering musician' who's played many a background music gig myself, I know that's hard to believe, but it's true. They're aware of the music on some subliminal level, but they're mainly concentrating on their meal. The only time they really pay attention to the music is when it stops, because they're aware—again on some subliminal level—that something has changed, and that makes them uncomfortable. So don't stop, and most people won't notice you've made a mistake."

Then I asked—again because I knew I could offer some good advice—if she was a voice major. (The answer to that one was a no-brainer since she clearly wasn't a piano major.) When she confirmed my obvious guess, I suggested that she sing while she played. "They don't want me to. They won't give me a mike," she lamented. "But you play better when you sing, don't you?" I asked. "So sing, even if it's only to yourself, even if no one else can hear you."

Relieved and thankful for the advice, she went back to the piano. I spent the rest of my dinner listening to some wonderful background music played by a much happier young musician who had found her confidence *and* her music by shifting the context within which she viewed her gig.

■ ■ ■

Before our conversation, this lovely young woman hadn't really known her gig. She didn't really understand that she wasn't supposed to be the center of attention. She was supposed to be providing background. She was supposed to be creating a pleasant but not intrusive ambience for the restaurant's patrons, and calling attention to herself in any way meant that she was not doing the job she'd been hired to perform. Not knowing her job meant that she didn't really know *herself* within the context of that particular moment in her secondary world. And her lack of self-knowledge was preventing her from forming a successful relationship with those in her secondary world—the diners in the restaurant—and from elevating her own meaning by enjoying the fruits of that success.

Have you ever had a friend call you to complain about something going on in his or her life? Quite often when that happens we want to help our friend by solving his or her problem. But if we fail to understand our gig, we might just be making our friend more upset, and his or her distress or anger might, in the long run, be directed toward us. Our gig, as defined by our friend, would be to listen empathetically, not to fix the problem, and if we misunderstand that, no solution we can come up with, no matter how persuasively we present it, will make him or her feel any better.

DEFINING YOUR GIG IN THE SPIRIT OF SERVICE

If, for whatever reason, you find yourself *uncomfortable* in a conversation with another person, try to determine what his or her definition of your gig might be. You feel yourself struggling to make a connection, and there's no power in struggling. Most of the time, whether he knows it or not, the person you're talking to is looking for validation. Remember, we're all more or less insecure, and we're all trying to validate our own meaning.

Try putting aside what the other person is *saying* and think about how he or she is trying to *feel*. If he needs to feel important, help him do that. If she's looking for empathy, empathize. Don't focus on your interpretation of the specific problem but on how the other person might be using that problem to connect with you and, through that connection, to feel a certain way. ■

How well you know your gig determines your value to others, which means that it determines how successful you'll be at making connections in your secondary world. It's through making those connections that we create our own happiness because, as John Donne so eloquently put it, "No man is an island." Life, in other words, is an interactive game, and it's not meant to be played alone.

Making Connections in Your Secondary World

Roger Dawson, renowned expert in the art of negotiation and author of *Secrets of Power Persuasion,* says that except for your health, your spirituality, and your happiness, almost everything you want in the future—be it love, money, respect, or anything else you can think of—is currently owned or controlled by someone else. And because almost everything we want in the future is owned or controlled by someone in our secondary world whom we can't control, the greatest power we have lies in our ability to influence other people so that they'll be willing either to give us what we want or to help us get it. And believe it or not, more often than not, their willingness to help us will be based on just one consideration—how much they like themselves when they're with us. In their primary world, it's all about them. And while you might think it's important that they like you, it's far more important that they like themselves when they're with you.

To illustrate how it works, here's a true story about how a $3.2-million business decision was based on just this principle.

I was attending the opening ceremony of a very large convention of travel managers from across the country. A few people recognized me from previous speaking engagements and approached me to make small talk. Among the group were four people, each of whom was responsible for making all the travel arrangements for his or her company, none of whom knew one another. In the course of our conversation, a manager named Lisa let everyone know that her company had just changed travel providers and that this was a $3.2-million contract. Everyone was properly appreciative of the scope of the decision, so I asked what I thought was an obvious question: "How did you decide whom you would go with?"

Lisa responded by proudly explaining the very sophisticated bidding process the prospective vendors had gone through. I let her know that I was duly impressed, but that her explanation still didn't answer my question.

"What do you mean?" she asked. "Do you want to know how we awarded point scores to the vendors based on various aspects of their offers?"

"No," I responded. "I'm not sure I could understand that even if you explained it to me. What I'd really like to know is much simpler. My guess is that after you applied your sophisticated scoring system to all these vendors, there were probably two or three who qualified. Am I right?"

"There were three," she confirmed.

"So now you're left with three qualified vendors; your system has done its job, and you still have to make the final decision. My question is, how did you decide who to go with?"

Everyone's gaze turned to Lisa, who was now furrowing her brow as she truly considered the essence of my question for the first time.

"Well," she said slowly, "I guess we went with the one we liked best."

The next day, I saw Lisa again and asked what she thought had swayed her decision more—how much she liked the particular vendor or how much she liked herself when she was with him. Her answer was emphatic. She said she'd liked all three of the leading candidates very much, but the one she'd chosen had made her feel smarter and more confident than she felt with the others.

Even in the cold, hard world of business, when decisions cost as much as $3.2 million, we still choose to help those who make us feel good about ourselves.

■ ■ ■

You can't, of course, *make* people like you. You can't *control* their reaction to you any more than you can control anything else in your secondary world. But if you'll stop trying to make people like you and concentrate instead on how you can make yourself more likeable, you'll discover the power that derives from understanding, accepting, and managing yourself in such a way that other people will *want* to form relationships with you because they value you. And they'll value you because you help them to value themselves when they're with you. And once they do that, they will also want to help you get what *you* want. That's the key to successful communication and the secret behind the Four Rules of Engagement.

The Four Rules of Engagement

1. Everyone is always right.

2. Everyone's greatest desire is to be right.

3. You can't change another person's mind.

4. You *can* help people shift their perspectives.

These are the four basic principles that are *always* in operation whenever one or more people are engaged in any kind of communication. I say "one or more" because even when we're alone, we're engaged in communication with ourselves—trying to talk ourselves into something or out of something, or seeking validation for something we already believe to be true. (In short, we all talk to ourselves.)

The rules are simple but incredibly powerful. They are based on the common human truths that drive us to think and behave the way we do. Over the last twenty years I've seen them work in both my professional and my private life. They are as true in boardrooms as bar rooms (or bedrooms), in every country and culture I've ever visited, without reference to age, sex, or ethnic background. In short, they are the driving force behind all human understanding and interaction. It would, therefore, behoove us all to master the rules and learn how to use them to our benefit, which means, ultimately, to the benefit of others, as well.

By learning to use them to our benefit, I don't mean learning to manipulate other people, because, as I hope I've made clear, we can't *make* anyone do anything he or she doesn't want to do, including like us. Nor do I mean using the rules to make us feel better about ourselves. If that's our primary purpose for forming relationships, it will be almost impossible to find the happiness we seek, because people will realize that we're really interested only in ourselves, and that will never make them want to be in our company. What the rules of engagement are really about is honoring the common humanness of others. People who need to count on these commonalities, like advertising and marketing executives, political advisors, and Hollywood directors, are very familiar with how to use these rules in their own way.

If you keep in mind that the person you're talking to is always the most important person in his or her world (just as you are in yours), you'll be honoring him or her. That's love, that's service, that's what allows other people to elevate their meaning, which will lead them to value you and thus bring greater meaning to your own life, as well. When we help people elevate their meaning, we are actually helping them to see themselves on a higher level. By "higher level" I mean that they will like themselves better. They will, to some degree, feel more positive and powerful about themselves and the world they live in, which may in turn help them to form more positive definitions and contexts for themselves.

If all of this sounds a bit too "touchy feely," for your taste, I'd like to tell you that I use these rules constantly as my guides for negotiating and communicating. When a client was about to sell his company for $25 million and almost lost the deal because he was feeling too cocky and forgetting to honor the guy who was going to write the check, it was adhering to the Rules of Engagement that allowed me to help him prevent the negotiations from going up in flames. And when a police officer—actually the friend of a friend, someone I didn't know at all—called me because she was sitting with her own gun pointed at her head and couldn't decide whether or not to pull the trigger, all I had to help me talk her through the crisis were the Four Rules of Engagement. Throughout our rather long conversation, I worked hard to stay focused on using the rules no matter what we were ostensibly talking about, and I was eventually able to talk her into putting down the gun so that she could get the help she needed.

There was even one occasion when the rules helped to save my own life. I had been to a late movie with friends and stopped to use the rest room before leaving the theater. Shortly after I entered, three tough-looking kids walked in. They were very boisterous and appeared to be high. I did my best to leave the room as quickly and calmly as I could, but before I could do that, one of them pulled a handgun that had been tucked into his waistband and began waving it at me as the others blocked the door. The situation quickly went from bad to worse, and the next thing I knew I was in a headlock with the gun pointed at my head while the four thugs laughed about "popping a cap" into me. I knew I couldn't overpower them, and it was perfectly apparent to me that the only weapon I had lay in the power of my words. I began to listen carefully to the words *they* were using and tried to consider what it was about those words that made them feel good about themselves. I then focused on trying to calmly reinforce that feeling while at the same time making my participation in their fun seem less important. After what seemed like an eternity (although I knew it was only a few minutes) they apparently decided I wasn't worth their effort and kicked me out of their bathroom.

So, as you see, I've staked both my life and my livelihood on the Four Rules of Engagement, and they haven't let me down yet.

Rule #1:
Everyone Is Always Right

According to Einstein, "There is no knowledge without experience," which really means that what we know or what we believe to be true is limited by our own experience, and as long as we believe it, it remains for us incontrovertible truth.

Before we developed the means to study matter on a subatomic level, classic Newtonian physics taught us that a particle was a particle and a wave was a wave. Now, however, quantum physics has confirmed not only that a particle will actually behave like a wave, and vice versa, if that's how they're measured, but also that both particles and waves can exist at different points simultaneously, depending again on how they're measured. In other words, how we choose to define or interpret the physical world on the subatomic level affects its actual reality. The observer becomes a participant in determining that reality. And the same is true for the human observation of everyday life.

Since each of us experiences the world from our own perspective, we are, from that perspective, always right about our own experience. And since we can define the world only as we see it, we are always, no matter whom we are talking to or what we are talking about, feeling a need to validate our story and make ourselves right. In other words, we are always in some way talking about ourselves. Once we can accept that, we can decide how to respond (talk about ourselves) to those in our secondary world in a way that will allow them to connect with us so that we can form mutually uplifting relationships.

Let's imagine for a moment that I'm sitting in front of my fireplace and talking on the phone. In the course of conversation, I mention how warm and cozy it is in front of the fire. Person A might respond by saying, "Oh, you use real logs? That's great." Person B might say, "I hate dealing with setting up and then cleaning up the mess of a wood fire, so I have a gas fireplace." And Person C might say, "Using real wood is too much of a hassle. I buy those prefab logs at the supermarket, and they work just fine for me."

Obviously, each of these people is really talking about himself, and what each of them wants is for me to validate his version of the truth. That leaves me with several choices. I could

- attempt to change his mind;

- decide I want this discussion to be about *me* and either redirect the conversation or change the subject;

- take a sincere interest in the other person's perspective (although I don't have to agree with it) and, by doing that, help him to edify his meaning.

If I want to develop a mutually satisfying relationship with any one of these people, there really is no choice. It's got to be the last. But how do I do that without compromising my own perspective? The most effective way is simply to ask them questions. "Oh, you prefer gas? Why is that?" "Do those prefab logs really work? Isn't that interesting?" By asking those questions, I'm allowing each person to tell his own story, to talk about *himself*. If I fail to do that, I fail to honor *him*. He'll hear that, and I'll have lost any chance of eventually getting him to consider *my* perspective, if that's my goal.

If I fail to understand that none of us is really talking about that fireplace and that each of these people, by offering his opinion, is actually presenting me with a piece of himself, I'll probably be missing the opportunity to honor his story about himself and his personal entitlement to be who he is. He will instinctively know that, and, in consequence, he won't want to be engaged in a relationship with me. Would you want to spend time with someone who was, in effect, belittling you by indicating that your opinion (and, hence, you) were less valuable or "true" than his own?

Here's another example to indicate how distinctly and completely each one of us is a collection of our own likes and dislikes. I was in a home-furnishings shop recently when I overheard a woman say to one of the salespeople, "I *hate* people who paint natural wood." I had to laugh to myself because it was so obvious that this woman's statement, were we to take it literally, would be patently ridiculous. Clearly she wasn't talking about hating thousands of people she'd never met. She was simply making a statement about her preference for natural, unpainted wood. But you can see how much that opinion was a part of her self-definition. How much chance would I ever have had of influencing her to consider a different perspective if I'd just barreled up to her and said, "Well, that's pretty dumb. I know some really nice people who use painted wood, and I think it looks just swell." Not much, right?

ASK, DON'T TEACH

Avoid trying to teach people. Instead, allow them to discover for themselves. I'm in the business of helping people learn, grow, and change. My income depends on how successful I am at doing that. While that may sound like a tough position to be in, I don't worry about it, because I don't try to teach or change anyone. Instead I've learned that my success depends on my allowing them to discover things for themselves.

I've learned to ask a lot of questions rather than give a lot of answers.

For example, when a client shows me how he or she approaches a certain element of his or her work, I first indicate that I am sincerely impressed. Then I ask questions like, How did you come up with that particular approach? What other ways have you tried? Does this approach offer any unique challenges for your internal or external customers? And so on.

Try it yourself.

Once you've practiced recognizing that everyone is always right, you can begin using this Rule of Engagement to facilitate communication.

Here are some tips that will help you to do that.

1. Remember to honor the other person's perspective. After all, he's right (from his perspective).
2. Ask the other person about his or her perspective. If you find it difficult to do that, you might want to think of yourself as an interested talk show host, as I suggested on page 49.
3. Practice offering other considerations only in the form of questions. (For a good example of this, remember how Jeannie got me to stop considering my death and start considering my life.) ∎

The first step toward forming a relationship with another human being, and thus having the opportunity to influence him or her in any way (to help you get what you want), must be to acknowledge his individual humanity and value because . . .

Rule #2:
Everyone's Greatest Desire Is to Be Right

If, as we already know, we are the stories we tell ourselves, we must, in order to validate our meaning, see the world as conforming to our story. Because, if we aren't right about our story, then who are we? It may be a lousy story, it may hurt rather than help us, it may bring us pain rather than love, but if it's ours, we'll cling to it with bonds of steel. In this way we go about our day with our subconscious adamantly saying, "That's my story, and I'm sticking to it," as opposed to, "That's my story, but I'll willingly and openly consider another version of me if you'd like." It's our personal driving myth, for us it's more powerful than truth, and for that reason we seek to make connections with people who will validate our myth and make us "right."

Individuals have been made miserable, and businesses have been destroyed by clinging to bad myths, and yet cling they have, and cling they will continue to do because neither people nor societies can act for any length of time in a way that is not congruent with their driving myth.

Carol Oleksiak is the Director of Child and Family Services at the prestigious Guidance Clinic in southeastern Michigan. She's counseled women, children, and families for more than fifteen years and has seen how some people's driving myths can affect their lives in very negative ways.

"A woman who has a background of neglect and emotional abuse will have a tendency to develop low self-esteem as a foundation for her personal driving myth," states Carol. "Often, this in turn gives her a propensity to find partners who will validate those messages she tells herself about herself. For example, if I felt that I were no good, it would be difficult to form a meaningful relationship with someone who tells me I'm wonderful, because I would think they were lying. Someone who is seductive enough to make me feel just good enough for me to want to be with him, yet who validated my driving myths about my low self-worth, would actually be more attractive to me on a psychological level. This is one of the reasons abusive men can find women to abuse, and abused women have trouble finding men who won't abuse them on some level. Of course, most people aren't even aware that they have a driving myth because so much of this goes on in their subconscious."

Sometimes we are victimized by some aspect of our own psychology without even knowing it. And those who would victimize us often use that same aspect of our psychology against us.

How does that happen? And how can we learn to protect ourselves from those who would prey upon us and use the power of our negative driving myths to hurt and victimize us? Let's just examine what we know about human interaction in the context of our driving myths and our psychological need to have them validated.

Since the middle of the last century, cognitive scientists have been studying the nature and limitations of our ability to send and process information. They have proved that we, as human beings, have the capacity to communicate—through gesture, expression, speech, and so on—up to 72,000 bits of information a minute, and we have the mental capacity to receive and process up to 7,560 bits per minute. The signals we send are always about ourselves—what we think, how we feel, and what we believe to be true. In other words, we have the ability to telegraph our driving myths on a regular basis to other people. And others have the ability to sense those myths on a number of levels. Counselors, psychologists, therapists, and social workers are quite familiar with the fact that, whether it is good for us or not, we will seek out those who will validate our myths and avoid those who contradict our myths. In other words, we will validate those who validate us.

■ ■ ■

While our personal myths are not the cause of other people's behavior, they can and do determine who we let into our lives and how we let them treat us. It's critical that we consciously understand how this happens and how deeply it can impact so many aspects of our lives. Although it would be nice, our greatest desire is not to be loved. It's to be right. Even if it hurts.

THE IMPORTANCE OF CONNECTING WITH YOURSELF

In order to start becoming aware of those times when your desire to be right hasn't served you, consider the arguments you may have had in order to prove you were right that, in retrospect, only caused you more distress or damaged a relationship to the point where proving your "rightness" simply wasn't worth the emotional turmoil. Think of the times you've said things you knew you shouldn't have because you just couldn't restrain yourself.

Now that you're aware of your own powerful desire to be right, try to use that awareness to become more tolerant of other people's need to be right and practice working harder to honor their perspective. You may find that your need to be right will not diminish (it is, after all, the foundation of the principle of congruency and essential to your understanding of the world), but you just might discover that you begin wanting to be right only about things that serve you and edify your relationships.

The more we become aware of when others do themselves a disservice by needing to be right all the time, the more we'll become more aware of how we ourselves may be guilty of the same thing. Then we can begin to work to make sure that our desire to be right helps us rather than hurts us.

My friend's twenty-year-old daughter, Lisa, did just that. Once, when we were talking about drugs, I asked her if she had any personal experience taking illegal drugs. "I used to," she said. "But I never will again." When I asked her why, she shook her head and said, "Because I watched how drug use made my friends change—and it wasn't for the better." ∎

Professionally, it's my job to help people shift their perspective and find better contexts; personally, it's my greatest desire since, if I can help them shift from a destructive or self-defeating perspective to one that is constructive and elevating, I'll have improved their lives and made my own more valuable. But I also understand that I must first acknowledge not only their right to their own point of view but also their need to believe that their view is the (one and only) correct one before I can introduce alternatives in a manner that might appeal to them.

I had the opportunity to do that recently when I was approached by Marilyn, a manager at one of the companies for whom I was consulting. She asked to talk with me, and I could tell right away that she was extremely upset about something. "Did you see that memo?" she demanded before I could even ask what was bothering her. The memo, which I had indeed seen, had to do with some aspect of corporate operations. "I'm going right in to talk to the VP of operations about it." And then she ranted on about how dumb the memo was and what she was going to do about it while I just smiled and nodded. I didn't have to say very much (she didn't stop long enough for me to respond); I just had to let her vent.

Finally, she ran out of steam. "Marilyn," I asked her, "did you know you are being considered for a team leader position? Do you want that job?"

"Of course I do," she said. "It's what I've been working for all this time."

"Well, then, isn't a team leader's job to bring solutions to people, not problems to management?"

She thought about that for only a minute before saying, "My goodness, I see what you mean. I can't do that, can I?"

"What can you do, then?" I asked.

She thought again before responding, "I can tell him some people might take that memo the wrong way. I could tell him that if he liked, I could review his memos before he sent them out."

"That's a great idea," I said.

I'd listened to Marilyn and honored her point of view, but I'd also allowed her to see that her perspective might not be serving her well in her particular situation. By the end of our conversation, she'd shifted that perspective to one that would serve her better. She no longer felt the need to prove the manager wrong, but she was still allowed to be right. She was just being right in a way that wouldn't hurt her. Happily, I did my job that day. I helped Marilyn find her power without denying her reality, and six months later, she was made a team leader.

What I didn't do was to try to argue her out of her planned course of action simply by telling her she was wrong. I knew I couldn't control what she was thinking because . . .

Rule #3:
You Can't Change Another Person's Mind

If we could change people's minds, we'd be controlling them, and we can't do that. In fact, even if we lock someone up, tie him hand

and foot, and torture him, we still can't control what he's thinking. And the harder we try to change someone else's mind, the more he's likely to resist. Why? Because of rule number two—everyone's greatest desire is to be right! Keep in mind that I'm not talking about things they care little about, like getting them to go to the 6:30 movie instead of the 7:30 movie. I'm talking about things about which they feel strongly and about which their minds are made up.

Our intentions may be totally honorable; we may want nothing more than to show this person how to be happier, healthier, more at peace, and more fulfilled in his life. It doesn't matter. We may think that if we're able to change the mind of someone whose life affects ours—a boss or a spouse, for example—we, too, will be happier, so we continue to try. But it will never work.

Wanting the people around us, especially those we love and admire, to agree with us—to see the world from our perspective—is the most human desire in the world, because we feel that if they understand the world the way we do they'll understand *us*—or at least appreciate, if not agree with, our perspective.

When someone shares our perspective or point of view, we feel connected to that person, and if, psychologically, being right is our greatest desire, spiritually, we all long for connection. Doesn't it then stand to reason that we'll feel our greatest connection with those who acknowledge the "rightness" of our point of view?

The only way to make those connections, however, is to *stop trying to change people's minds*. When we stop doing that, we'll be able to discover the power of influence as a method for making connections in our secondary world, because . . .

Rule #4:
You *Can* Help People Shift Their Perspectives

If someone agrees with your perspective, it's usually because hers lines up with yours, not because you have made her "change her mind." Have you ever stood with someone on a terrace or a hillside and said, "Wow, look how beautiful the sun is, sinking behind that building [or mountain, or tree]," and the other person says, "I can't see it."

"Come, stand over here," you say. "You've got to see this. Look, over there." And you get him to move to your position and, effectively, stand in your shoes, until he can see the sun as you do because his perspective lines up with yours. Until you can get him to do that, he won't see what you're seeing. No matter how much you say, "Don't be ridiculous, what do you mean you can't see it, just look up there," he won't see it until he's able to change his perspective. If he can't see it, it isn't reality for him, and you won't be able to make him change his mind. Once he does see it, his perspective will have changed completely, and so will his view of reality. He may not think the sunset is as beautiful as you do, but he *will* be able to see it. While you've certainly helped him shift his perspective, his conclusion remains his own—and you can't control *that*.

It probably doesn't take much to influence someone to take a couple of steps to his left or right in order to view a beautiful sunset, but influencing him to change his belief system (his driving myth) may be a bit more problematic. We do that by honoring the first three rules of engagement and then expressing ourselves in a way that will influence him to shift his perspective. The influence itself is not something we can claim to "own," but it is something we can affect.

Orchestra conductors and CEOs both depend on the power of influence. A conductor can't touch the music, he doesn't play a note, he can't actually control anyone else's playing, yet he's responsible for the sound of the entire orchestra. A CEO is probably the one person in his or her company who does the least to directly affect the product or service provided by the organization, and yet he or she is ultimately responsible for its success or failure. There are, nevertheless, critical differences between conductors or CEOs and most of the rest of us—the conductor has an entire orchestra looking at a common musical score, and the CEO has the power of rank and position. For most of us, however, the power to influence lies almost entirely in the power of our expression.

Expressing yourself effectively is the art of communication, which is how we make connections and develop meaningful relationships in our secondary world. This is true on every level, from the most personal to the most universal.

Think of the powerful and effective world leaders of modern times who have influenced nations by means of their oratory: Winston Churchill, whose inspiring speeches lifted the spirits of the British people throughout World War II; Franklin Roosevelt, who had Americans glued to their radios to listen to his fireside chats; John F. Kennedy, who won a presidential election largely because his power to communicate on television outshone Richard Nixon's; Ronald Reagan, the Great Communicator; and Adolf Hitler, who ignited the nationalistic pride of the German people. (We may despise what he did, but there's much to be learned from how he did it.) Successful leadership depends on the willingness of others to follow, and the only way leaders have to get others to do that is through their power of expression. A dictator might get his subjects to *behave* in a certain way by using threats or intimidation, but he still can't make them his followers. He can't change what his subjects think, and eventually, if he can't influence them to accept his point of view, they'll rebel. This is why history has shown us that most dictators have relatively short careers. Many people confuse authority with leadership; leadership is determined by just one thing: the willingness of others to follow. If you think you're leading, and then you turn around and there's no one behind you, your "leadership" is only your illusion.

The same is true of any communication. The power to influence is passive; someone else has to be actively willing to allow you to influence her. Galileo said that you can't teach anyone anything; they have to be willing to learn. If they learn, you will have taught. If they shift their perspective, you will have influenced them. In conversation, when you hear someone ask, "Do you follow me?" he's checking to see if you're willingly considering his perspective. To follow is always a choice. And so, it's the follower who defines the leader. Most people, because they are threatened by their out-of-control experience, crave the "controlled" and "safe" role of leadership. What they don't realize is that it is the follower who actually determines the leader. Leadership, because it is determined by those in our secondary world, is an out-of-control experience.

■ ■ ■

Whenever we're communicating, we're selling or pitching a point of view—our own perspective on a situation, an issue, a product—and if we can influence others to share that point of view, we'll have formed a relationship with them, and they'll be willing to follow our lead. If we effectively honor the rules of engagement and honor their perspective, we'll have helped them to elevate the meaning of their lives, and we'll have enhanced the value of our own. Or, to paraphrase Confucius, there's no greater sight in the world than watching someone walk down their path alone after you've shown them the way.

In business, politics, or on the world stage, our enhanced value derives from persuading others to buy our product or elect us to office or follow our leadership. On a personal level, our enhanced value comes from the happiness of enjoying the love, companionship, and respect of someone we value and with whom we want to connect.

It's Not Important that People Like You

At the risk of repeating myself, there are very few people in this world who will ever really know you, certainly not in the way you know yourself. To do that, they would have to try to step inside your primary world, stand in your shoes, and look out through your eyes.

On the other hand, there will be many people who like you—or at least I hope there will be. But how can they like you if they don't know you? The answer, as we've already discussed, is really quite simple. People like you because when they're with you they *like themselves better*. They like you because being with you elevates *their own* meaning. That's the key to all successful marketing.

Did you know that *Wheel of Fortune* is the most successfully syndicated television game show in the *world*? It's not fast-paced, it doesn't have a lot of bells and whistles; in fact, watching *Wheel of For-*

tune can sometimes be as exciting as watching grass grow. So what's its undeniable universal appeal? It's really very simple. As we watch those contestants trying to guess the phrase by calling out letters, we very often "see" the answer before they do. We get to yell out, "No, dummy, there's no *s*! How stupid can you be!" We feel smart, we feel good about ourselves, and that's why we like the program.

We're drawn to people for the same reason we're drawn to *Wheel of Fortune* or to a particular product—because it makes us feel good about ourselves. We may be convinced that everything we buy and every program we watch is "the best" and that we're buying or watching it for good reasons. In fact, we watch what we watch and buy what we buy because something about that program or product validates the way we feel about ourselves—and marketers know that. In each of the following instances, how we feel is what we know, and what drives our behavior—in this case, our buying decisions. Michelin, for example, doesn't sell tires to men; it sell tires to *parents*. And parents buy the tires because they like themselves *as parents* when they're with Michelin. (Think of the Michelin commercial with that cute little baby and the voice that tells you, "There's so much riding on your tires.") We buy Nikes because wearing them makes us feel "cool." (Their commercials never even bother trying to tell us about the shoes. They just focus on getting us to like ourselves when we're with the "swoosh.") We buy Healthy Choice products because eating them makes us feel that we're doing something good for our bodies. Good marketers know we can doubt what they say, and we can even doubt what we know, but we can't deny our feelings.

That's the concept behind "branding." No manufacturer can "make" us purchase his product. (Even the telephone company has plenty of competition these days.) Rather, successful marketing, like forming a successful relationship, is always reciprocal: The manufacturer provides something another person wants, and the degree to which he wants or doesn't want it helps the manufacturer to determine its value. The manufacturer's only way of creating a successful relationship with us, the consumer, is to know his gig and pitch his product in such a way that we'll like ourselves when we're with it. He does that, as we all do, by using the power of expression.

Conversation as Context

Whenever two people are engaged in conversation, whatever the ostensible topic, that conversation is always, on a psychological and emotional level, the context within which each of the people involved is seeking validation of his or her selfhood.

Just as context is a general that lends meaning to the specific, conversation (as context) lends meaning to the individual.

The more aware we can become of this model as we talk with others, the more we will be able to see how they use conversation for validation, regardless of the subject. This realization will, in turn, help us to understand that if they are talking about themselves and we want to connect with them, we should be talking about them, too.

At a party some time ago, a gentleman approached my wife and me and began telling us about his recent trip to Paris. He went on for almost fifteen minutes, talking about what a terrible time he had and how rudely he felt the French people had treated him. When he left, my wife asked me why I hadn't told him about our own wonderful trips to Paris and about the fact that I had proposed to her at the top of the Eiffel Tower at sunset. "He didn't ask," I said. "Besides, I didn't want to change the subject. He was talking about *himself* and *his* trip to Paris, and he was right."

I had just finished explaining this concept of conversation as context at a music broadcasters' convention when a gentleman named Dave raised his hand and, with a very concerned look on his face, said, "All of this makes a lot of sense, and I can see how it works, but I find it quite depressing. I mean, when do I get to talk about myself?"

I quickly apologized to Dave for ever implying that he couldn't talk about himself. In fact, I told him that if he wanted to, he could talk about himself all the time. It's just that no one else would care. Everyone, including Dave, laughed at my little joke. But to be sure that its truth wasn't lost on anyone, I added this clarification: Even the people who truly love and care about us are always alone in their primary world, and because that is the world where they experience and process their reality, it is the world they care about the most. If we like, we can choose to ignore that model for communication and choose not to make use of it. But if we do that, we need to keep in mind that the principle will be working anyway.

Harnessing the Power of Conversation as Context

Whether you find yourself in a conversation about cars, movies, politics, the weather, or any other subject, no matter how apparently trivial or profound, practice bringing all of yourself to the other person by keeping yourself out of the discussion. In other words, talk to that person about him, not about you.

At a seminar in Windsor, Ontario, I was working with a number of sales reps for a group of radio stations. A gentleman in the back raised his hand and told me he respectfully doubted that what I was saying about conversation was true. He said he'd been in sales for years and had a great deal of experience and success talking with people. It was his experience, he went on, that most people would actually feel less rather than more comfortable if you talked about nothing but them.

I walked back to where he was sitting and told him he had a good point. I said that it was important to bring yourself into the conversation in order to allow the other person to feel a sense of commonality with you, but that it was equally important to then return the focus to him. I added that if you bring the conversation to something the other person cares about and actually identifies with, you can light up most people like a Christmas tree.

"Well," he said in a rather skeptical tone of voice, "maybe some people." I agreed that it's sometimes hard when people don't want to be engaged.

I'd noticed that this man was wearing a golf shirt, so I asked him if he golfed. "Yes," was his short reply. I then told him that I'd recently moved into a new home and that there were two golf courses very close by but that I didn't golf. I went on to say that my wife and I wanted to learn together, but a golfer friend had said the best way to learn was to spend a week or two at a golf camp. "What do you think?" I asked.

"Well," he said, "I think that's really good advice. That way you won't pick up any bad habits you'll have to unlearn later."

Then, as the rest of the audience watched and listened, he went on to tell me that he'd been a golf pro before taking this current job. I said I was impressed and asked him what that job had been like and why he'd left. Those words were the last I was able to contribute to our conversation. The gentleman began talking about the circumstances that had prompted him to change careers, about his wife and kids, and about his current golfing abilities as compared to his previous proficiency. And he went on talking. I simply nodded and smiled at the appropriate times. After a minute or so, I could see some of the members of the audience pointing at him and whispering to each other. A few minutes after that, they began giggling and commenting a bit louder. All the while my new golfing friend kept right on talking to me, oblivious of anything going on around us.

When he was starting to wind down, I thanked him again for his question. He paused for a minute, as if he couldn't remember what his question had been, and then he kind of laughed and said I was welcome. The whole room broke into applause and laughter, and we spent the next few minutes sharing our perspectives on what had just happened.

■ ■ ■

When I talk to people about themselves and they become truly engaged, the conversations are almost always more fun, and the person I'm talking about becomes extremely interesting to me. It can be a bit difficult to do, because most of us have spent years bringing ourselves into the subject matter of every conversation, but I think you'll find that with a bit of concentration and diligence you'll soon have people liking themselves when they're with you. You might also find that whether you're at work or at home, it's a bit easier to get what you want a bit more often. And that's not such a bad thing either.

Using the Power of Expression

Manufacturers, like all of us, influence others by telling them stories, in the form of commercials or print advertising. They don't give you facts and figures about how many stitches go into their sneakers or how much rubber is used to make each tire. Rather they create little vignettes or stories about their products in which we recognize something about ourselves that allows us to make a connection with those sneakers or those tires.

The best way to be sure that we *don't* succeed in influencing people is to lecture them, bombard them with facts and figures, and tell them what they're doing wrong. As I've already said, the only way to get people to listen to us is to first honor their humanity by acknowledging the "rightness" of their own point of view. Lecturing them would be trying to change their minds, and we've already discussed the fact that doing that is the quickest way to get them to cling even more tenaciously to their own perspective.

The surest way to influence them is to share the examples of your own life and tell them stories that touch upon universal icons and images that will reveal a part of themselves to themselves. In the moment when they're able to do that they experience a revelation that allows them to see something new, something that changes their own meaning and therefore the meaning of their world. That's what I do in my work every day. If I can, through my storytelling, get a group of executives to see themselves differently in the context of their world (or their work) they will automatically begin to behave differently. I don't need to know what their job is, I don't need to tell them how to do their job differently, I just need to provide them with the tools that will allow them to change the driving myths that determine how they react within their secondary world.

■ ■ ■

Remember that when Jeannie allowed me to find a way to shift my own perspective—the context within which I defined my illness—she didn't do it by lecturing me or telling me I was wrong. She really asked me a series of questions that both validated my own "rightness" about the nature of my illness and provided a way for me to change my opinion about what that illness might mean. Influencing someone to change their perspective is a process, and Jeannie walked me through that process by honoring my perspective and using her power of expression to help me to change it. What she did, really, was to allow me to rewrite my own story in a way that would serve me better.

I thank God that, many years later, I was able to do the same for the woman who was to become my wife.

■ ■ ■

Carol and I weren't yet married when she was diagnosed with breast cancer. Luckily it was caught early and the prognosis was that with local surgery followed by radiation, she'd probably be fine. She was strong and positive from the beginning, determined to get through it and get on with her life—until the evening she called me, clearly very upset. I asked her to come over to my house so that we could talk about what was bothering her, and, after we'd settled down with cocktails and snacks, I put on some music and asked her what was wrong.

"They marked me today," she said quietly, and went on to explain that the radiologist had tattooed her body to indicate the spots they'd be hitting with the radiation therapy, and that she'd been told the marks would be permanent.

I wasn't really sure exactly why those tiny markings seemed to be more upsetting to her than the fact of the cancer itself, but, as I listened to her talk, I tried to think how I could connect with what she was experiencing and find a way to help her. Finally, I went into my office and returned with a permanent marker, a pen, and a piece of paper.

"Let's play a game," I suggested.

"A game?" she giggled, a bit confused. "What game?"

"Tick tack toe," I said, drawing the diagram on the piece of paper and making an X in the middle box. Like most tick tack toe games, ours ended quickly in a tie.

"That was silly," she said.

"Perhaps," I said, putting down the pen, "but now I want to play another game, only this time I want to play with your radiation therapists."

"Joe," she said. "You know you're much too busy to go to the hospital with me every day and sit with me through these treatments. Besides you couldn't possibly alter your speaking schedule. I certainly appreciate the offer, but you can't possibly do it."

"You're right," I agreed. "But I don't have to go with you to play this game. I want the game to be *on you*."

"What on earth are you talking about?" she asked, now thoroughly confused.

"I want to use this marker to draw a tick tack toe game on your left side, where they'll see it. And I want to write under it, 'Your turn.' Can you imagine the looks on their faces when you slip out of your gown? Who could resist tick tack toe?"

Both laughing and crying by now, she finally agreed. And the next day she called me from her car on her way home after the treatment. "Guess what," she said. "They laughed so hard when they saw what you'd done that they ran around bringing everyone they could find into the room to have a look. And then they started to argue about who would get to go first. It was so much fun, I couldn't believe it."

■ ■ ■

In the moment when it was most important to her, I'd been able to express myself in a way that would influence Carol to see her treatment from a different perspective. I couldn't change the specifics of her situation. The tattoos had been necessary, and they would be permanent. But I knew that with a bit of creativity—and the grace of God—I could help her to see those markings in a positive rather than a negative context. I helped to change her context that day, as Jeannie had helped me to change mine, and by doing that, I allowed her to gain power in a situation over which she had no control. She felt much better about herself, and by helping her I elevated my own meaning. Fortunately, I really knew my gig that day, I followed the Four Rules of Engagement, and I enhanced my own power by understanding that I couldn't control or change Carol's mind. As a result, both of us were happier, both of us felt better, and both of us had brought greater meaning into our lives. But the story doesn't quite end there.

Of course, that one game of tick tack toe didn't last through the entire course of her treatment, and before long she was telling me that her therapists were asking for another one. When I started this gig, I didn't really think about the impact my little idea might have on Carol's therapists; I was really thinking only of her. But when she asked again for another "round" I knew I'd have to think of something.

"Okay," I said, and, getting out the marking pen, I began to draw lines and slashes on a piece of paper. "This time we're going to play a different game, Hangman."

"What's the answer?" she asked, barely controlling her laughter as I showed her what I'd written on the paper and began to reproduce the lines and slashes on her side.

In the days and weeks that followed, Carol continued her treatments, and each day her therapists would gather in her room to take turns guessing a new letter and trying to figure out the answer to my puzzle. The result of that game, and also of Carol's own charm, was that she became one of their favorite patients. Finally, with just a few treatments left, her therapists were able to solve the puzzle. They laughed and joked about how much they'd miss her, and on the day of her final treatment, she brought them each a gift, a small, framed pen-and-ink sketch of a half-drawn man hanging from a gallows. Under the drawing, the inscription read

> "I've/left/tit/up/to/you"
> Thanks for everything,
> Love,
> Carol

In this instance, although my original intention had been simply to help change Carol's perspective on her therapy, I realized that, as an added benefit, I'd also helped to change the perspective of her therapists, who were so inured to the harsh realities of their chosen profession that they'd learned to resist making real connections with the people they treated, and rarely had the opportunity to get a laugh out of their job.

When someone close to us is hurting or in distress, we want to deny nature, grab control, and make it right. But that's exactly the time when we most need to grab reality, let go of our ego, and find our own power in it. It wasn't my job to analyze *why* those tattoos had such a negative meaning for Carol and try to make her emotions agree with my logic. Rather, I had to realize that I had *no* control over how she felt about the specifics of her situation—and I didn't need to. I merely needed to help her shift her context so that she could create a better meaning for the permanent ink someone else had put on her skin.

Welcome to the Real World

In the preceding chapters I've been talking mainly about how you function within yourself—in your primary world. But, as I hope I've made clear by now, all of us live every day in the context of our secondary world. It's in that world that we succeed or fail in finding the happiness we seek, and the tools with which I've tried to provide you in this chapter are intended to increase your chances for success—and hence for happiness—in the real world.

In the following chapter, I try to help you let go of those beliefs and contexts that may not have been serving you well and that may, as a result, have been preventing you from making the changes that will allow you to grow and flourish.

Chapter 5

If the Horse Is Dead . . . Get Off

> *Peace immediately follows surrender.*
> —the Bhagavad Gita

he universe is change; our life is what our thoughts make it," said Marcus Aurelius Antoninus in the second century A.D., and it's a statement that's as true today as it was then. We, as well as everyone and everything around us, are in a constant state of change, and yet, change is what most of us fear most in life. It's our thoughts about change, however, not change itself that causes our problems. And our fear of change is directly related to our need to maintain the illusion of control.

How many people do you know who are clinging to unproductive ideas and attitudes, dead-end jobs, or moribund relationships simply because they fear what might happen if they just let go and moved on? What we've got is known, even if it's less than ideal; what we don't have is the unknown and, therefore, fraught with danger—or so we think.

What we really need to figure out is twofold: whether what we're clinging to is really within our control and, if it is, whether it is actually serving us well. If the answer to either of those two questions is no, then we need to let go of it.

The truth of the first part of that statement was demonstrated to me very clearly when I was a sophomore in high school. I very much admired our Spanish teacher, Mr. Garcia, who was strict but fair, with a great sense of humor and enormous patience for his less-than-linguistically talented students.

One day, for some reason that was a mystery to us, he was late for class. The door was locked, and all twenty-eight of us were waiting for him in the hall when someone got the bright idea to jam the lock with the point of his pencil just to see what would happen when Mr. Garcia finally arrived. But if this wise guy thought the teacher would blow his stack, he was about to be bitterly disappointed.

When he got there, Mr. Garcia apologized for being late and proceeded to try to fit his key in the lock. When he realized it was jammed, he simply put away his key, took out his Swiss Army knife, and began whistling quietly to himself as he worked the lock. He got it open in no time, let us all in, and started on the day's lesson as if nothing had happened.

Admiring his cool and wondering what he was really thinking, I approached him after class. "Señor Garcia," I started out nervously. "I felt bad about the lock being messed with today."

He replied, shrugging, "These things happen."

"Well, the reason I bring it up is that a lot of us were really surprised when you didn't get angry. In fact, it didn't seem to bother you at all. So, I'm curious, were you just covering it up, or were you really as unfazed as you seemed to be?"

"That's a good question, Joe," he replied. "But, you see, I have a rule in my life that I always try to follow. When something happens to me, it falls into one of two categories: Either I can do something about it or I can't. If I can, I need to gather myself together and do what I can. If I can't, then I need to accept that and focus on something I *can* do something about."

Mr. Garcia had made a clear distinction between things he could control and things he couldn't, and he used that distinction as a context for everything he faced in life. In effect, he'd defined the power of letting go. By doing that in this situation he'd also found his power as a teacher. He'd won the respect of the class and taught me, personally, a valuable lesson that would serve me the rest of my life. His distinction became a powerful context for me to use in even my most unhealthy and out-of-control times. When I was struggling with the ravages of chemotherapy, I applied it to virtually every symptom, pain, and side effect. And in those times where energy seemed like a luxury, it was invaluable in helping me to accept what I couldn't control and bring what little energy I had to what I could control.

Taking the Plunge

Imagine for a moment that you're in a rowboat a mile from shore when the boat springs a leak. The bottom is quickly filling with water, and the boat is about to sink. At this point you have three choices: You can stay with the boat and surely drown. You can jump out, abandon the boat, and swim for shore. Or, you can jump out and swim for shore dragging the boat along with you.

Put in those words, the third choice sounds pretty ridiculous. But that's exactly what many of us do. We slog through life dragging along outworn ideas, false assumptions, and relationships that we've outgrown or worn thin, and all the while, we're exerting a lot of effort. If you can picture all that stuff as so much useless baggage, I bet you'll also be able to see that it's no more than dead weight that's keeping you from moving through life as effectively as you would if you just let it go. In the sport of ballooning, it's ballast, or dead weight, that keeps the balloon on the ground. Once that ballast is jettisoned, the balloon begins to soar. Your own dead weight may take many shapes and forms—including people and dead-end relationships. If you let go of it, your hands will be free to grab opportunity when it arises.

It's difficult to let go of anything we define as valuable. Many people, for example, have trouble throwing things away. My advice to these people is to throw away everything in their desks, closets, garage, and so on that they haven't used in more than two years. But even that seems too difficult for some. To those people I suggest lovingly wrapping all those same items, carefully labeling the boxes, and storing them away so that after they die, their kids can throw them away.

That example may seem like something of a joke, but I use it simply to illustrate the fact that as long as we define anything as being in any way valuable, it's difficult for us to let go of it. That's why it's so important for us to clearly identify the cost of whatever it is we're holding on to. What does it cost us in time, energy, money, unhappiness, anxiety, and so on? We need to find a way to understand how the things we're holding on to might be preventing us from getting something else we really want.

The son of a friend recently earned a college degree for which he'd paid dearly with much hard work and tens of thousands of dollars in student loans. Upon graduating, he chose to continue working at the same job he'd had while he was in school, with only a small increase in salary. At some point, he became dissatisfied with the work or his salary or both, and he came to talk with me about how I might be able to help him find the kind of work and pay that would be commensurate with his degree.

As he explained that he wanted to take a lot of time off in the summer, not have to drive too far, and not relocate, it didn't take long for me to realize that he wasn't going to be leaving his job any time soon and would probably be facing difficult financial times for the foreseeable future. While he admitted that he didn't like being "poor" and that he really wanted to make a lot more money, he also didn't want to stop hanging out with his friends and partying as often as possible. At that point, I reminded myself that his diploma indicated only that he'd graduated from college. It didn't say he'd graduated into maturity.

More often than not, before we can let go of a habit, a bad relationship, a dead-end job, or any other weighty baggage, we first have to let go of the idea that what we're holding on to is more valuable than whatever it is we desire.

■ ■ ■

Another friend recently told me of a conversation he'd had with his daughter, who is a junior at a prestigious East Coast college and who is dating a classmate who is attending the school with the help of a combination of grants designed to help lower-income students attend such institutions.

It seems that she had been talking with her boyfriend about the career he'd recently decided on and had pointed out to him that, while she believed he should work at what he loved, he'd have to accept the fact that he wouldn't be able to do a lot of things he enjoyed because of the low wage he'd be earning in his chosen profession.

His reply to her was angry and even a bit hostile as he began to rant about the unfairness of the system and vehemently declare that it wasn't his fault some jobs paid much better than others in our society.

When he was done, my friend's daughter responded very calmly and with great conviction. "You may want to check the way you think against the reality you live," she said. "The very fact that you're able to attend this college is proof that the system is not only fair but that it's also working to your benefit."

After a long pause, he acknowledged that what she'd said made a lot of sense and that he'd have to rethink the way he'd learned to define his opportunities.

■ ■ ■

Whether I'm speaking at a convention, to senior-level managers, to employees, or to a volunteer group, I always try to point out the responsibility we all have for making sure that the cost of having me there was worthwhile. I do this in a number of ways. First, I ask the participants to estimate the cost per hour, based on their salaries, of gathering everyone in that room. I then remind them that I'm the only one who is actually doing his job at the moment. In addition, I ask them to consider what I call the "opportunity cost."

The opportunity cost is the total cost of all of the opportunities we're all missing by being in that room. While I realize it's not possible to actually measure that cost, the suggestion helps people to recognize how expensive the meeting really is.

What I do with the participants in those meetings is very much like what we all have to do when we know we need to let go of something. We need to begin to evaluate the way we define that "something" with relation to what it costs us. Only once we recognize how expensive it is in terms of opportunity cost will we truly understand whether we can afford to hold on to it for the sake of habit, sentiment, or even old times' sake.

By the same token, it's also helpful to imagine the value of having what you want and realizing how good it will be to bring whatever that is into your life. For example, if you want to quit smoking, you might weigh the value of lighting up against the value of living to see your grandchildren. In other words, do everything you can to understand as fully as possible that the expense of your current reality may well be more than it's worth.

Acceptance Is Not Resignation

If you see what is small as it sees itself,
And accept what is weak for what strength it has,
And use what is dim for what light it gives,
Then all will go well.
This is called acting naturally.
—Lao-tzu (604 B.C.)

Central to the paradox of the power of losing control is the indisputable fact that the degree to which we are able to accept our current reality has a tremendous impact on our ability to be happy in it. Lao-tzu's poem brilliantly points to the fact that at any moment the world is what it is, our circumstances are what they are, people are who they are, and to try to deny that is to deny reality. In the last line of the poem, he implies that not to accept reality for what it is, is to act unnaturally.

A viable working definition of *sanity* might be understanding and accepting what is real. If we don't see our situation for what it really is, we're demented, disoriented, and doomed to live in a world of illusion. We're flirting with insanity. If that person in the rowboat, for example, hadn't accepted the fact that the boat was sinking, he wouldn't have been able to assess his options realistically.

But accepting our current reality doesn't mean resigning ourselves to perpetuating that same state of affairs. In fact, the degree to which we're able to correctly assess our current reality determines our ability to change it—to create a better reality for ourselves in the future. In other words, we can change the way we respond to "what is," which will effectively change its meaning.

In *The Road Less Traveled*, M. Scott Peck defined the measure of mental wellness as how quickly one is able to define a crisis. To test that definition, let's imagine what might happen if you were sitting in a room that suddenly caught fire. There might be three possible ways you could react. You could say, "The room's on fire; I'm going to die." You might think, "I can't believe this is happening; this can't be happening." Or you might say to yourself, "The room's on fire. I need to get out of here as fast as I can, help others get out, and call the fire department."

In the first instance you'd certainly be accepting reality, but you'd also be resigning yourself to the perpetuation of that reality, and, as a result, you'd probably burn to death unnecessarily. In the second example, you'd simply be denying reality, and, again, you'd burn to death. Only by accepting reality *and finding your power in it,* can you affect what happens in the future.

I was struck again by how true this is when, shortly after the attack on the World Trade Center in New York City, I was watching—along with the rest of the country and much of the world—ongoing news coverage on CNN. Mayor Giuliani and his entourage were walking through the streets of New York on their way to a safer location. He didn't have much information yet, no one knew what had really happened, much less what might happen next, but he was being grilled by reporters as he walked. One particularly persistent reporter kept asking questions, to which the mayor finally answered, "I don't know, but I do know you need to cover your mouth and nose." He accepted the reality of the tragic situation and dealt with what he could in the moment. By doing that, he found his power when others were panicking and denying what was happening. That was the moment when he started to transcend his mere mayoral status and started to become a hero in our national consciousness. To have the presence of mind to let go of what we can't control and to focus on what we can is a trait that can transform victims into heroes and heroines.

Defining the Problem Is Part of the Solution

Letting go is really no more than an approach to a problem. Since, by definition, we are active participants in creating our own reality, the number of solutions we'll see to any problem is limited by the way we define the problem in the first place.

If you went to see a chiropractor because your feet hurt, he'd probably find a problem with your spine; a surgeon would, more often than not, find a surgical solution; a dietician would tell you to change your eating habits; and an orthopedist might suggest that you need orthotics. Before we consider the solution to a problem, we have to consider how we've defined it, because that will determine the kinds of solutions we allow ourselves to see. That is, in effect, the law of congruency.

At one point in my career, I decided to do an informal study of people who wanted to lose ten pounds, to see if I could determine why some succeeded while others failed. Weight loss is a $33-billion industry in the United States with a 95 percent failure rate. I wanted to know how that could be, and why. I discovered that some of the people I was studying lost some or all the weight and then gained it back, some had less than good results and simply quit trying, and some actually succeeded in losing all the weight and keeping it off.

It didn't matter which one of the thousands of different diets they picked. A diet is nothing more than a list, and trying to change people's behaviors, and the outcome of those behaviors, by merely giving them a list is really an exercise in futility. We've all made lists. We all know what we're *supposed* to be doing, but that doesn't mean we're going to do it. We can always move an item from the top of the list to the bottom, or from one day to the next. And even if we did complete everything on our list, it wouldn't change our behavior, because we'd still be using the same old approach to the problem instead of looking at it in a different, more effective context. If lists helped to change behavior, we wouldn't always be making new lists for the same problems.

What finally made the difference for those who were successful was that they actually asked themselves, "What do I need to let go of in order to lose ten pounds?" The answer might have been, "I need to let go of French fries." Or, "I need to let go of eating after seven o'clock at night." Or, "I need to let go of chocolate." But it was that commitment to letting go that made the difference because it allowed them to shift the perspective from which they viewed the problem, and their reality shifted to line up and become congruent with their view of it. In effect, they were using the fourth rule of engagement—you can help people shift their perspective—on themselves.

To put that concept in another context, let's say that what you define as your problem is your career. Is it bringing you a sense of fulfillment? Does it make you feel good about yourself? Do you like getting up to go to work every day, or do you dread the sound of the alarm?

The first thing you need to do if you're not happy in your job is to determine what's causing your unhappiness. If the reality is that your job is really the problem (it's boring, it's unfulfilling, it's repetitious, whatever), and you're staying in it only because you need the paycheck and because knowing that a certain amount of money will be coming in each week allows you to maintain some sense of control over your life, I have to ask what it is that you're really controlling. You must realize that, in reality, you could lose your job at any time—and not because of anything you did or didn't do. So whatever sense of "security" it gives you is really no more than an illusion. If you let it go, you might find yourself unemployed. But you also might find yourself in a brand-new, exciting, soul-satisfying, even financially more lucrative position.

But maybe it's really you and not your job that's the problem. Perhaps you have a problem accepting authority, and your ego is preventing you from forming productive relationships with your supervisor and your coworkers. Or perhaps you go to the opposite extreme, lacking the assertiveness to promote your ideas and allow others to recognize your true value. I've certainly seen people in both those situations, who blamed their jobs for their lack of success and then went into business for themselves. The ego-driven person found himself no more able to work productively with clients than he'd been able to work with his boss—because his ego was still getting in the way. And the unassertive underachiever found it just as difficult to promote his ideas to potential customers as he had to his coworkers.

In both those cases, the job hadn't been the problem at all. It was the person's attitude that had been making him unhappy and thwarting his success. And when he left his job, he took that attitude with him.

Once again, the bottom line is the realization that all we can control is ourselves. And so, if we're not as happy or successful or effective as we think we can or should be, we need to first assess the reality of our present situation. Is our job really the problem? If so, we need to let it go. But if *we* are the problem, we need to understand what it is about *us* that's causing the problem—a bad attitude, a mistaken idea, a less-than-positive driving myth—accept that as reality, and then *let it go*. That's what it means to understand, accept, and manage yourself. That's what it means to know your gig in your secondary world and find the power of losing control.

We are always responsible for our own success and happiness, and our best chance for real growth lies in our ability to first accept what is and then figure out how to change it for the better. That's the secret of learning to let go. It isn't always easy because, as M. Scott Peck said in *The Road Less Traveled,*

> Life is difficult.
> This is a great truth, one of the greatest truths. It is a great truth because once we truly see it as truth, we transcend it. Once we truly know that life is difficult—once we truly understand and accept it—then life is no longer difficult. Because once it is accepted, the fact that life is difficult no longer matters.

Practice Doesn't Always Make Perfect

I can't promise that all change is always positive, but I can promise that nearly everything positive happens as a result of change. And I can also promise that change *will happen* no matter how hard you try to prevent it.

It's fear of change that causes us to try to control things we can't. And because that sense of control is only an illusion, maintaining it becomes increasingly stressful. Either we don't see the reality of our situation—the fact that we really aren't controlling anything—in which case we're deluding ourselves, or, we really *do* understand that our illusion of control could slip away at any moment, in which case we're fighting to ignore that which we know to be true. Either way, being a control freak is not a happy way to live.

I know a woman who prides herself on the wonderful Christmas party she gives at her house every year. The tree is always decorated just so, and the other decorations in the house are perfectly displayed. The food and drink are planned with great attention to every detail. The invitations are perfect, and so on for each and every aspect of the event. While there is nothing wrong with paying attention to detail, I think you'll soon begin to see the problem. As soon as her guests arrive, this hostess begins to inform them exactly how the evening will be orchestrated—when they'll eat, how to get their drinks, when they'll *all* sing Christmas carols, and in what order.

Each year everyone obediently plays the perfect guest by complying with all her requests. Then they all write her a thank-you note effusively commenting on how perfect her party always is, even though nearly all of them dislike being told what to do and when. In other words, her "perfect" party is perfect only for her.

Her motivation for all that perfect preparation is the problem. The reason she wants the decorations, invitations, food, drink, and entertainment to be perfect is that she needs to be in total control of the perfect party. And for that reason her guests must also perform perfectly. One year, a couple of guests actually had the temerity to refuse to sing carols and were summarily dropped from the guest list the following Christmas.

■ ■ ■

Attempts to achieve some sense of control come in many different guises. Those who delude themselves into believing that they really *can* actually control what happens in their secondary world might try to do so by manipulating those around them. They might tell you what they know you want to hear, say one thing to your face and another behind your back, or make promises they can't or don't intend to keep. I'm sure we all know some of these people. If they're good at their game, they might fool us for a while, but they're always found out eventually. And when that happens, all the enormous energy they've been putting into playing their manipulative games will turn out to have been wasted after all.

A salesperson who worked for one of my clients once told me he's always believed he was so good at manipulating his customers that he could get them to do whatever he wanted. The reason he wanted to talk with me was that he'd begun to notice that his sales numbers were going in cycles of feast followed by famine. Whenever he had a period in which he exceeded his goals, it would be followed by a period of barely making them, if he made them at all. The pattern was so consistent that he was finally convinced he himself must be doing something to cause it.

As we talked, it didn't take long for me to see that he behaved one way when his numbers were up and another way when they were down. When they were up, he was full of stories and anecdotes about how he'd manipulated his clients to do whatever he wanted. He was so proud and full of himself that you'd have thought he would burst. And when his numbers were down, he was angry. While he directed some of that anger toward the company for one reason or another, he reserved most of it for his clients.

I asked him to consider whether or not his taking full credit for his high numbers, to the exclusion of anything the clients might have done to contribute to the situation, could possibly be affecting the way he communicated with and treated them. He thought my question was reasonable and said he'd consider the possibility. I then went on to suggest that he might also consider whether or not his clients deserved at least some of the credit and quite a bit of gratitude for "his" successful numbers.

Three months later he called to tell me that his numbers were up to record levels and he thought he'd broken the cycle. I said that perhaps he had, but I also wondered to what he attributed his success. "Isn't it obvious?" he responded. "I've got the best clients in the world!"

Isn't it interesting that when he stopped trying to manipulate his clients (and perhaps when they stopped resenting his attempts at manipulation), his sales went through the roof? I'm happy to report that today this very same salesman is vice-president of sales for his company.

■ ■ ■

In addition to the manipulators like the salesman described above, there are also those who might try to hold on to relationships by chaining other people to them in some way. For example, there are parents or spouses who try to keep their children or marital partners bound to them by controlling the purse strings. There are people who do favors just so the recipients of their so-called good deeds will be beholden or feel obligated to them. There are some who make it clear they'll withhold favors if you don't behave in a particular way. But what these people don't realize is that by attempting to chain others to them, they are enchaining themselves, as well. Every chain has two ends, and both ends are binding. So both the manipulator and the one who allows himself to be manipulated are, in a sense, agreeing to be chained. If either end is dropped, both people are freed.

Again, it's important to emphasize that any attempt to control anything other than oneself is always driven by fear—the fear that if we lose control even for a minute, something "bad" is sure to happen.

At the most extreme level, the need to believe in absolute control manifests itself as the anxiety disorder known as obsessive-compulsive disorder (OCD). The unfortunate people who suffer from OCD are compelled to ritualistically keep repeating simple acts because their delusion causes them to believe that this endless repetition will give them greater control over their lives and that *not* to engage in those repetitive acts will result in some unnamed disaster. PET scans of the brain have shown that the area known as the cerebral cortex is larger and more active in OCD patients than in the general population, and that in 70 percent of patients who are treated with Prozac, an antidepressant and anti-anxiety drug, the compulsions are alleviated and the cerebral cortex returns to normal size and activity. The brain abnormalities return, however, as soon as the patients stop taking the drug.

In his book *Brain Lock,* psychiatrist Jeffrey M. Schwartz offers an alternative, drug-free program combining cognitive self-therapy and behavior modification techniques that allows OCD patients to develop new patterns of response to their obsessions. In Dr. Schwartz's study, 60 percent of patients (almost the same number as those who respond to Prozac) who used the therapy had a diminished frequency of compulsive moments and were able to handle them more easily when they occurred. And scans of these people's brains showed that Schwartz's therapy had the same physical effects as Prozac. In short, Schwartz's patients were able to use their minds to fix their brains.

Clearly, the need for control that manifests itself in OCD patients is delusional in the extreme, but I would urge anyone who thinks he or she can control anything beyond him- or herself by persisting in a behavior or thought that hasn't served well in the past to take a page from Dr. Schwartz's book. He didn't try to counsel or train his patients to let go of the thoughts themselves, because that would have been like telling them not to think of pink elephants—it would have ensured that they were unable to think of anything else. Rather he taught them to examine those thoughts, see how they attached to emotions, and then to let go of the notion that those thoughts had to drive their behavior.

As an example of how we can do that, let's consider another of my clients, a gentleman who was a very successful CEO but who suffered from panic attacks. Because he was a proud man, he didn't want anyone to know about his problem. He also refused to take any medication and, for whatever reason, the professional counseling he'd been in for almost a year was yielding him no positive results. When he asked if I thought I could help, I told him that I had no idea, but that I'd be glad to talk with him about the attacks. I asked him to describe them and to tell me what brought them on. He said that they didn't come at any specific time, nor did they seem to be related to any specific event or circumstance. He also said that they were not all equally powerful. We talked at great length about what made some episodes more or less powerful than others and what caused them to dissipate. I made sure that we always spoke about them with the greatest possible detachment, almost as if we were merely interested observers.

Eventually we got around to the subject of who might have coined the term "panic attacks." With a little guidance, and to his credit, my client decided that whoever it was probably had little or no interest in helping people deal with them. When I asked him how he'd come to that conclusion, he said, "Well, look at the words. Why'd he pick the word *panic*? While these incidents sometimes escalate to sheer panic, more often than not, they're really just levels of anxiety. And look at the word *attack*. The implication is that you're some kind of helpless victim who's unable to defend himself in any way."

It was obvious that this last concept was contrary to my client's personal myth. He liked to be in charge and to have some level of power in every situation. I told him I agreed with his assessment of the term as one that almost forced a definition that did not serve anyone. "What would be a more accurate name that might allow someone to have more power in the situation?" I asked. After much discussion, he decided on "moments of anxiety." I could tell that he was quite happy with his new definition, and we agreed to use it whenever we referred to his "situation" in the future. (We also agreed that to call it a *condition* would be giving it too much power.)

Because my client had much more experience with this problem than I, and because he was a very intelligent person with a highly developed understanding of how to find power in the human condition, I asked him to suggest ways that others might deal with their own moments of anxiety.

"Well," he said, "I'd definitely start by reminding them that it is just that—a moment in time—and that it will pass. I'd remind them that their experience has proved this to be true—the moments always pass—and that they can't deny their experience.

"Next," he went on, "I'd ask them to think of something they love to do that requires a great deal of concentration over time, like playing a specific song on the piano, or rock climbing."

We spent a bit more time chatting about how much we'd enjoyed our conversations and how pleased my client was with the advice he'd come up with. In fact, he said, he was going to try it out on himself the next time the opportunity arose.

It wasn't too many months later that this same gentleman called to let me know his anxiety moments were becoming fewer and farther between as well as much less powerful and, in fact, they were no longer at all difficult to manage. That was more than two years ago, and I never brought the subject up with him again until this year. When I did, he paused, looked at me, and said, "They don't happen anymore. Maybe it was just something I was going through at the time."

I don't want anyone to think that my having used this particular example is intended to indicate that I believe medications are unnecessary or in any way bad. To the contrary, there are times when drugs are very necessary. Drugs played a major role in saving my life. But I also know that the mind is also a very powerful tool and that we can harness that power to improve and enhance the meaning of our lives.

If a bad or delusional thought is driving your behavior, that behavior will never be productive. You need to examine it and then refocus on a thought that will serve you better because, as author and motivational speaker John Alston has so succinctly put it, "What works works. What doesn't work, doesn't. And working harder at what doesn't work won't make it work."

Surfing the Waves of Change

Once we accept the truth that change *will happen* and that it's beyond our control to prevent it, we can be prepared to respond to it in positive ways.

I remember once sitting on the sand at Maui watching people approach the water. Some of them were just trying to avoid the waves, standing near the shoreline and either running back toward to the beach every time one approached, or getting smacked by every wave because they were afraid to move beyond the place where the surf was breaking. Their behavior was driven by fear, which meant they weren't really having any fun, and they were actually getting more beaten up by the waves they couldn't control than they would have if they'd overcome their fear and moved farther away from shore.

On the other hand, those who swam farther out, kept an eye on the rollers, and caught the waves were able to bodysurf all the way to shore, riding the crest instead of getting knocked down. They weren't able to control the waves any more than the people who feared them, but their fearless attitude allowed them to grasp the opportunity each one presented and use it to their advantage.

If you've ever watched a surfer—or been one yourself—you'll know that your only chance to ride the curl rather than end up sucking the sand is to anticipate the changes in those waves and make the constant adjustments that are necessary if you're to maintain your balance. You know you have no control over the water, but you do have the power to respond to its ever-changing patterns in ways that will allow you to continue riding high. It's called going with the flow!

To put that metaphor in a different context, consider the dramatic changes that have taken place in corporate culture during the past several years. Mergers, takeovers, reorganizations, and downsizings are common, everyday reality. If you haven't been involved in one, I suspect you know someone who has. Who do you think would be most likely to survive and thrive in that kind of situation—where change is clearly beyond his or her control? The person who persists in doing things the way he's always done them, or the one who is able to adapt to new procedures and ways of doing business? The one who keeps his gaze firmly focused on the past, or the one who is able to look to the future? The one who feverishly tries to dam up the waters of change, or the one who goes with the flow? The one who insists on maintaining his illusion of control by repeating unproductive behaviors, or the one who is willing to let go in order to grow?

I'm often asked to speak to people who've been out of work and in job-counseling programs. After dozens and dozens of conversations with those who are still out of work up to a year after leaving a job, I can tell you that they are consistently the ones who refuse to let go of the past. They're still talking about the company they've left as "us" and defining themselves in terms of the job they used to do.

Letting Go in Your Primary World

The changes we fear occur in our secondary world, which is where we all function every day. But since we have no control over those changes, and our only power lies in the way we respond to them, what we really need to do is constantly check our definitions, attitudes, and ideas against our current reality in the context of what we want for ourselves. Then we need to let go of those that might be preventing us from thriving in that world and from forming the kinds of relationships that will enrich, enhance, and elevate the meaning of our lives. If we're not doing that, it's only because we're not using the tools we already have to at our disposal to better understand, accept, and manage *ourselves*.

Too many of us are afraid of taking the first step, which is to take a really honest look at ourselves and recognize what it is we're trying to control and why. What is it we're afraid of? Once we figure that out, we can take a step back and say, "Gee, isn't that interesting?" Creating that space between who we are and what we fear provides the objectivity we need to let go of the thought or idea or attitude that isn't serving us and concentrate on what it is we *can* do that will make a difference. We'll then be better positioned to *create* the changes within ourselves that will allow us to respond more positively to the changes we can't control.

Letting Go of Bad Definitions

Whenever we define anything in our world, we are really defining ourselves. So it stands to reason that if we can let go of our bad self-definitions, we'll also be redefining the way we see the world around us—and the way those in our secondary world define us. We project to the world (at the rate of up to 72,000 bits of information per minute) our own definitions, and the world responds in kind.

Take, for example, the story of a woman who attended one of my weekend seminars because she wanted to better understand why she seemed so unable to form a long-term relationship with a man. She was a divorced mother and a successful career woman with a bad self-definition. When I asked her, she admitted that she was successful—"Yes, I am. I have a wonderful job with an encouraging career path ahead of me. I exercise and take good care of myself. I've been told I'm quite attractive for my age. I'm raising my kids, and they're doing really well. I own my own home. I feel on top of it, self-reliant and self-sufficient."—But she was still unhappy. When I asked her why, she said, "Well, I don't have a life partner. I'm all alone, and I need someone in my life to make it better."

"I thought you just said you had a great life," I reminded her gently. "If you're self-reliant, why do you think you need a man in your life to complete you?" I didn't want to imply that she shouldn't want to form a relationship with a man—or with anyone else, for that matter. To do that would be to suggest that relationships are unimportant when, in fact, it's through forming meaningful relationships that we enhance our own meaning. What I *was* trying to do was to help her shift her perspective so she'd be able to understand that she didn't *need* that other person to be happy. In fact, if she did need a man in order to be happy, she would be doing her relationship with him a great disservice by making her need rather than her love the basis for their relationship. Because any relationship based on need is created out of fear, and therefore doomed *not* to produce the happiness we seek.

Following our conversation, and over the course of the weekend, this woman was able to shift her context and let go of her bad self-definition (I'm a woman who needs a man to complete her) in order to grasp on to a new one (I'm quite capable and attractive just as I am. No one has more power to make me happy than I do myself).

As you might imagine, this new self-definition changed not only the way she viewed herself but also the way she saw the world around her and the attitude she projected to others. The happy ending is that within just a few weeks she met a man who was attracted to the beauty of who she was rather than to her neediness. They fell in love and now have been happily married for several years.

Letting Go of Bad Ideas and Attitudes

Remember the woman in the previous chapter who "hated" people who painted natural wood? If so, you'll also recall that we discussed how much of her self-definition was wrapped up in that statement.

Our ideas and attitudes are all self-reflexive, psychological projections of ourselves, and are "driven" by our own driving myths.
Our self-definitions determine our ideas and attitudes, and our ideas
and attitudes determine the way we view ourselves and the world.
In fact, we must interpret the world in order to understand it. As
we've already noted, quantum physics has taught us that we affect
what we observe simply by the process of observing it. So we really
need to let go of the notion that *anything* exists separate and apart
from our interpretation of it. The world is not the concrete place we
think it is. We don't create the world, but we do create what it
means to us.

But that doesn't mean we're doomed to the reality we've created,
because anything we've created we have the power to change. If it's
true that we're each responsible for our own happiness, it's also true
that we're each responsible for our own victimhood or unhappiness
or failure to make positive connections in our secondary world. We
can change all that by accepting our current reality, letting go of
past mistakes, and creating new and more positive ideas and attitudes.

The Top Ten Ideas and Attitudes We Need to Let Go Of

Nearly all of us have something that's preventing us from being as
successful, happy, and fulfilled as we might be. The possibilities of
what that might be are as endless as the differences that make each
of us unique. But, in my experience, the ones listed here are those
that are the most common and the most debilitating, and letting go
of them offers us the greatest opportunity for growth.

#1 Regret

He who regrets loses twice. We can't change what is and we can't
change what was, and if we spend our time losing sleep over what
we can't change, we'll be too tired to change what we can. Regret,
therefore, is always self-defeating. If you missed an opportunity—
whether it was to accept an invitation to dinner, to study harder for

a test, to get to know someone better, or to sail around the world on a yacht—the opportunity of that moment went with that moment and no amount of regret is going to get it back. By living with regret, you're reliving the same loss, which makes it an even greater loss than it was in the first place. But if you can take a step back and figure out what it was that kept you from seizing that opportunity when it was presented—in other words, define what you were afraid of—you'll be able to let go of that fear so that it won't be holding you back the next time an opportunity arises.

MAKE YOUR OWN TIMELINE

Take a piece of paper and draw a line across it from left to right. To the left of the line write the word *birth*. To the right put the word *death*. Now pick a point anywhere along that line. Make an *X* above the line and write, "You are here."

We are all creatures of the moment, and regret causes us to try to live in the past. When we try to live in the future, we'll experience anxiety. Trying to live in either the past or the future puts stress on the psyche because it means we're attempting to live in two or more places at once. And that stress manifests itself as either regret or anxiety. So, to let go of regret, practice being "in the moment." Teach yourself the powerful lesson that to bring all that you are to all that you do is all you'll ever need. ∎

#2 Anger

Anger, we know, is always based on fear. If we're angry at some*one* or about some*thing*, it's because we fear that person or circumstance is likely to harm us or has harmed us in some *way*. What we really fear is that we're losing control. We're casting ourselves in the role of victim, but that's a self-definition, and since we've created it, we also have the power to change it. We can't control other people's actions or attitudes, and we can't control external circumstances or events, but we can control the way we respond to those things. We don't have to be angry, because we do have other choices. The way we respond is always a choice—in fact, it's the only thing that's always a choice. So why would we choose to respond with a self-defeating attitude instead of one that would serve us better?

FIND THE FEAR

When you feel angry, try to find out what it is you're afraid of. In the heat of the moment, it's always easier to deal with fear than it is to manage anger. The more you think about being angry, the more you'll validate your "rightness," and in doing so you'll try to manage your anger and thus become "righteous." And you'll only become angrier later. I call this "banking your anger," which means saving it up to use later in an even bigger way. Sooner or later you'll begin looking forward to making a big, righteous withdrawal from the bank, and eventually you'll blow up. It won't be pretty, and it won't serve you—or anyone else.

Looking for the fear allows you to

1. take the psychic energy off your anger,
2. arrive at a higher level of self-understanding,
3. get to the real source of the problem,
4. find your power in it,
5. refocus your psychic energy to respond in a way that serves you rather than with an automatic "fight or flight" surge of involuntary adrenaline.

Consider your fear, consider what you want, consider what you can do about it, and do it. We can only act *beyond* our fears, not worry ourselves past them. ■

#3 Blame

Blaming others for our situation or our unhappiness is a sure sign that we're feeling out of control, which means we're feeling afraid. If someone is treating us badly—well, they get to do that. We can't control the behavior of others. (Heck, there are times we don't even control our own behavior as well as we should.) It's rational to blame someone for something in our past or even our present, but more often than not, it is irrational to blame someone for our future. And what has happened to us is always less important than what we can do for ourselves. Blame keeps us from focusing our psychic energy on what we can do for ourselves and thus helps to perpetuate our pain.

IT'S ALL IN HOW YOU KEEP SCORE

Fact: Other people can and will do things that negatively affect us.

Fact: Other people can and will do things that positively affect us.

Fact: People will sometimes do things *on purpose* that negatively affect us.

Fact: People will sometimes do things *on purpose* that positively affect us.

Fact: They get to do that.

We live in an interactive world, and all living things affect all other living things. They always have, and they always will. To accept that fact is, as Lao-tzu said, acting naturally.

■ ■ ■

But, if we pay attention, we'll begin to notice that, contrary to what we believe, more often than not we're the victims of unintended blessings. Start to look for the unintended blessings you receive. That's learning to keep score differently.

Look for ways other people's actions have created opportunities for you. Notice that far more people have done things that have had a positive effect on your life than have hurt you or negatively affected you in some way. Consciously spend more of your energy being grateful to those who have helped you and less of it blaming those who have in some way done you harm. It's important to remember that your energy is a blessing. It is the very stuff of life. Why would you want to give it to someone you don't even like? ■

We don't get to control other people's behavior, but their behavior can't control us either—unless we allow it to do so. And so, in the end, we have no one to blame but ourselves. Which leads to the next thing we need to let go of . . .

#4   Guilt

If we're blaming ourselves for something, it means we're feeling guilty. And if we're under the delusion that our guilt isn't self-inflicted, it means we're allowing someone else to determine how we feel about ourselves. They can't do that unless we let them, and letting them means relinquishing our power to respond positively and productively to the people and circumstances in our world.

NOW IS ALWAYS PERFECT

Wherever you are right now may not be ideal, but it is always perfect, because it is perfect reality, and for you to be where you are, everything in the past had to have happened exactly as it did. Any reality at any point in time is always the culmination of everything that's transpired up to that point.

Webster's New Collegiate Dictionary defines *perfect* as "having all the properties that naturally belong to it." And the perfect tense of a verb expresses "the action or state as completed at a time denoted." Our problem occurs when we begin to associate what is perfect with what is ideal. The ideal is a projection of our desire, based on our definitions of ourselves, but that is not always (not even usually) what's occurring in the present. And since as sentient human beings we are always in the process of growing and changing, there can be nothing more perfect in the future than what is right now.

Seen in that context, you can't have done anything wrong, and you don't have anything to feel guilty about. You may have done something wrong in the past—something that was wrong at the moment you did it—but whatever that was, it's now part of the perfect reality of the present. That reality could possibly be more ideal, but it isn't. And so, to feel guilty is to not accept reality, which is only self-defeating.

We can always look back to reconsider what was, or ahead to imagine what will be. But since, as author and chronicler of traditional British country life Ronald Blythe has said, "The most important thing in the world is always what a man is doing at this moment," anything you feel guilty about having done in the past has to be *less important* than what you're doing right now. So, instead of wasting psychic energy dwelling on what was, the question to ask yourself is always, "Okay, this is where I am, so now what?" ■

#5   Pride and Ego

Lord, make me an instrument of thy peace.
Where there is hatred, let me sow love;
Where there is injury, pardon;
Where there is doubt, faith;
Where there is despair, hope;
Where there is darkness, light;
Where there is sadness, joy.

O Divine master, grant that I may not so much seek
To be consoled as to console,
To be understood as to understand,
To be loved as to love;
For it is in giving that we receive,
It is in pardoning that we are pardoned,
It is in dying to self that we are born to eternal life.
—Saint Francis of Assisi.

That prayer asks that you focus your psychic energy on making other things more important than your own egocentric desires. If we interpret the word *self* in the last line to mean *ego* and the words "eternal life" to mean "eternal wisdom" it becomes clear that to achieve eternal wisdom we need to look at and interpret reality in its natural state, without the interference of our own ego, devoid of our own bad definitions, without the distortions created by our own fears, pride, emotional baggage, and insecurity. Whether or not you believe in God or in any kind of higher power, these words can help to provide you with a better context when you feel your ego is getting in the way of your interpretation of reality.

Whenever I'm asked to speak before a large group of people or to help resolve the differences between two high-powered executives, I have to remind myself that I need to set aside my ego and think of *them,* that I am there to serve them, and when I do that, my role—my gig—is suddenly clarified for me. Fritz Perls, the world-renowned psychoanalyst who developed and popularized Gestalt therapy, once said, "Human beings are the only creatures with the capacity to get in their own way." We do that by allowing our ego to define our place in the process—our moment in time, our gig of the moment. While pride may be the opposite of guilt, they are both driven by ego. If we're feeling guilty, we're making ourselves feel bad about ourselves; if we're feeling proud, we're just feeding our ego. But, paradoxically, the only way we'll ever *really* feel good about ourselves is by letting go of our ego and thinking not of ourselves but of others. It's by putting others first, by honoring their humanity, and by acknowledging their value that we get to make the connections that elevate our own meaning and bring us genuine fulfillment. Letting go of ego is at the heart of love and of all spiritual practice; man's ability to do that is at the core of his humanity.

#6 Insecurity

I like to say that we're all insecure because we came into this world without an owner's manual and we're afraid that if something happens to us—and it will—or if something breaks, we won't know what to do or how to fix it. But just because we're insecure doesn't mean we have to allow that insecurity to drive our behavior.

YOU'RE INSECURE—ADMIT IT!

We're insecure because we don't know the future and we live in an out-of-control world. That's okay. Simply being aware of that truth allows us to become secure in the knowledge that, no matter what happens, we'll be able to guide our mind and emotions in a way that will serve us.

So, practice learning to get comfortable with your insecurity. Make it a point to try to become aware of when it is driving your thoughts, emotions, or behaviors. Learn to recognize the various triggers. Perhaps your insecurity is triggered by your definition of your appearance, your definition of how smart you are, or your definition of your sense of humor. Learn to get comfortable with the fact that your goal is not to eradicate your insecurity but to recognize that it is driven by your own definitions, and to remember that you are in charge of your own definitions. ∎

If life were a game of chess and we were constantly making defensive moves driven solely by our fear of losing, we might not lose, the game might end in a draw, but it would surely not end in a victory. Constantly being on the defensive, acting out of insecurity, is tiring and debilitating, and over the long haul it will surely wear us down and tire us out. It's a loser's attitude driven by the context that says, "I can't win, therefore . . ." It's more fun to play any game with the intention of winning than it is to play driven by the fear of losing.

#7 Jealousy

Jealousy is an emotion born out of both pride and insecurity. We see other people as happier and more successful than we—that's our insecurity talking. And we want what we think they have because we don't want to see ourselves as "less" than they are—that's pride. And so, we're jealous. What we're doing once more is allowing other people to determine how we feel. And, as I keep saying, they only get to do that if we let them. It would be much more productive for us to claim the control we have—to determine what we think and how we respond to circumstances—in order to let go of that unproductive emotion and create a better context for ourselves.

TEN REASONS NOT TO BE JEALOUS

If we're covetous (or jealous) it's only because we don't have enough appreciation for ourselves and what we've got. To help shift your context, sit down with a pencil and paper and make a list of the ten things people most often compliment you about, reasons they like and respect you. Now make a list of ten things you like and respect about yourself. Can't think of any? Call your best friend and ask him or her. Now read your list and think of as many supporting facts as you can for why those assessments are true. Notice that when you do that, your psychic energy shifts from a context of fear to one of love. ■

#8   "What If" Scenarios

These are the fear fantasies we create for ourselves that prevent us from letting go of what's not serving us well in order to grab on to better ways of thinking that will allow us to grow. If we let ourselves, we could probably scare ourselves to death, but why would we let ourselves do that?

Most of what we worry about never happens anyway. Take a look back and think of all the time and energy you've wasted by worrying about things. If they happened, your worrying didn't stop them from happening; and if they didn't happen, there was no reason to worry about them in the first place.

THE DIFFERENCE BETWEEN CONCERN AND WORRY

To understand the difference between concern and worry, go back to the story of Mr. Garcia, my high school teacher who didn't get upset when he found that a student had jammed the lock on the classroom door so that his key wouldn't work. He didn't worry about what had happened because he couldn't change it; so he focused his concern on doing what would serve him in the current situation.

Concern is valuable; worry is debilitating. Concern focuses on the moment; worry focuses on a future that might not even happen and therefore leads to nothing but anxiety and stress that may well be unnecessary. Because we are powerful creatures of the moment, concern is a natural and important context to use as a guide for channeling our energy. But when our energy is guided by worry, fear is in charge. When we worry, we're wasting the very energy we need to help us avoid that which we fear. ∎

#9   Debilitating Myths

If we are the stories we tell ourselves we are, and if our stories are self-defeating, we need to let go of those old stories and write ourselves new ones.

We need to learn to recognize that stories are nothing more than devices we use to create meaning. If, for example, you had a traumatic experience in your past that is still troubling you today, your problem in the present is not so much the experience itself as it is the meaning you give to it or the story you tell yourself about it. The meaning you give it will last much longer and will have much greater impact than the event itself. That's the good news. Because while you couldn't control the event and can't do anything to change the past, you are completely in charge of deciding what it means.

WHY CAN'T I HAVE—?

Is there something you want that you think you can't have? Peace, love, happiness, joy, adventure? Write down whatever it is you think you're lacking in life, and then list all the reasons why you think you can't have it. Now, make a big *X* through that list and write down all the reasons why those reasons are totally wrong, absolute garbage. What you've just done is to rewrite your story so that it will serve you better. Whatever story you tell yourself is right, because it's yours—that's the first rule of engagement—and that rule helps to feed the process of rewriting, as well. ■

Accepting yourself doesn't mean making excuses for yourself. It means seeing yourself clearly so that you'll be able to manage yourself better in the future. It means finding the power to elevate your meaning by making better, more fulfilling connections in your secondary world.

#10 Debilitating Definitions

All our definitions are self-reflexive because whenever we define anything we are always defining ourselves. And so, whenever we recognize that a definition isn't serving us well, we can, by examining ourselves, discover what it is about *us* that's driving our definition. By reframing that definition, we'll also be letting go of whatever negative thoughts we'd been having about ourselves.

WHAT DO YOU HATE?

"I hate that!" We've all said it at one time or another. But hate is not a useful emotion; it doesn't serve us well. And in that thing we hate—whatever it is—there's a debilitating definition. So, try to become aware of how it is you're defining what you hate, and you'll be better able to let go of the emotion that's attached to it. "Hating" something isn't a matter of taste; we hate something (or someone) because of the underlying definition we've given to it that reflects something we don't like about ourselves. And hate never serves us well, because it's an emotion based on fear. ■

Rome Wasn't Built in a Day—And Neither Were You

Chance favors the trained mind.
—Louis Pasteur

Your life is a work in progress, and the tools I've been offering you in this chapter are ways to help you become more aware of yourself. Emotions, definitions, attitudes, and ideas—both negative and positive—are part of the human condition. You'll be dealing with them on some level as long as you're alive and cognizant. But the more you're *aware* of how they impinge upon *your* life, the more power you'll have gained in controlling them. And remember that the only control you really have is over yourself, your thoughts, and your emotions. You can't control what happens *to* you, but you can control your response.

Gaining that control is a goal that serves us, even though we'll never attain it absolutely. Newborn babies have no control over when they laugh or cry. As the baby begins to mature, however, he or she begins to become "socialized" and gains some mastery over those emotional responses. The older we get, the more control we gain, but we never achieve "total" mastery. It's a process. To be alive is to grow, and our growth is directly related to our willingness to let go—to the degree we are able—of responses that don't serve us.

Look at the foregoing list of "The Top Ten Ideas and Attitudes We Need to Let Go Of." Are there some items there that resonate with you more than others? Are there others you can think of that might be more pertinent to your particular circumstances? Why not pick one item at a time to concentrate on, and see if just for a day you can let go of that particular idea, thought, or definition. Aristotle said, "Excellence is not an act but a habit." If you can practice making letting go a habit, the process will take hold and your perspective will shift. Your world will still be out of control, and you may still be insecure—but you'll be much better equipped to accept what happens and find power in it to create the life you want.

Chapter 6

Faith Is the Antidote to Fear

*Not truth, but faith it is
that keeps the world alive.*
—Edna Saint Vincent Millay

Imagine that you're skydiving. You stand in the open doorway of the plane, parachute strapped to your back, and look out at— nothing but sky. And then you jump. You can't be certain your parachute will open, and you probably can't even see the spot where you'll be landing. That's what I call the ultimate leap of faith. You can't see where you're going, but you have faith that your chute *will* open and that you'll be able to make the necessary adjustments on the way down in order to wind up in the place you want to be.

Or, for another high-flying image, think of yourself as a trapeze artist. You let go of that bar with ultimate faith that your partner on the next bar will be there to catch you. Without faith, you'd never jump from that plane or let go of that bar—because you'd be too afraid. Faith is the antidote to fear.

■ ■ ■

It's fear of the unknown or unfamiliar that too often makes us cling to what we know and prevents us from being able to let go of whatever is creating negative outcomes in our lives. While it doesn't make us want to cling to what we *feel*, that is, ironically, the result. Fear is seductive in that we don't want to cling to the fear itself, but it makes it impossible for us to let go of everything else, which means we'll continue to be fearful.

Faith is the most powerful tool there is for achieving the power of letting go. It's daunting for us to decide to let go of anything (like the bar of the flying trapeze) unless and until we know there will be a "next thing" to grab on to. The problem is, of course, that we can't know the future, and so we are constantly faced with either having to take that leap of faith or continue to try to cling to what we know. Doing that dooms us to more pain, discomfort, and unhappiness because to try to remain static in a dynamic and changing world is not natural. In fact, it's not even possible. Nobel Prize—winning philosopher Henri Bergson said,

> [F]or a conscious being, to exist is to change, to change is to mature and to mature is to go on creating oneself endlessly.

Life requires that we learn how to continuously step boldly into an unknown world that is beyond our control. While we are biological creatures of the present, living forever in the "here and now," our lives will be shaped by the way we approach the next present moment to come our way.

If you remember what I asked you earlier about whether or not you'd whisper that baby's future into her ear, you might want to consider what you *would* tell her if you could. In fact, it's what we all whisper to babies all the time, "There, there, it's okay, it will be all right." Sound familiar? We whisper that to babies even when they're not crying and are perfectly content because we know on some visceral level that it's all they really need to hear. They don't need to know *what's* going to happen in the future, just that, whatever it is, it will be okay. To have faith is *not* to know that whatever happens in the future will be everything you *want* but to know that whatever it is, you'll be able to accept it as reality and move forward.

While fear can seduce us into perpetuating negative outcomes, faith allows us to participate fully in the process of becoming, and to own our own determination. The word *determine* comes from the Latin root *terminus,* meaning "boundary," and it means to set boundaries or limits. We can choose a life bound by fear or a life bound by faith.

Fear, Faith, and Psychic Energy

The Nobel Prize–winning physicist Werner Karl Heisenberg wrote, "[T]here is only one fundamental substance of which all reality consists. If we have to give the substance a name, we can only call it 'energy.'" However, he went on, "Nothing is really known about energy itself. No one has ever contacted it except through its effects." In other words, until we put it to use, energy remains an unknown potential, and the ways we use it, mentally and emotionally as well as physically, are determined by one of two forces—love or fear. Only when we have faith can we truly use the energy of love; without it, we are susceptible to living a life diminished by the negative effects of fear.

■ ■ ■

In addition to making us cling to old habits, beliefs, and behaviors, fear can also be a powerful motivator. It can scare us enough so that we either start or stop doing something, and sometimes whatever it is we start or stop doing can have a positive effect on our lives. I remember, as a kid, thinking that my grandfather must have been a very brave man to leave his native Sicily and come to the United States to start a new life. He didn't really know where he was going, couldn't speak English, and would have to leave his wife and first-born child behind and send for them later. As I grew older, I learned that in the early years of the twentieth century, the simple, poor farmers and fishermen of Sicily who'd been living under oppression for so many years really had only one hope for a better future—emigration. In fact, in the first fourteen years of the twentieth century, my grandfather was only one of one million Sicilians who abandoned their homes and headed for America. I still think my grandfather must have been very brave to undertake that journey, but I now understand that the catalyst for his emigration was primarily fear.

But despite the fact that fear can be an effective motivator and serve us well by forcing us to create change in our lives, the choices we make when driven by fear may not be the best choices. If you remember the person who discovered that his boat was sinking a mile from shore, you'll see the difference between acting out of fear and acting out of faith. The fearful person would be the one dragging that boat along with him, while the person with faith would be able to jump overboard and leave the boat behind, thus greatly improving his chances of actually reaching shore. When we're at the point of decision, fear can make us want to cling or leap (although not necessarily in the right direction). Faith, on the other hand, allows us to think more clearly and act with conviction; it allows us to step boldly in the direction of our choice, which will greatly increase our chances of arriving in the place we want to be. That's why it's so important for us to understand how to use faith as our tool to help us create the life we want.

Baby Steps, Giant Steps, and the Leap of Faith

Taking the leap of faith is a commitment to letting go of what is in order to arrive at something new. That's how all of us grow. If you've ever played the old game Mother, May I, you know all about baby steps and giant steps

The more faith you have, the bigger the steps you'll be able to take on the road to growth and self-fulfillment. But taking a step of any size still leaves you with the chance to change your mind—it's not quite letting go. When we're walking, we don't lift our back leg until the front one is on the ground, which means that, at any time, we can pull that front leg back and return to our starting position.

When we leap, on the other hand, both feet are in the air at the same time, and there's no possibility of going back. To take that leap requires full faith and absolute commitment.

Most of us, however, don't go leaping through life, letting go of one thing after another. We tend to move forward more slowly, and there's nothing wrong with that, as long as you've made the decision to burn the trail behind you, to commit fully to your destination (the last step) before you take the first. That, too, is a form of faith. If you are willing to burn the trail behind you, you *have* let go, mentally and emotionally. And when you take that first step with that kind of conviction, it may be one small step physiologically but it will be one giant leap mentally and emotionally—a leap that will provide the momentum to keep you moving confidently on your way.

Faith in Things We Can't Control

We all, to some degree, practice faith every day. Every time we step off the curb to cross the street, we have faith that the drivers on the road won't lose control of their vehicles and run us down; when we put our money in the bank, we have faith that it will still be there when we go to make a withdrawal; each time we put a stamp on an envelope and mail a check to pay our bills, we have faith that the postal service will deliver it to the proper address.

If we didn't have faith that things we can't control would behave in the way we've been taught they should, we wouldn't be able to function at all. We'd be terrified to step off the sidewalk, deposit a check, or mail a letter—among millions of other everyday activities we all take for granted. We, and the world, would stop functioning.

To a certain degree, our every human interaction is based on a kind of faith. If, for example, I'm describing to you a blue chair I've seen in a shop window, I must have faith that when you picture that chair in your mind, you're seeing "blueness" and "chairness" in the same way I do. I have to believe that your reality, on some basic level, is congruent with mine.

The kinds of faith I've been talking about so far, however, are all based on past experience. The last few thousand times we stepped off the curb or cashed a check or mailed a letter, we got the same results, and so we can safely assume that we'll get those results the next time we engage in those activities. The last time you showed me a blue chair, it really was a blue chair and not a green table, so I have to believe that your concepts of blue and chair really are the same as mine. That kind of faith is absolutely necessary to get us through life day by day, but it's not enough to allow us to let go of bad definitions and elevate the meaning of our lives.

The Difference between Belief and Faith

When we act "as if" something will happen in a certain way because it's always happened that way before, that's belief. Our beliefs are truths we've come to accept because of past experience. And when those beliefs are related to proven and repetitively experienced natural phenomena such as the rising and setting of the sun, functions like turning on the lights or turning off the gas, or the commonality of meanings, they are the foundations upon which our understanding of reality is based.

Our beliefs, however, can also be created by our driving myths, and if our driving myths don't always serve us, beliefs that derive from negative driving myths won't serve us any better. Beliefs based on our driving myths are also based on, or at least reinforced by, our past experience. But because these myths are self-created, we have great power in being able to perpetuate them and continue to use them as a basis for reality or to make them irrelevant by changing them.

While our driving myths obviously can't prevent the sun from rising and setting or the rain from falling, they can and do create many repetitive outcomes that we then come to think of as normal. Remember the story of the woman who thought all men were jerks and the exercise of believing the rich are different? Those kinds of beliefs are debilitating because they don't serve us well and are preventing us from creating a better reality for ourselves in the future. Belief, in that sense, requires clinging or grabbing on to the past, and is actually the opposite of faith. Life is all about growth and change, and what we don't want to do is limit our potential for optimum growth by resigning ourselves to perpetuating what happened in the past, which is an attitude based on fear.

Becoming aware of how our contexts work and why our definitions are always reflective of ourselves is the first step toward being able to let go of the negatives, but awareness in and of itself isn't enough. We also need to have commitment, and true commitment requires a leap of faith. We can use logic and reason to help us create change, but only up to a certain point—and then we must take the leap of faith. Because, as the nineteenth-century English poet Philip James Bailey has said, "Faith is a higher faculty than reason."

What faith does is to allow our fundamental desire to be right (the second rule of engagement) to work for us rather than against us, because our desire to make a *new thing* right requires that we have faith in it before we can commit to it.

True Faith—The Ultimate Let-Go

True faith requires that we relinquish any attempt to control the future at those times when we have no past experience upon which to base the probable outcome. I first discovered how powerful a context that kind of faith could be when my father's eldest sister, my Aunt Josephine, who was then eighty-four years old, was scheduled to go into the hospital for surgery to correct a hernia. Josephine was the eldest of fourteen children, she'd virtually raised her youngest siblings, and for them, losing her would be like losing their mother all over again.

My father went to visit her a few days before the operation, and I knew how frightened he and everyone else in the family was about how a woman of Josephine's age would withstand the trauma of surgery, so, when he returned from his visit, I asked him how she was doing.

"Oh, she's doing great, as usual," he responded.

"But," I said, "how's she doing with the upcoming surgery? Is she scared?"

My father stopped in his tracks and looked directly at me. "Don't you understand?" he asked.

"Understand what?"

"Josephine's got faith," he said, smiling. "She doesn't worry about anything."

That was a very powerful lesson for me because, for the first time in my life, I saw faith as the powerful tool it really is. Here was an eighty-four-year-old woman about to undergo potentially life-threatening surgery, which was scaring her entire extended family out of their wits, and *she* wasn't worried because she had faith. In that moment, I knew I wanted that thing called faith.

■ ■ ■

Today, Josephine is ninety-seven years old, and while her memory may be failing, her faith is stronger than ever.

To have faith like Aunt Josephine's is to have trust in something greater than oneself. It allows us to let go of trying to control the unknown future out of fear that if we don't, things might not be "okay." Faith is our reason to believe that things *will* be okay, even though they are beyond our control. It's empowering because it allows us to let go of our fears and devote our psychic energy to acts based on love.

■ ■ ■

In contrast to Josephine, consider Debbie, a forty-two-year-old client who came to discuss with me the fact that she had recently been plagued with excessive fear and anxiety. From previous conversations, I already knew that she defined herself as a very religious person with a strong and unshakable faith in God.

"You believe in God, don't you, Debbie?" I asked.

"Absolutely," she replied with a sense of pride.

"Well, in your mind what is God's job?"

"Well—" She paused. "I guess God's job is to be in charge of everything."

"Absolutely everything?" I asked.

"Absolutely everything," she chimed back.

"Debbie, would you call God a failure?"

"Certainly not," she stated quite emphatically. "Just what is it you're getting at?"

"Well, Debbie, I'm just trying to understand you. You say you have faith in a powerful God who is in charge of everything, and who doesn't fail, and yet you're worried about him doing his job. Perhaps you're focusing on the wrong problem."

After some consideration, Debbie quietly said, "Wow. I never thought of it that way. I guess my problem isn't my anxiety after all. My problem seems to be that I need to work on my faith."

■ ■ ■

When it comes to faith in God, there are those who have what I call full faith and those who have empty faith. My aunt Josephine would fall into the first category because so much of her psychic energy was invested in her faith that there was none left to feed to her fears. On the other hand, Debbie, at least at the time of our conversation, had an empty faith. She was dedicating and directing so much of her psychic energy to her fears and anxieties that she had precious little left to feed her faith.

To have empty faith is to proclaim a belief in God but to still be anxious and fearful and constantly petitioning God on your own behalf. Empty faith is not really faith at all, because it's driven by fear. And to be fearful is to fly in the face of all that faith implies.

DEVELOPING FAITH AS A TOOL

If you see yourself as a person of God and you'd like to develop your faith as a tool for helping to overcome your fears, you can do the following:

1. Make your God bigger.
   The Socratic nature of my dialogue with Debbie revealed to her that while the God she believed in was big and powerful, the God she actually had faith in was small and weak.

2. Cultivate your faith.
   Practice attributing every good thing in your life, the large and the small, to God, and make it a practice to thank him as often as you can think to.

3. Keep in mind that there are plenty of sources for fear in this world, and grow your faith. That's your job. Let God worry about his. ■

Faith and Religion Are Two Different Things

While Aunt Josephine's faith was certainly based on her deep-seated religious belief in God, it's not my intention—or my job—to preach religion to you or even to tell you what you should or shouldn't think about God. Faith in God is certainly one version of faith—and, in fact, I believe it's the most powerful version—but it's not the only version there is, or the one that will necessarily speak to your own belief system, and that's okay. God, faith, and religion can be touchy and sometimes difficult concepts for many people to consider, and I have no interest in telling anyone he or she is right or wrong about such a personal matter. My responsibility with regard to faith is to simply help you become highly aware that God, faith, and religion are three distinct and different concepts that should not necessarily be linked to one another. Some people have so much emotional baggage when it comes to God and religion that they can't consider the concept of faith in and of itself. And experience has taught me that this can be as true for people who claim to be religious as it can be for those who claim to be agnostic or atheist. If you find yourself responding a bit emotionally to the concepts of God and religion or feeling a bit uneasy about reading a chapter on faith, let me remind you that this chapter is about learning to use faith as an antidote to fear and as a tool for facilitating personal growth. If you can stay focused on that as your context, you'll be well positioned to make use of the information in this chapter and learn how you can use faith to alleviate the problems that fear may cause in your life. For my part, I will do my best to keep that information as relevant as possible for you regardless of your religious beliefs by talking about different kinds of faith and the various things in which we can have faith.

For example, did you ever consider that, in addition to being the basis for religion, faith is also the basis for all scientific discovery?

Belief . . . is the insistence that the truth is what one would believe or wish it to be. . . . [F]aith . . . is an unreserved opening of the mind to the truth, whatever it may be. Faith has no preconceptions; it is a plunge into the unknown. Belief clings, but faith lets go. . . . Faith is the essential virtue of science, and likewise of any religion that is not self-deception.

>—Alan Watts, author and renowned interpreter
>of Asian philosophies in America

In the case of both religion and science, we must walk up to the very edge of the known, and then leap. "God" is an intangible concept—we can't see, smell, taste, or touch it—and yet we *can* believe in God's existence. Scientific experimentation and discovery is also the result of faith in the unknown. If Copernicus hadn't taken that leap of faith by embracing his belief in a new system of astronomy, we might still be clinging to the belief that the sun revolves around the earth; it took a leap of faith to believe that by sailing into uncharted waters we wouldn't be falling off the edge of the world; we can't see subatomic particles, and yet we "know" they exist because of our faith in scientific principles.

■ ■ ■

If you find it difficult to have faith in God or some version of a higher power, or even in a natural, cosmic order, you can still use faith as the powerful tool that it is, so long as you have faith in someone or something else, such as a person in whom you really believe or a strong and positive myth about yourself and your place in the world.

Why Faith Isn't Optimism

It's very important that we draw clear distinctions between the concepts of faith and optimism. In his book *Good to Great*, author Jim Collins identifies what he calls the Stockdale Paradox. It's named for Adm. Jim Stockdale, who was the highest-ranking American soldier captured during the Vietnam War. For eight years he lived in the Hanoi Hilton under brutal conditions, and the soldiers who were imprisoned with him proudly tell stories of how the admiral's faith got them through. During an interview with Mr. Collins the admiral said, "I never doubted not only that I would get out, but also that I would prevail in the end and turn the experience into the defining event of my life, which in retrospect I would not trade."

The admiral had a term for those soldiers who did not live to make it out alive. He called them the optimists.

> Oh, they were the ones who said, "We're going to be out by Christmas." Then Christmas would come and Christmas would go. And then they'd say, "We're going to be out by Easter." And Easter would come and Easter would go. And then Thanksgiving and then Christmas again. And they died of a broken heart. This is a very important lesson. You must never confuse faith that you will prevail in the end—which you can never afford to lose—with the discipline to confront the most brutal facts of your current reality, whatever they might be.

That is the essence of what Jim Collins calls the Stockdale Paradox. It's also an effective context for us to use when considering the distinction between the power of faith and the seduction of optimism. We don't have to know with any certainty whether or not Admiral Stockdale believes in God or what his religion might be in order to see how his faith helped him survive through incredible difficulties. His undying faith in the end of his story was mythical in its power to edify him and pull him through his most difficult moments.

While optimism certainly isn't all—or always—bad, it can't substitute for the power of faith. In this case the admiral called those who perished optimists because their psychic energy wasn't focused on the end of their story, but rather on when they *wanted* the story to end. They were wasting their psychic energy trying to control something other than themselves. The admiral, on the other hand, had a clear understanding of the power of losing control. He *knew* he couldn't control *when* the story ended, so he let go of trying and instead found his power in directing his psychic energy toward his faith in *how* it would end.

■ ■ ■

Another man whose story embodies the meaning of true faith as well as any that I know is Gerry Staton. Gerry was born on New

Year's Day in 1925, the oldest of three boys and one younger sister. When he was four years old, his three-year-old brother died of typhoid fever; three months later his dad died of typhoid, and a month after that his mother died of the same illness. He still remembers her last words to him: "Be a good boy, and God will take care of you and guide your way." A month later, Gerry helplessly watched as a drunk driver ran over and killed his one remaining brother, leaving him and his little sister totally alone in the world. During those Depression years few people could afford to feed an extra mouth for very long, and so Gerry and his sister were, for the most part, separated and raised in a series of foster homes.

At the age of seventeen, Gerry enlisted in the marines. As a marine, he participated in landings at the Solomon Islands, New Guinea, and New Britain. In New Britain he contracted scrub typhus and was put in a mosquito-ridden tent with thirty-two other guys who also had typhus. For the next week he lay on his cot listening to his tentmates petitioning and bargaining with God for their lives. Seven days later there were three men, including Gerry, left alive.

After the war, he returned home, married, started a successful insurance business, and became the father of a son and two daughters. Three years ago, I married his eldest daughter.

As I listened to Gerry tell me his story, I had to ask him what it was he thought of in that tent, and this is what he told me. "Well," he said, "I was praying, too, but just the regular prayers I always said. What got me through was thinking about how good a Coney Island hot dog would taste when I got back to Ohio. I used to really love Coney dogs."

If there's anyone who had good reason *not* to have faith, it was Gerry Staton. But all his life he had carried with him and trusted the faith he'd received from his mother. Faith is *knowing* that which you have no real reason to believe. Based on his past, Gerry had good reason to justify mythical fears about "the fever" and think about how ironic it would be for him to travel halfway around the world only to die of a disease similar to that which had killed his mother, father, and brother. But instead, he had faith in a different story. And because of his mother's promise, he didn't focus his energy on anything except what he would do when he got home. He was driven by faith rather than by fear, and, while we can't know for sure, that faith may well have played a significant role in his ability to survive while so many of the other men in that tent died. Given the workings of the sympathetic and parasympathetic nervous systems, it isn't hard to understand how Gerry's faith may have helped him physically as well as emotionally.

Trust and the Big Lie

No matter what kind of faith you decide to use as your tool, it will require trust—trust in God, trust in an outcome, trust in your myth, or whatever you're placing your faith in. And just as there are many misconceptions about faith and how it works, there are also misconceptions about trust.

Trust comes up as an issue for most of the companies I work with, especially when I'm brought in to help a group of people work together more effectively. Each time the issue is brought up, it's not long before someone says in his or her most authoritative voice of experience, "Trust . . . has to be earned," and then he shoots a glance at the coworker he trusts the least. That is the biggest misconception about trust, and usually the first reason offered when trust doesn't exist.

Given the number of times you may have heard the words, "Trust . . . has to be earned," spoken by authority figures like your parents and your teachers while you were growing up, and given the chance that you yourself have probably used the phrase once or twice as a parent, I'm not about to deny that it has some validity. That said, however, all the "earning" in the world will never be enough to create trust.

Trust can't exist until it is given. Trust is born of giving, not of earning. And that giving requires a leap of faith. The power of both trust and faith is not determined by the recipient but by the giver. And while I contend that there is a causal relationship between how the giver defines the recipient and how much faith or trust he or she is willing to give, both faith and trust derive their ultimate power from the giving, not from the earning.

INCREASING THE POWER OF YOUR TRUST

To raise your awareness that the power of trust is determined by the giver, think of a situation in which you could have given your trust, but didn't. Was your lack of trust justified, or can you see that by increasing your willingness to trust you might have experienced a better outcome? If the latter is true, try to remember to give trust more freely the next time an opportunity comes along. ■

With the blockbuster movie *Star Wars*, the phrase "May the Force be with you" entered our vocabulary and our collective consciousness. In the movie's climax we heard the wise old teacher tell Luke to "Trust the Force." Doesn't that really mean "Have faith in the Force"? The implication of that phrase, and the main theme of the movie, is that in order to harness the power of the Force for your own personal use, you first have to have faith in its power. That kind of faith requires trust. And the level of your trust in turn determines the power of your faith. So, while the Force in which you place your faith can have great power, the degree of power you get to harness for yourself lies in your willingness to give yourself fully to the Force.

The Paradox of Faith

The essence of faith is always, out of love, to give yourself over to the service of something greater than yourself, which is, paradoxically, also the essence of faith *in yourself*.

To have faith in God is to give yourself over to the service of God. To have faith in scientific principles is to give yourself over to the service of science. And, in effect, to do that is to have faith in your worthiness to serve. Whenever we give ourselves over to the service of something greater than ourselves, we are paradoxically reconfirming our faith in ourselves. We can see that if we return once more to the story of Mahatma Gandhi. Gandhi gave himself totally to the service of improving the lives of his people, but in order to do that, he had to believe that he would be able to make a difference, and to have enough faith in his principles to cling to them in the face of dire adversity. Herein lies the greatest paradox. When we commit to subjugating our shallow egos and selfish desires to something more compelling, more attractive, and more powerful, we become more powerful, as well. One would think we'd become weaker, yet the more submissive we are able to become to the mythical power of that which we serve with our faith, the more power we are able to draw from it. And that kind of power can be scary to many people—with good reason.

Faith as a Weapon

As any successful writer or producer knows, the stories that make the greatest books, movies, and plays great are, more often than not, those vehicles whose foundations are based solidly on common universal or cultural myths. While the story lines, characters, and settings may vary, it's the underlying common cultural myth that really attracts us, because it's a myth that reflects our reality back to us, and, therefore, we connect with it.

The main reason *Star Wars* became such an important movie in our culture isn't the power of its dazzling special effects, although they helped feed our initial desire to see the film. The real reason for its lasting popularity is the fact that it reflects our myths with such true clarity. In *Star Wars*, we both related to and understood how Darth Vader could use the same Force for evil that Luke was told to trust in order to be more powerful. That made perfect sense to us on a very basic level because we know that the power of faith can be harnessed for evil as well as to do good. To my mind, that's the very reason why the subject of faith evokes such strong emotions in so many people.

On September 11, 2001, followers of Osama bin Laden purposefully flew jet airplanes directly into the twin towers of the World Trade Center in New York and into the Pentagon. During World War II,

Japanese kamikaze pilots willingly flew their planes into the airstrips and battleships of the American army base on Oahu. Undeniably, these were acts of will fueled by a tremendous faith.

While some in our culture may have difficulty accepting the validity of using a term like *faith* to describe the motivation for such evil, it's nonetheless true that the individuals who perpetrated those acts were working with the power of faith and trust in their own way. And I believe that the reason so many of us are so reluctant to accept the concept of faith is more complicated than simply wanting to protect our right to believe in one god, many gods, or no gods at all. Acknowledging the power faith can have over human behavior is scary in and of itself. Throughout time, faith has fueled both great acts of goodness and heinous acts of evil.

We've already discussed the fact that energy, in and of itself, is not power but merely potential. Energy expressed, however, *is* power. And expressed energy that is fueled by faith is very powerful indeed.

The power of faith can easily be ignored, but it cannot reasonably be denied. For that reason, it's important that we learn to take the energy we may be expending on fearing the power of faith and devote it instead to making sure that our faith is being fed by love and results in positive and loving outcomes. As individuals and as a society, to attempt to shy away from or muffle the power of faith is as dangerous as it is to use its power to harm others. We have a responsibility to become all we can, and that responsibility is greater than ourselves and greater than our fears. It's a responsibility that requires the power of our faith.

Faith, Fear, and Compensatory Behavior

In terms of what many of us do every day, parenting may be the greatest act of faith there is. Good parenting is always acting out of love. And to do that, we must believe (or have faith) that we are worthy of being parents—that if we bring all we have to all we do as parents, it will be all we need. Without that faith, we'll always be afraid that if we don't control our child every minute of every day, something terrible will surely happen. We'll be creating "what if" scenarios and fear fantasies, and our actions will always be dictated by our fear of what *might* happen: We'll yell at our child *before* he does something for fear that he *will* do it at some point in the future, or we'll allow him too much freedom for fear that he'll rebel or won't love us if we refuse him anything. We'll be too strict or too lenient. In other words, our behavior will always be compensating for our fear.

TAKE STOCK OF YOUR UNNECESSARY FEARS

Get out your pad and pencil and think back to five things you were afraid *might* go wrong, but didn't actually happen that way. Did you do anything that actually prevented them from happening? Could you have controlled those outcomes? Did your fears help you think smarter or feel better or find power in the situation?

Does looking at your fears logically help you to develop the faith that the next thing you fear won't happen either? Can you see that acting out of those fears of negative outcomes rather than faith in positive ones might have prevented you from acting in a way that would have served you better?

Now think of something you feared would happen that actually did. Are you still okay? Can you still experience happiness? Do you still have your faculties and the power to choose who you want to be?

The next time you're afraid of something that "might" happen, see if you can act *beyond* that fear with the faith that whatever happens, it will be okay. ∎

We've already talked about the fact that fear can act as a powerful motivator, but we also know that human biology dictates our physical and psychological reactions to fear. When the sympathetic nervous system reacts to fear, adrenaline starts rushing through our body and to our brain, affecting all our perceptions, which, as you'll recall, is what happened to the poor frightened woman who lost her child at Disney World and then was too terrified to even see the child sitting in front of her. Fear distorts the way we see the world, which means we might be looking at something that appears attractive without recognizing its inherent dangers—or, just as bad, we could be looking at the very answer to all our problems yet be unable to see it for what it is. In other words, we'd literally be blinded by fear.

When we base our actions on perceptions generated by fear, we're reacting out of pure emotion, and those reactions may not necessarily be the ones that are most natural or that serve us best, because emotion simply doesn't recognize logic. Remember Lao-tzu's admonishment that to see things as they really are is to "act naturally"? To do anything else is always compensatory behavior.

STEPPING BACK FROM FEAR

Unless the house is burning down around you, in which case your fear can be a powerful and positive motivator, it's usually better not to act at all until you've been able to step back from your emotion and let reason guide your way.

First, create some distance between yourself and your fear by saying, "Isn't that interesting!"

Next, determine what it is that you're afraid of.

Now, ask yourself how you can use that fear in a way that will serve you.

Commit to that decision, and take the leap of faith. ∎

The Power of Faith as a Tool for Personal Growth

Just in case you're still hesitant about accepting the power of faith as a tool in the context of personal development, you may want to consider that at this very moment you are holding in your hands the result of just that sort of power.

When I first promised myself to commit to studying the greatest, most powerful truths ever written about the human experience, I didn't know if I'd be smart enough to pick the right books and the right teachers—let alone understand, assimilate, and process the information I found in them. Years later, when I sat down to write this book, I knew no one in the publishing business, I had no literary agent to represent me, and I really had no idea how to go about getting a book published. So the fact that you're now holding this book in your hands is an undeniable testament to the fact that an action fueled by the resolve that comes from faith can manifest significant realities. I thought of writing this book before anyone thought to publish it or read it. And then I acted on my faith. I had no reason to believe that your reading these words would ever become a reality. Yet it is a reality that can't be denied. And it is a reality that was created by one man taking action based solely on faith.

Faith Is Not the Only Solution

There is an old Spanish proverb, *"A Dios rogando, y con el mazo dando,"* which translates to, "Pray to God, but hammer away." We cannot, in other words, pray and simply expect God to do our work for us. Although cultivating faith is one of the tools we can use for doing the work of learning to better understand, accept, and manage ourselves, it is not, in and of itself, all we need to find the peace, power, and happiness we seek. And I'm certainly not suggesting that anyone just sit back and let things happen as they will. If true faith is a combination of ego and humility—a faith in our worthiness to serve something greater than ourselves—it follows that to have that kind of faith, we also have to know our gig at any given moment. Or as that great golfing philosopher, Sam Snead, once said, "Prayer works if you know how to putt."

I take a leap of faith every time I'm called upon to find a solution to the problems of high-powered corporate executives even though I might not know anything about how their specific business works. I have to have faith that what I know works and that if I really listen to what they have to say, I'll have the clarity to perceive what they can't in order to help them. I know the "what" of my gig, and I have the faith that, if I bring all that I have to any given situation, I'll also uncover the "how."

I suppose that could be seen as the corporate version of leaping with both feet into the fire. Each time a firefighter rushes in to fight a blaze, he's putting his life on the line to serve a greater good. But he's also well trained, he knows he's got the skills to do what he's doing, and he has faith that he'll have the ability to know how to do it in that specific situation. And even though he has absolutely no experience fighting the particular fire that he's currently fighting, he has something going for him that's more powerful than specific experience. He has faith in his training. And that is more than enough to overcome any fears he may have. While fear can be incredibly powerful and quite often even justifiable, applied faith can always overcome it.

Faith Is Transferable

If part of our purpose in life is to elevate our own meaning through service to something greater than ourselves, then one of the most valuable gifts we can give is, through our own faith, to help others find theirs. My father did that for me during the most difficult time of my life, when I was undergoing chemotherapy.

I was feeling sicker than I ever had in my life. I really understood at that moment what the doctors meant when they told me that if I didn't die, I'd probably wish I were dead. My hair was falling out in clumps, I was weak as a baby, totally exhausted all the time, vomiting uncontrollably, and in constant debilitating pain. I remember trudging out to the kitchen one evening to talk to my father, carrying the big blue plastic bowl that had become my constant companion because I never knew when another bout of nausea would hit. I don't remember anymore what it was I could possibly have wanted to ask him, but I'll never forget my father's response. He said, "Joe, once you get through this cancer thing, we'll deal with that. But for now, don't worry about it."

With that, I turned around and slowly made my way back to

bed. But halfway down the hall I did an about-face. My father was still in the kitchen, finishing his evening cup of tea. "Dad," I said, "don't take this the wrong way, but you just said 'when you get through this.' I don't want to bum you out or anything, but haven't you been listening to the doctors? They've been saying I'm probably *not going to get through this*." I felt bad having to tell him this, but I was very concerned that he might have been in denial of that reality or simply putting up a brave front for me.

"Joe," he answered thoughtfully, "I've been there every time the doctors talked to us, and I'm perfectly aware of what they've been saying. Now I want you to listen to *me*. I have no doubt that you're going to get through this."

I was struck by the fact that he didn't say it emphatically or melodramatically. He was just very matter-of-fact. I can remember my thoughts as I once more started back down the hall and up the stairs to my room as if it were yesterday. *My dad wouldn't lie to me. My dad isn't stupid; in fact, he's the smartest guy I know—even smarter than my doctors. I don't understand how he could possibly know I'll get through this, but if he's so certain I will, maybe I actually will.*

I had absolute faith in my father's integrity and intelligence. My faith in him was mythical in proportion. I had faith in the value of his positive contexts and definitions and, therefore, I had faith in his faith. There was no reasonable evidence to prove him right. In fact all the circumstantial evidence indicated that he was wrong. But I now had something more powerful than circumstance. In effect, he had transferred the power of his faith to me, and, from that day on, I didn't worry about the cancer or what my future would bring.

Like many people, my first real experience with the power of faith came through transferable faith. Now, when I work with CEOs, I never fail to emphasize how important it is for them to have conviction in their vision, because it's in that conviction that their employees, customers, and stockholders will find their faith. One of the greatest attributes of faith and the human experience is that faith is transferable.

A Cage in Which to Be Free

Self-improvement, growth, enhancing the meaning of our lives—these are natural, innate human drives. In our most candid moments, most of us will admit that we want to become better people. To do that, we have to be able to let go of whatever it is that's been holding us back from making the changes we want in our lives. To quote Joseph Campbell, "We must be willing to get rid of the lives we've planned so as to have the life that is waiting for us." We'll never be able to do that if we continue to act out of fear, and we'll never be able to overcome our fears if we don't have faith that whatever happens in the future will be better than what was. Faith is what helps us to overcome our insecurities and holds up a mirror that reflects our potential.

Each of us lives according to specific myths, contexts, and definitions that we, in effect, have *chosen* (consciously or subconsciously) and that determine the limitations we set upon ourselves. Since truth is limited by our perception, and whatever we believe to be true is true for us, the concepts by which we choose to live become the boundaries of our potential—the bars of the cage in which we live our life. Our insecurities might be leading us to believe that we are naturally driven to perpetuating pain and anxiety, but that's only because we're allowing ourselves to be controlled by our fears. By picking good myths, contexts, and definitions—the ones that serve us best—as our boundaries, we can ensure that the cage we've built for ourselves will provide us with whatever we need in order to grow and enhance the meaning of our lives.

Paradoxically, we all need the rules and boundaries that define our reality in order to feel free. The times we're most likely to panic and become paralyzed by fear are when we can't see any boundaries at all, when we're totally at sea or lost in the woods or stranded in the desert. We need to see where we are in the world in order to function. But we also have the ability to fix our own boundaries, to create roomier, more positive contexts that allow us to grow rather than those that limit and confine us. Given that choice, wouldn't it be better to be bound by a context of faith than by one that is driven by fear?

By working to develop your faith, you'll be honing one of the most powerful tools there is for letting go of the concepts that keep you confined and pushing out the bars of your personal cage so that you can soar.

It won't happen miraculously, in a single "aha" moment, accompanied by a chorus line, flag-waving, and full orchestral accompaniment. Everything in life is a process, including the development of faith. It's a habit we need to practice and work at every day, like manners, love, and regular physical exercise.

There's an old Buddhist aphorism that says, "After ecstasy, the laundry." To me this means that the happiness, peace, and power we seek in life are natural aspects of the human experience that nevertheless require the focus of our will and attention. In other words, we have to work for the happiness and love that we feel. And some of us have to work a bit harder than others, depending on how willing or unwilling we are to let go of the things that don't serve us.

As human beings, we all want to know our potential, what we're capable of, which means that there's a part of us that wouldn't mind having a crystal ball that would show us our future. But we don't have that crystal ball; we can't see into the future, and so we must have faith—the ultimate trust—that we'll have the power to respond to whatever the future brings in a way that will help us to move closer to fulfilling our potential. Again, in the words of Joseph Campbell, "The world is a mess. It has always been a mess. We are not going to change it. Our job is to straighten out our own lives." There is no job more important. No one can do the job for us. It is a job that requires faith.

Chapter 7

The Difference Between Knowledge and Wisdom

*Knowledge, if it doesn't determine action,
is dead to us.*

—Plotinus

A lot of us know a lot of things, but if we don't use what we know in order to act, our knowledge remains, in effect, no more than mere potential. Only by using what we know to elevate the meaning of our lives and the lives of others do we become wise. In other words, putting knowledge into action is wisdom.

Generally speaking, we Americans love to show off how much we know. As soon as we become aware of something new, we want to tell it to someone else. I'm sure we've all said, shortly after we've picked up a bit of new information, "Hey, did you know that—?" and then off we go, sharing our so-called knowledge with another person. But I would suggest that "awareness" is only the first step on the path to real knowledge—that, in fact, there are actually five steps we must take before we can claim to have true wisdom.

Consider, if you will, how many of us are overweight. We now have more information than ever before about health and proper nutrition. We have access to more varieties of healthful foods; the menus in our restaurants tell us which meals are better for our hearts or how many calories or fat grams there are in certain dishes; we have more dietary supplements, aids, and guides at our disposal than ever before in the history of this country. And yet, as a nation, we're getting fatter and fatter. So, how many of us are really profiting from our knowledge? And what good is knowledge if we are unable to use it? To take the five steps to wisdom is to go from becoming aware of something to actually being able to profit from our knowledge.

The Five Steps to Wisdom

1. Awareness

2. Consideration

3. Experimentation

4. Experience

5. Commitment

These are the five steps each and every one of us must go through if we are to put knowledge into action. For the most part, we aren't even aware of what we know; we don't truly consider much of what we know, and we never experiment with what we know. (We sometimes think we do, but I'll explain in a bit why we're not truly experimenting.)

Instead, most of us have learned certain roles and certain scripts, have taken on specific responsibilities and roles, and have become accustomed to certain habits and feelings. When we become aware of something, we weigh it against our experience and play out whichever familiar script seems to best fit the new situation, and then we wonder why we keep repeating our experiences and having the same negative outcomes.

In learning to understand, accept, and manage ourselves, it's critical that we understand how we learn and what are the distinctions between mere awareness, true knowledge, and real wisdom. Recently, I became acutely aware of taking these five steps myself when I spent an evening in Hawaii on the island of Maui. I was lounging with friends on a grassy cliff overlooking Kapalua Bay.

"This is about as good a day as anyone could hope to have had," someone remarked as we gazed up into the star-filled sky. After a few moments of silence, someone else spoke up. "Look, there's the Big Dipper. And there's Cygnus and Orion."

Uh-oh, I thought to myself, *now the trouble starts.* Because, you see, I happen to be "constellationally challenged." No matter how many times I've tried, or how often people have tried to help me, I've never been able to "see" any constellations except the Big and Little Dippers. What usually happens is that, after much pointing on their part—do you have any idea how many stars a finger can *appear* to be pointing to at once?—and much squinting on mine, I just give in and say, "Oh, yeah, sure, I see it now." Except, of course, I don't really. Now I was having flashbacks to all those previous occasions, realizing that I'd probably have to lie again. I hate to lie, but I've learned that it's the best way to make people stop trying to get me to see what I can't and a way to cut short the escalating frustration my perceptual handicap always creates for both me and my teacher of the moment. For some reason, however, on this beautiful night, after such a perfect day,I decided to try again.

"Okay, you guys," I said, "I have a confession to make. I've never been able to see what you're talking about. I'd love it if you could help me try to see Orion, but you have to promise not to get frustrated if I can't."

Needless to say, my friends were eager to help. They started the same way everyone else had, pointing up at a sky full of stars, which were—to me, anyway—virtually indistinguishable from one another. "Okay," someone said, "follow my finger. You see those three stars very close together?" I was already squinting and trying to decide whether I should just say, "Oh, sure, I see them," as I'd done so many times before, when suddenly, for some reason, I really did think I saw what my friend was pointing at. "Okay," I said, "that's his belt. Now where do I look?"

They went on to show me the rest of the constellation, and—lo and behold!—I really saw it. For the first time in my life my constellational challenge had been cured! I could see Orion! I was afraid that if I looked away, I'd never be able to find those particular stars again, but I knew that so far I'd followed only the first four steps to wisdom, and that I still had to complete the fifth.

I'd become aware of the constellation.

I'd considered that the three stars I saw could actually be Orion's belt.

I'd experimented by trying to construct the rest of the constellation.

As a result, I'd experienced actually seeing the constellation.

Now I knew that if I truly wanted to be able to say that I knew how to spot Orion, I'd have to commit to my new knowledge by looking away and then repeating the process.

■ ■ ■

One of my clients had a similar experience, in a moment of reflection, as she was watching her granddaughter dive fearlessly into the water at the family's lakefront summer home. This client, Katherine, had come to one of my programs and for the first time became aware of the five steps to wisdom. Afterward she began applying what she'd learned to her own experience. Now, watching her granddaughter, she remembered that as a child she herself had been afraid to dive into that very same lake, and she realized how, without being aware of it, she'd used the five steps to overcome her fear and teach herself to dive.

First of all, she watched the other kids and became *aware* that they were all diving. She *considered* that some of those kids were actually younger than she. She began to *experiment*, first with jumping in feetfirst, then with bending over, hands above her head, and just letting herself fall into the lake. As a result, she *experienced* diving, and *committed* herself to continuing to dive based on what she'd learned.

■ ■ ■

Gaining true knowledge, whether it's in order to learn to see a constellation, to dive, or to change unproductive behaviors, always requires that we take those five steps—from awareness to commitment.

Awareness—The First Step to Wisdom

Clearly, we have to become aware of something before we can "know" it in any way at all. On the simplest level, you might, for example, be aware that Paris exists out there as the capital city of France without ever having visited it yourself. You may be aware that French exists as a language without being able to speak it. Having become aware that Paris exists, you can decide whether or not you want to go there. Having learned that there is a French language, you may or may not choose to learn it. But until you make those decisions, you've still taken only the first step toward wisdom (at least as it relates to Paris and the French language).

Now, let's take that concept one step further and think about how it relates to our ability to gain power in situations over which we have no control. Until we become aware of something, there's no way we can know it. But things of which we're not aware can still influence our lives for better or worse. Again, on the simplest level, we're all influenced by the laws of science—whether or not we're aware of those laws. In fact, for centuries, men were ruled by the laws of gravity and astronomy without knowing what those laws were. And, in the same way, because both our primary and secondary worlds are ruled by the psychological principle that requires us to seek congruency, we may be ruled by our own unconscious definitions and contexts simply *because* we're unaware of them. To become aware of this principle as it relates to the issues, challenges, outcomes, and behaviors in our lives can be the first step toward liberating ourselves from the self-imposed constraints and restrictions created by those debilitating definitions.

A powerful example of how this can happen would be the way we are unable to control our anger until we become aware of the underlying fear that is creating it. Once we are able to take that step back and become aware of what we're afraid of, we're that much closer to being able to let go of our anger and begin to act out of love. That in itself can create a dramatic improvement in our lives. And it begins with mere awareness.

DON'T GET UP MAD

Have you ever gone to bed in a perfectly good mood and awakened the next morning grouchy or apprehensive, or just generally feeling "off"? It's happened to me on many occasions, and when it does, I simply don't allow myself to get out of bed until I've become consciously aware of what it is that's bothering me so that I can shift my context and once again be in control of my feelings. If you wake up in a bad mood, you need to be aware that *nothing* has happened during the night to cause your mood change. You're simply directing your psychic energy to something negative. Get hold of your emotional steering wheel, and redirect that energy toward something that will serve you. You can do this through prayer, meditation, clearing your mind, or simply thinking about something you love—whatever works for you. Remember—the one thing we *can* control is ourselves, and this is much more easily achieved if we're *aware* of what's driving our feelings and behaviors. ■

The essence of learning begins with an awareness of ourselves. Until we do what's necessary to bring unproductive definitions and contexts to conscious awareness, it will not be possible for us to take the next step. Like everything else that leads to human growth, acquiring wisdom is a *process*.

Consideration—The Second Step to Wisdom

Going back to Paris and the French language, it should be clear that once you are aware of something, you have the opportunity to decide how you want to act on that awareness. In other words, you are able to bring *consideration* into the process. Does Paris sound like a place you'd like to see for yourself? Do you think it's worth your time to learn the French language? Will visiting Paris or learning French enhance your life and bring it greater meaning? If you reread the preceding sentences, I think you'll see that what you're doing in those instances is relating your awareness of certain information to yourself—that's the distinction between awareness and consideration, and just making that distinction is a tool for growth. To consider something is to see your awareness in the context of yourself.

How does this work with relation to scientific principles? We can't change them, but having become aware of them, we can consider how we might use them to our advantage rather than allowing them to rule us unconsciously. We can gain a certain amount of power simply by being able to consider an idea or a fact that is beyond our control.

But if the one thing we *can* control is ourselves, it stands to reason that by bringing our unconscious definitions and contexts to awareness—by becoming consciously aware of the self-created myths that are governing our lives as surely as the laws of gravity and physics—we can consider whether they are helping or hindering our growth.

CREATE YOUR OWN WALDEN POND

Sometimes as I idly sit on Walden Pond I cease to live and begin to be.
—Henry David Thoreau

We all sometimes focus too much on the reality we've actually helped to define and not enough on the source of our definitions. I believe that every one of us needs time—at least fifteen to twenty minutes a day—to just be, to contemplate our contexts and behaviors and try to become aware of the connections between bad definitions and bad outcomes. As the poet Lao-tzu wrote,

There is no need to run outside
For better seeing.
Nor to peer from a window.
Rather abide at the center of your being;
For the more you leave it, the less you learn.

Take that time for yourself, and, once you've brought those possibly less-than-positive definitions and contexts to conscious awareness, see if you can find a connection between them and the outcomes they are creating.

See if you can uncover the fear you're projecting onto particular situations that may be causing you problems.

Consider how that fear might be driving your desire to control things you can't.

Consider the fact that by not accepting reality, you may be engaging in compensatory behaviors.

Try to use your heightened awareness to find better definitions and contexts—that is, to find your power in a world over which you have no control. ■

Very often, after I've given a talk, at least a few people will come up to me and say something like, "I really enjoyed your talk. Thanks for the good reminder." When I hear those words, I realize that they must already have been aware on some level of the information I shared with them. And my response is first of all to thank them for coming and listening and then to ask them if they're going to think about what we've discussed, because I know that if they'll just give it due consideration, they'll be positioned to take the next step.

Ever since I was fifteen years old, I've enjoyed teaching music to young students. Anyone who has ever helped anyone learn anything will know how good it feels when a student "gets it" and his or her eyes light up. That light lets me know they're really "turned on" by what I've suggested because they can relate it to something they love and are, therefore, validated by it. But sometimes I'm met with a blank stare that tells me either that my students can't connect to what I've said because they just don't see any relationship to themselves in the example I've used, or that something about what I've suggested denies them something that's important about themselves. When I see that second response, I realize it's my job to back off and reframe my suggestion so that they *can* see it as a personal validation and will, as a result, be willing to consider it. By getting them to the point where they'll be willing to consider a new idea, I'm helping them to change their perspective in order to see their music in a way that will be more edifying for them.

True consideration is the second step we must take in order to profit from any new awareness. It allows us to think about how we might use our new information in order to form a more positive and edifying context that will allow us to shift our perspective and create a better outcome for ourselves.

Experimentation—The Third Step to Wisdom

Many of us these days have become voyeur chefs by watching Emeril Lagasse or Jacques Pépin or Paul Prudhomme cook up a storm on the Food Network, but no matter how many times we watch one of these culinary artists turn out a perfect soufflé or a perfect bouillabaisse or a perfect chocolate cake, we won't really know how to make one until we've gone into the kitchen and tried it ourselves.

Or, if you prefer sports to cooking, consider this: Barry Bonds might teach you everything you need to know in order to hit one out of the park—how to hold the bat, where to place your feet, how to judge the speed and height of the ball, and so on—but you'll never really know how to hit a home run until the first time you stand at the plate and knock one over the fence. That's always the "aha" moment, when it all comes together and you really "get" what it means.

The word *experiment* is defined in *Webster's New Collegiate Dictionary* as "an operation undertaken to discover some unknown principle or effect." In other words, experimentation is the process of gaining knowledge or learning through trial and error—we can't truly know the outcome until we've tried it, and we won't always succeed the very first time. That's true whether we're experimenting in the kitchen, with hitting home runs, or with trying out new definitions and contexts. We are, at this stage, dealing with something that, by definition, we don't yet "know," because, by definition, if we knew, it wouldn't be an experiment.

> *We would rather be ruined than changed.*
> *We would rather die in our dread*
> *Than climb the cross of the moment*
> *And let our illusions die.*
> —W. H. Auden, *The Age of Anxiety*

Experimenting on ourselves takes courage. I call my life the great experiment. Mine is the only life I have the right to experiment with. And in order to know myself, personal experiment is required, because we can't "know" until we experiment. I don't get to experiment with anyone else—my clients, my wife, my friends, or you. Not only can I experiment only on myself; in fact, it's my responsibility to experiment with myself and my truths if I'm going to learn how to be happier and find my higher meaning.

When we experiment with ourselves, however, it's important that we begin by acting "as if" the new concept or context or definition were true—even though its truth may still be unknown to us. When a scientist starts an experiment, she begins with a hypothesis—a conjecture, a presumed but unproven truth—and the purpose of her experimentation is to *prove*, not to *disprove*, that assumption. If we allow our desire to cling to the old truth to color or skew our experiment, we'll only be sabotaging our chances for proving what we, in theory, have set out to prove. We'll be giving the old truth an unfair advantage, which flies in the face of the spirit of experimentation.

Whenever we experiment with a new truth, the old one will inevitably have the edge because of the laws of congruency and the first rule of engagement—everyone is always right. That old truth is what we know, it's what we've experienced, and, therefore, it's true! But if a new truth offers up hope of better outcomes in the future, we have to help the experiment along. Simply being aware that our desire to be right may be making us less than completely objective will help us to work a little harder. It will allow our desire to be right to work for us rather than against us.

■ ■ ■

Several years ago, a young woman named Heather came to talk to me about the difficulties she was having in her relationship with her mother. It seemed that whenever she wanted or needed to take some time to do something for herself, Heather's mother would create a situation that demanded her immediate attention.

In the course of our conversation, I helped her become aware of the fact that if she was already doing everything her mother wanted her to do and if neither she nor her mother was happy, then doing everything as her mother would like was not making—and never would make—either one of them happy. This new awareness encouraged Heather to consider that it was her responsibility to make *herself* happy and, by the same token, that her mother was responsible for creating her own happiness. She considered that if she started to do whatever it was that would make her happy, she'd at least be making one of them happy, and her mother would probably be no less happy than she already was.

Heather started to experiment with setting boundaries, such as letting her mother know when it was all right to call and when it wasn't. She had to learn to listen to her mother and honor her feelings without falling victim to her bad definitions and contexts. She needed to understand that while she'd never make her mother happy, she could, if she committed to maintaining those boundaries over time, be happy herself, and their relationship could be better than it was—but that would be up to her mother. She couldn't control that relationship, and if her mother continued to be unhappy, it wouldn't be Heather's fault. Years of doing things the old way had already proved that making her mother happy wasn't in Heather's power in the first place.

Today, Heather's mother still doesn't celebrate her daughter's victories the way Heather would like her to, but she no longer negatively affects her daughter's thinking and outcomes. Once she realized she could no longer control Heather, she stopped voicing her criticisms and offering her opinions, and mother and daughter now find other things to talk about. As a result, their conversations are more pleasant, their relationship has improved greatly, and they now call each other friend.

By becoming *aware* of the ways in which her mother was impacting her happiness, *considering* how she could counteract those negative effects, then *experimenting* and *experiencing* better outcomes, Heather was able to *commit* to continuing her relationship with her mother in a way that was healthier and happier for her. She had arrived at a kind of wisdom regarding the possibilities that were open to her, and, by doing that, she had made the power of losing control work for her.

■ ■ ■

In another, similar situation, two women who were business partners came to consult with me for a weekend in order to assess where they stood with regard to their business and how they might become better at what they did. At the end of our session I asked the question I usually put to my clients before they leave: "Is there anything else you'd like to discuss?"

One of the women rather reluctantly admitted that there was. "What's the problem?" I asked.

"The problem," she admitted, "is my mother. She's just always so negative, and she's never supportive of me."

I explained to my client that the definition of a problem is the difference between what "is" and what "should be." In this case, the problem was really her definition of the problem. The problem was not her mother, but what she thought her mother should be. We talked about the fact that she had no control over her mother and no power to change her. What she did have was the power to *redefine* her mother in her own mind so that she would begin to be able to accept her for who she was.

As soon as my client became aware of her ability to redefine the situation, she was able to consider her options. She decided to let her mother just "be" who she was. When she was able to do that, her perspective and expectations changed, she stopped trying to control her mother, and, as a result, their relationship inevitably improved.

Experience—The Fourth Step to Wisdom

It's important to understand that the *only* place where experience can come before experimentation is in the dictionary. When we experiment, we learn firsthand what it's like to make a soufflé, to bake a cake, or to hit a home run. We see for ourselves what it's like to view our world from a new perspective. You may remember that at the beginning of this chapter I said that we never experiment with what we know. That's because, by the word's very definition, we can only experiment in order that we *can* know. Acquiring the kind of real knowledge that can come from personal experience requires questioning and experimentation.

It's absolutely critical when we're experimenting with a new truth that we arrive at this stage, because, until we've actually experienced something for ourselves, we can still always deny it. In my work, I can help people take the first three steps to wisdom, but experiencing the new truth is something they must always do on their own.

While we're experimenting we still have one foot on the ground, and we can always pull back and return to our old contexts and definitions if our experimentation causes us too much anxiety or does not provide the positive changes we thought it would. If, however, our experimentation shows us that this new "truth" works better for us than our old one, we'll become more and more willing to raise that second foot off the ground and commit ourselves to it fully. While we can easily disregard that which we consider, it's very difficult to deny our actual experience.

Commitment—The Fifth Step to Wisdom

Committing ourselves fully to a new concept, idea, or truth always requires a leap of faith. It means that we've determined there's no going back, and it's that wholehearted commitment that puts knowledge into action. Once we're truly committed, we won't keep sticking our toe in the water and then pulling it back. We'll dive right through the wave and come out wiser for it on the other side. As the Scottish writer W.H. Murray put it in *The Scottish Himalayan Expedition*,

> Until one is committed, there is hesitancy, the chance to draw back, always ineffectiveness. Concerning all acts of initiative (and creation) there is one elementary truth, the ignorance of which kills countless ideas and splendid plans: that moment one definitely commits oneself, then Providence moves too. All sorts of things occur to help one that would never otherwise have occurred. A whole stream of events issues from the

decision, raising in one's favor all manner of unforeseen incidents and meetings and material assistance, which no man could have dreamed would have come his way.

When you make a commitment, you set the world moving in the direction of that to which you've committed. And so, it's imperative that you are sure your commitment will serve you.

THE ZEN OF COMMITMENT

Write down one guiding principle you know to be true beyond a shadow of a doubt. Be sure that it's one that is edifying and serves you, and commit to it fully. To invest ourselves fully in what we know, we must focus on it for periods of time over periods of time. The process of writing something down forces us to really concentrate on it. Think of it as a mantra you repeat to yourself until, through conscious repetition, it serves to empower your life and guide your actions. ■

There's an important distinction to be made between decision and commitment. Decisions are firm but not binding; they allow us to "change our mind." A commitment, on the other hand, is backed by the power of will and has the effect of becoming a way of life. Aristotle said, "Excellence or virtue is a settled disposition of the mind that determines our choice of actions and emotions." Excellence requires commitment. It's commitment that allows us to bring all that we are to all that we do.

COMMIT TO A GOOD DECISION

Consider good decisions you've made in your life that you probably should have committed to, but haven't yet. What steps can you take to begin to profit from those decisions by turning them into commitments?

Put them in the order of importance starting with the one that would have the most powerful and positive outcomes for you. Circle that one. Cross all the others out, and focus on committing to the one that's left. ∎

A decision can be made in a split second, as an immediate reaction to a particular situation. Commitment is a considered response rather than an immediate reaction, and it requires our continued vigilance and energy. A decision takes place in one moment in time while a commitment consists of many consistent decisions made over time.

CONSIDER THE DIFFERENCE

How do you commit to responding rather than reacting?

- Try to become aware of those times when you're responding and when you're reacting. Make a point of keeping score.
- In the morning, promise yourself to be in the moment and to look for every opportunity to respond rather than react.
- Try to heighten your awareness of the ways in which reacting fails to serve you well.
- Become highly aware of the negative repercussions of reacting.
- At night, review your day. Accept whatever you did as reality. It happened. It's okay. Don't judge yourself for reacting. Simply play back the tape of your day in your mind. If you punish yourself, you'll lose twice, but you can turn a negative into a positive by becoming aware of when you started to react and considering how you might have responded. Tell yourself that whatever triggered you to react in the past can also remind you to respond in the future.
- Experiment with that a couple of times by playing out scenarios in your head.
- Commit to letting that trigger be your reminder in the future. ∎

Wisdom Is Knowledge in Action

Notice that wisdom is not something we seek directly; rather it's what results when we take the five steps that lead to committing ourselves fully to a better "truth"—one that provides us with better outcomes and thus improves and elevates our life.

Reading this book, for example, won't make you wise. It might, however, make you aware of at least a few new ideas and concepts, and if it does, that awareness will put you in the position of being able to consider whether or not they might be useful to you. If, after true and serious consideration, you think they're worth experimenting with, you might have an experience that's different from what you've experienced before. And if that experience proves beneficial, you can then choose to commit fully to the concept and become a bit wiser about yourself, your relationships with people in your secondary world, and your power to positively affect your life and the lives of others.

The 80/20 Principle and the Power of Losing Control

In 1906 Vilfredo Pareto, an Italian economist, observed that 20 percent of Italians owned 80 percent of the country's wealth, and in the years since, the observation of that ratio has been used in a variety of contexts and situations to describe the fact that the relationship between input and output is not necessarily balanced. This has come to be known as the 80/20 principle.

Chances are that not everyone who reads this book will agree with everything in it. In fact, if Pareto's Principle applies, each of you may agree with 80 percent of what's in it, because it will in some way validate your own truths about yourself, but you may also disagree or not connect with the remaining 20 percent of the concepts and theories in this book. And I would suggest that your greatest opportunity for growth lies in that 20 percent.

Renee Haynes wrote in *Seeing Eye Seeing I,*

In all investigations the answers you get depend on the questions you ask; the questions you ask depend on the assumptions you make, and the assumptions you make depend on how much you think you know. Even more on how much you take for granted, and most of all, in serious investigations, on how willing you are to accept what William James called "the pain of a new idea."

There are two possibilities for why you might disagree with a new idea: Either it's wrong, or you're not aware of this truth—and the truth you *are* aware of invalidates the new one. In either case, you are right. Because I live by the rules of engagement, I believe in my heart that you are right. But the relevant and critical question to consider is whether your "rightness" is serving you well. The four rules of engagement have taught us that the "truth" is that which we believe to be true. And so, in the consideration of new and different ideas, it would serve us to be less interested in "what is truth" and more interested in which truth might serve us better.

When we experiment with a better new truth and experience a better outcome, we'll become that much happier and more peaceful. Our happiness depends upon our ability to understand, accept, and manage ourselves, and, clearly, we can't manage what we don't understand. But by applying the five steps to wisdom to the truths we hold about ourselves, we *can* arrive at greater understanding and happier outcomes.

■ ■ ■

Several years ago I was called in to work with a company that had been suffering not only from an unproductive veneration of its own history—a commitment to doing things the way they'd always been done—but also from an undeclared war between its production and customer service departments. These two departments were on different floors, and the staircase between them was known as the DMZ.

The vice presidents in charge of each of these departments mirrored (or possibly had created) the hostility that existed in their departments as a whole. I never know, when I begin to work with a new group, who the champion of the "new way" will be. Quite often, it turns out to be the quiet cynic rather than the demonstrative cheerleader who becomes the undeniable new leader, and that's exactly what happened in this situation.

I worked with the management staff over a period of time, discussing the various concepts in this book—the power of myths and contexts, the rules of engagement, the fact that one's past needn't predict one's future, and so on. After a while, one of these two vice presidents, whom we'll call Jane, was able to repeat to me every one of the concepts I'd presented. She even bragged to her clients about what she and the organization were learning, and started to use my terms and catchphrases in her e-mail communications. She was clearly aware of what I'd been saying, but her pride in what she thought she knew got in the way of her actually experimenting with those truths in any personal way.

Bill, the other vice president, was also aware of the words and concepts I'd been sharing with the leaders of the organization. The difference between him and Jane was that Bill actually considered them in terms of himself and then went through the experimentation process, experienced better outcomes, and, as a result, *committed* to these new truths. Because of that, he was able, through his own example, to help the staff become aware of new ways of thinking and experiment with new ways of behaving that led to extraordinarily different results. The employees were so impressed with these new outcomes that they committed to them willingly. He shone in their minds as the representative of all that was now good about the company, and so they committed their loyalty to him personally, as well. The company as a whole became a very different place to work. The DMZ became a thing of the past, and departments began to cooperate rather than stonewalling one another.

Jane, who was still living in that old world, had lost much of her ability to influence the other employees. Bill, however, could have influenced people to walk through walls for him simply because he was the embodiment of the path they'd all taken. The CEO had previously treated the two vice presidents equally, and had even determined to divide his duties between them when he stepped down. In the end, however, that didn't happen. Bill had become such an undeniable leader, and had been able to lead the company so effectively, that he became the new CEO.

Notice that Jane, who was able to parrot back and toss around the terms and concepts I'd introduced, was actually prevented from using the five steps to wisdom by priding herself on the assumption that she already "knew it all" while Bill truly traveled the path and, as a result, arrived at the commitment that comes with experience. Whenever we embark on learning something new, it's important that we remember to humble ourselves to our lessons rather than to take pride in our learning because, more often than not, real learning is impossible in the presence of pride. As Roger Bacon put it,

There are in fact four very significant stumbling blocks in the way of grasping the truth, which hinder every man however learned, and scarcely allow anyone to win a clear title to wisdom: Namely, the example of weak and unworthy authority, longstanding custom, the feeling of the ignorant crowd, and the hiding of our own ignorance while making a display of our apparent knowledge.

Humility, on the other hand, is a tool we can use to aid us in our journey through the five steps to wisdom.

Getting Started on the Path to Wisdom

Sometimes getting started is the hardest part of a process. Once we've found a starting point, everything else just seems to fall into place. If you're now wondering how to begin applying the principles of the five steps to wisdom in your own life, I suggest that you might start by becoming a voyeur.

The fact that we're all in this together alone implies that we're each unique—just like everybody else. If that weren't true, cultural references, movies, plays, and books wouldn't be transferable; we wouldn't be able to relate our own experiences to the experiences of others. But the fact is that we all have common experiences, and if we concentrate on what we have in common, we'll be able to learn something from virtually anyone in our secondary world. If you'll recall the promise I made to myself back there in the hospital, it was to discover the wisdom of simple, common, timeless, human truths, not of esoteric, nontransferable knowledge.

Sometimes it's easier to see things in others than it is to recognize them in ourselves. Being a voyeur, however, is just the first step, because after recognizing a behavior in someone else, we may be aware of it, but we still need to apply it to ourselves. My advice is to make *everyone* in our secondary world our teacher. Not only those we admire and respect, but especially those who display behaviors we *don't* respect and who experience outcomes that are obviously negative.

If, for example, we can see that someone is acting out of fear and recognize what he or she is afraid of, we can then apply that awareness to ourselves, consider how we can replace that fear with a better context, and experiment with ourselves in order to have a different experience. We may be tempted to simply sit back and psychoanalyze that person, but doing that won't serve us at all. Our job is to look at his or her behavior and see if we can recognize it in our own life—see if we can find similar fears, negative contexts, and definitions that may have been creating our own negative driving myths. Having done that, we can consider them and experiment with new ones that might be more edifying. That's allowing another person to become our teacher. That's truly humbling ourselves to our lessons, and it's a good way to learn to better understand, accept, and manage ourselves.

LOOK AROUND YOU FOR A TEACHER

Take a look at the people you're with every day—perhaps in your office or among your friends. Is there someone whose behavior you believe to be driven by a fear he or she doesn't recognize? Pick one of these people, and commit yourself to allowing him or her to become your teacher. Can you see how her fear is driving her to try to control what she can't? How is it affecting her physically? Observe his expression, his speech, his gestures. Do you see that he is in a constant state of "fight or flight," and that this is creating, for him, a vicious cycle of action and reaction? By becoming aware of that behavior in someone else, you can take the five steps to wisdom by considering how it might apply to your life, experimenting on yourself, seeing if you have a better experience, and committing to the new truth you've discovered about yourself. ■

If, on the other hand, we observe that someone else is having a better outcome than we are, we might determine that his or her driving myth is better than ours. We can't deny our experiences, because they've already happened, but we can learn to let go of the truth or truths that drove those experiences in order to arrive at others in the future.

It's possible to commit to a bad truth, but that bad truth will inevitably lead to bad outcomes. And if, as the old saying goes, it's just as easy to marry a rich man as a poor one, I would like to suggest that it's just as easy to commit to a truth that will lead to a richer future as it is to commit to a truth that will lead to a poor one.

■ ■ ■

It's also possible for one person to *consciously* become the teacher of another and help him or her along the path to wisdom. If you're like most people, you've probably already thought of at least a few individuals who could profit from some of the ideas in this book. But I suggest that you might want to do yourself a favor by not thinking about them until after you've finished reading it yourself, because while you're reading you'd be best served by considering yourself. Then, after you've finished, it would be appropriate and would serve you to consider how you might help others to experiment with a new idea by guiding them through the five steps.

As I've said before, my father was one of the smartest people I've ever known. He was a great teacher, and whether or not he was conscious of the five steps to wisdom, I've rarely seen anyone help others go through them better than he could. One of the most brilliant displays of his ability to do that occurred when my brothers and I were all still in our twenties.

My father, Mick, was an accomplished trumpet player, and my three brothers and I began playing music together when the eldest of us was just about ten or eleven. We played our first paying gig when I was fourteen, and by the time we were in our early twenties, we were about to embark on our first extended road trip. Mick had been on a few road trips himself, and he must have known the many temptations that would be awaiting his four sons. But he was also smart enough to know that he wouldn't get very far by simply giving us a list of things we were "forbidden" to do. What he did instead was to call us all into the kitchen. When we'd gathered round, he started out by asking if there was anything we needed for the trip.

"Nope, we're all set, but thanks," we said, proud of our forethought and independence.

"Well, that's great." He beamed. "So, tell me, do you guys have a sign or a banner or something with your name on it?"

"Sure," we said, proudly displaying the banner with the name CARUSO that we'd had specially made.

Dad nodded his approval. "Nice sign," he said. "So, where do you hang it?"

"We hang it right behind us on stage," said Rob, who was my youngest brother and the drummer in the group. "We want people to look at it while they're listening to us so they'll remember our name."

"That's pretty smart," Mick agreed. "It seems like you guys really have a lot of things figured out."

Of course, we blustered with pride, thrilled that our father had recognized our genius.

"There's just one thing," he went on. "That name, Caruso. It's a good name for the band and it's probably good marketing, but, you know, it's not just *your* name. Caruso was your grandfather's name for more than seventy years. He gave it to your grandma in a cathedral in Monreale, Sicily, more than fifty years ago. Then he and your grandma brought it over to this country and gave it to each of my thirteen brothers and sisters before giving it to me on June 25, 1924. When I turned forty, I gave the name Caruso to your mother in a church in Wyandotte, Michigan. Then, one at a time, we gave it to each of you."

He paused, looked at each one of us, and smiled his big Mick smile.

"I just wanted to tell you that before you went on your trip. So, have a good time, be safe, take care of each other, and play well."

That brilliantly timed little story had just the effect Mick knew it would. Without preaching in any way, he'd helped to raise our awareness of the meaning of our name, and the method he used to introduce us to that new idea compelled us to consider it in a new context. He'd provided us with a new truth that was undeniable and would ensure—as no lecturing could—that we would be vigilant about guarding the good name we shared.

CREATE YOUR OWN "MICK MOMENT"

Consider Mick's perspective as his boys were getting ready to leave. While many parents might be tempted to let their fears about what they couldn't control and what could happen direct their words and actions, Mickey displayed a true understanding and command of the power of losing control. Because his thoughts and his words were inspired by his love for his sons and his acceptance of what he couldn't control, he was able to find tremendous power in the moment.

Consider a time or situation in your own life when you might be afraid that someone you love would do something that wouldn't serve him. Rather than allowing fear to direct your energy, consider how you might respond in a more Mick-like fashion by using what you now know about the five steps to wisdom. ■

The Circle of Life Spirals Upward

The German philosopher Hegel noted that when it comes to personal growth, our movement is not linear. Rather, he suggests that we move in a series of ever-ascending circles, like a spiral. To see how that works, let's consider the concept in the context of what we've learned about the five steps to wisdom. First, we define everything in our primary and secondary worlds in the context of our self-definitions; then we behave in a way that is congruent with those definitions. As a result, we experience outcomes and are met with circumstances that we, in turn, again define in the context of ourselves and that again result in congruent behavior. Unless and until we become aware of how our self-definitions create our own outcomes and go through the five steps that will elevate self-knowledge, we'll be traveling in a vicious circle rather than spiraling upward. Awareness is the seed of knowledge. Knowledge is born with experience, but it's still just a baby. We need to commit to its nurturance so that we can arrive at a higher level of awareness in order to continue spiraling upward. Each time we begin that cycle of awareness, consideration, experimentation, experience, and commitment, we'll be starting at a higher level than we did the time before, which means we'll be acting with more knowledge and gaining more wisdom. Wherever we are at any point in time, our search for higher meaning, greater happiness, and a greater sense of peace in our lives must begin with achieving higher levels of awareness and consideration.

While it's easy to be seduced into believing that personal growth comes from seeing something new and finding in it something familiar, the truth is that real growth begins only when we can learn to see something familiar and find in it something new. Having been around ourselves roughly since birth, we have no more fertile ground for finding the familiar than in ourselves. When we can learn to master the process of looking inside and seeing something new, we'll have begun to master the game of personal growth, and we'll have put ourselves on track for reaching our true potential.

The process is largely about going back to basics in the most basic way. That may not sound very exciting or enticing, but the level of commitment we make to the basics will indicate and eventually determine the level of mastery we are able to experience. Even the most successful, most experienced athletes in the world begin each new training season with a renewed commitment to relearning the basics—at the next level.

Chapter 8

Cherish the Chase as Much as You Treasure the Trophy

If I were called upon to state in a few words the essence of everything I was trying to say both as a novelist and a preacher, it would be something like this: Listen to your life. See it for the fathomless mystery that it is. In the boredom and the pain of it no less than in the excitement and gladness: touch, taste, smell your way to the holy and hidden heart of it because in the last analysis all moments are key moments, and life itself is grace.

—Frederick Buechner

We're all in the chase throughout our lives, for two quite simple reasons. First, we can't stay where we are, because, no matter how comfortable we might be, the world around us will change, and will *make* us uncomfortable. It's not natural to try to remain static in a dynamic world while inhabiting a body that knows only how to grow or how to die. And because we are driven by our will to live, we *must* continue to grow. Second, we all always desire something more than we have. That's just human nature. And there's nothing wrong with that.

All forms of life, from single-celled animals to spiritual masters, are goal-oriented. The extent of our human capacity for growth can never be determined and, for that reason, we are all always in pursuit of something more. The good news is that the more we try to discover what we're capable of, the more we *become* capable of. As John F. Kennedy indicated in *Profiles in Courage*, we must always try to do our best because our best will always get better. We'll never reach the limits of our ability. We can discover the capacity of our heart and lungs by taking a stress test, and we can reach the limits of our ability with regard to a particular set of skills, but our human capacity will always exceed our grasp.

That may not be very appealing to those who treasure trophies, but it's a fact that becomes more attractive when we consider that where we are right now doesn't determine where we can go. From the lowliest depths, there's always a path to the loftiest heights. While we may not be able to see the top from the bottom, we don't have to. Further, we don't need to judge our chances of being able to get there by what we now perceive as viable or "realistic." As we climb, our ability to go yet higher than we'd previously imagined will increase as we grow and become more capable.

Our problems arise when we have our eyes so firmly glued on the trophy that we believe lies somewhere in our future that we forget to pay attention to, enjoy, and cherish wherever we are right now. We're used to thinking that there's only one trophy, and that it will go to the one who crosses the finish line first. But that's not the way it really works. The true measure of our success and happiness in life is who gets there *best*, and the winner of that race is determined over time, one step at a time. Or, as James Taylor so beautifully put it, "The secret of life is enjoying the passage of time."

What distracts us from doing that—our two greatest barriers to living in the moment and enjoying the passage of time—are our obsessions with our past and our future.

The Value of the Past

Remember that he who regrets loses twice, and that the past has already happened. It can't be changed, and it doesn't serve us to spend our time and expend our psychic energy on trying to exert control over something that can't be undone. To do that is to create "if only" scenarios that will never come true.

The past can be costly if you spend your precious energy dwelling on what-ifs. But it can also have value. What determines the value of your past is not what happened but how you processed what happened—what you may have learned from it. If your past is serving you because you learned something that's now bringing you more happiness, you're getting a good return on your investment. But if it's still costing you psychic energy, you're still paying for it, and its value is, therefore, diminished. Because we are creatures of the moment forever living in the present, none of us can change the past. But the good news is that we don't have to change it in order to be happier, more peaceful, or more powerful. All we have to do is make the past work for us rather than against us.

We Are Creatures of the Moment

Energy exists only in the now, and because it is only of the moment, it is best spent *on* the moment. One of the ways we can learn to cherish the chase is to make sure we're expending our physical and psychic energy on the moment we're in, the step we're on right now.

In addition, the peace, happiness, and meaning we seek also exist in the now, so our power to bring those qualities into our lives lies in focusing on our ability to experience them in the present.

When you are on a journey, it is certainly helpful to know where you are going or at least the general direction in which you are moving, but don't forget: the only thing that is ultimately real about your journey is the step that you are taking at this moment. That's all there ever is.

Your life's journey has an outer purpose and an inner purpose. The outer purpose is to arrive at your goal or destination, to accomplish what you set out to do, to achieve this or that, which, of course, implies future. But if your destination, or the steps you are going to take in the future, take up so much of your attention that they become more important to you than the step you are taking now, then you completely miss the journey's inner purpose, which has nothing to do with *where* you are going or *what* you are doing, but everything to do with *how*. It has nothing to do with future but everything to do with the quality of your consciousness at this moment.

—Eckhart Tolle, *The Power of Now*

Too many of us, in our zeal to improve the quality of our lives, have forgotten (or never learned) the wisdom expressed in those words. And, as a result, we've been sabotaging our own best efforts to arrive at the success and happiness we've been chasing.

If we're constantly looking toward some time or circumstance in the future when, we've determined, we *will* be happy, how can we ever be happy in the present, which is where we'll always live? And if we aren't happy, we certainly can't be successful no matter how much we've achieved.

The process of living in the moment isn't always easy. Sometimes it's a struggle. What we must understand, however, is that the struggle will never be over. Our problems may change, but we'll always have problems—count on it. We may achieve our goals, but we'll always have more goals. The risks we have today may not seem so risky in the future, but there will always be new risks. We may learn to feel more secure about the things we fear losing, but we'll always have other fears. And so, if we in any way attach our happiness to solving any of these issues, we are, in effect, sentencing ourselves to an unhappy life, a life sentence that we'll serve one moment at a time.

WHAT'S GOING TO *MAKE* YOU HAPPY?

Sit down quietly with a pencil and paper and make a list of all the events or situations that you've thought would make you happy.

When I have enough money so that I don't have to worry about my
     future.
When I can retire.
When I get married.
When I have a baby.
When I move to a bigger house.
When I get my next promotion.
When my kids are settled.

These are just suggestions. The possibilities are virtually endless.

Now look at your list. How many of those things have already happened? Are you happy now?

How many of them may never happen? Does that mean you'll never be happy?

Now think of the people you know who *have* those things. Are they stress-free and happy?

Surely you can see that constantly postponing your happiness for some future time is truly an exercise in futility. ■

Practicing Happiness

While struggle is the law of growth, and we often have to experience discomfort to get to greater comfort, we can't just take stress and struggle to the First Bank of Happiness and cash them in. We also need to *practice* seeing and cultivating the happiness, peace, and meaning that can exist in the now. The more we practice doing that now, the happier we'll be in the future.

In high school, as an aspiring clarinetist, I was very familiar with practicing. And I remember one particular occasion when I'd been practicing a long and difficult passage in preparation for a competition. In order to be able to attend a state college, I would have to win a scholarship, and to do that I would have to get a first-division rating at both the district and the state levels for the solo ensemble competitions. I absolutely could not get this passage right, and as the days went by I was becoming more and more frantic. A lot was riding on this, and I could already see failure looming before me.

As I was plugging away one afternoon and making very little headway, I heard my father call down the stairs, "Hey, Joe, listen to what's coming out of the end of your horn."

My first reaction was to be furious with my dad. He'd gotten all first-division ratings in high school and surely knew what I was going through, so why was he being so nasty? And then, I listened to those words in my head again: *He got all first-division ratings in high school and surely knew what I was going through. . . .* And my perspective shifted. Obviously he knew how important this competition was for me, and therefore, he was trying to help me. Lost in my efforts to master the fingering and phrasing of the passage, I'd stopped paying any attention to the actual sounds I was making. And my father knew that if I didn't begin to listen to the music I was making, I might become an accomplished technician but I'd be making really bad music. I was actually practicing hours a day, day after day, how to sound terrible. In the course of my struggle with the technique of the piece, I'd lost track of what I was working for.

That can happen when we become so involved with our struggle to grow that we lose sight of what the struggle is for. We can become so involved in doing our job that we forget what our job really is. We all have difficult passages in our lives. Even after dedicating my life to practicing all the concepts described in this book, I still have difficult passages. But when we struggle with these passages, we can try to remember to listen to what's coming out of the end of our horn. We need to practice going through difficult passages as harmoniously as possible because, if we don't do that, we'll be practicing being miserable.

Some time ago, I had occasion to speak to a group of nurses working with terminally ill patients. These were people who, undeniably, got to reevaluate the value of life in the context of death every day. After my talk, one of the nurses came up to speak to me. She'd gone into nursing, she said, because she wanted to help people, but she just wasn't finding her job to be as fulfilling as she'd hoped and believed it would be. She told me that listening to me that day had helped her to discover why. In her efforts to help one individual in need, she said, she sometimes hurt several others—often family members or other hospital staff—in the process by being rude or curt or expressing annoyance at being interrupted. She'd never thought about it before, but she now realized that doing that didn't make her happy, it didn't make the people she'd hurt happy, and so, in the end, what was she really achieving? And if she was hurting as many people as she helped, how could she be fulfilled? If, on the other hand, she could go to bed saying, "I helped people today without hurting anyone," she *would* be fulfilled, happy, and at peace with herself. That, after all, had been her motivation to become a nurse in the first place. She promised me that from then on she would find a way to redefine her job so that she'd be able to do just that.

Worrying Is Overrated

There's an old joke in which two guys meet in the street. When one of them expresses his anxiety over some inconsequential possibility, the other responds, "What are you so worried about?"

"I'm Jewish," says the first guy. "I worry."

"Well," says his friend, "I'm only half Jewish, so I guess I only worry half as much."

We can all always find something to worry about, and justify why and how much we should worry, but it would be futile to worry about everything, and far more useful to practice directing our energies toward our happiness. You may think that's easier said than done, but where we direct our psychic energy is always, in the end, our *choice*. While we don't have control over much in this world, no one and nothing has more control over where we decide to direct our psychic energy than we do. It's absolutely critical that we commit to making that fact of life work for us by using the control that we have in a way that will serve us.

I remember clearly calling a client one day and asking how she was doing. "Hanging in there," was her reply. When I inquired what she meant by that, she went on to tell me that her company was in the midst of an audit; they were preparing for the arrival of a new CEO, to whom she would report, she was in the throes of a divorce, her daughter was about to graduate from high school, and she was moving—all in the course of a single year.

"Sounds like you've got a lot on your plate," I agreed. "So, does that mean you're not going to have time to be happy until next year?"

It seemed clear to me that she had decided she had enough excuses not to be happy until the following year, but she herself hadn't had any idea she'd made that decision. By acknowledging that she had a lot on her plate, I'd validated her reality, but by asking the question, I helped to shift her perspective so that she became aware for the first time that she *had* made a decision. She also realized it was a bad decision that would drive an undesirable outcome. And, as a result, she began to see that there was a possibility of being happy within the context of being busy, so she started to think about how she could decide to be happy in the process.

As it turned out, she went through all her changes successfully and is now better off for having done so. But had she gone through her year the way she'd originally decided, she'd have spent an entire year practicing *not* being happy.

Learn to Celebrate

There have certainly been times in my life when I wondered what I could possibly have to be happy about. During my struggle with cancer, it sometimes appeared that there would be no happy moments at all between the present and my ultimate death. And yet, at the same time, I became acutely aware of the fact that life was a precious gift that ought to be celebrated. I was so sick for so much of the time that it was difficult to find anything about my life to celebrate, but I decided that I'd just have to practice looking harder for cause to be grateful. On those days when I had enough strength to brush my teeth, I celebrated that. And on those rare occasions when I felt well enough to actually take a shower, the absolute pleasure of standing under that water was a celebration in itself. Still, there were times when I caught myself really feeling sorry for myself and forgetting to celebrate. My own private method for getting over those times was to take a mental step back from my misery and ask myself, "Hey, Joe, are you celebrating?"

Even in the depths of our most miserable moments, there's always something to celebrate. Not too long ago, I was driving through northern Michigan, where I was to give a presentation. It was the dead of winter, and it was *freezing*! The wind was howling, it was snowing sideways, and I was at a service station pumping my own gas. My teeth were chattering, and my hands were so frozen I could hardly hold on to the nozzle. At that point I thought I must be crazy for doing this. I quickly became aware that I was drowning myself in righteous misery and that it wasn't serving me in any way. So I stopped myself short and asked myself, "Hey, Joe, are you celebrating?" The familiar question served as a context that reminded me to think of the positive aspects of my immediate situation. I quickly reminded myself how lucky I was that these people actually wanted me to come, and that they thought what I had to tell them was valuable enough for them to pay to hear me.

When times seem tough, we need to remember that those times will pass. We need to remind ourselves that we *can* shift the context within which we view the specific circumstances of the moment by reminding ourselves to celebrate, or to listen to what's coming out of the end of our horn.

We all need these reminders because the danger is that we might allow ourselves to become so focused on our misery that we're unable to discover and celebrate what's good. The problem is that the good things, more often than not, just sit there quietly waiting to be noticed while the bad things jump up and down, waving their arms and frantically demanding our attention. I'm not suggesting that you should learn to fake a good mood when you're feeling anxious or low. I'm suggesting that you need to shift your context to one that forces you to consider your blessings.

I'll never forget the time my friend Alex asked me if I was always happy. His question surprised me because I didn't realize I was perceived to be perpetually happy. After considering his question for a moment I said, "Although I'm not always happy, I guess I could say I'm mostly happy. But some days I have to work a lot harder to get there than others."

The Difference between Goal-Setting and Suffering for Success

There's nothing wrong with setting goals. In fact, as I've said, we human beings are naturally goal-oriented creatures. But success cannot be measured simply by the number of goals we've managed to achieve or by how many brass rings we've grabbed; true success is always a combination of achievement and what I like to call the "enjoyment factor." In other words, it's not simply what you get, but also how much you enjoyed getting it that will determine the quality of your life.

Just as the past is something we can't change, the future is something we can't control. We have no idea what could possibly happen in the future, so wouldn't it make more sense to do everything in our power to live in the moment and make ourselves happy in the present? Many wise men have made this observation in many different ways.

There's only one meaning in life; the act of living itself.
—Erich Fromm, *Escape from Freedom*

The best thing about the future is that it comes only one day at a time.
—Abraham Lincoln

Let the motive for the action be in the action itself.
—*Bhagavad Gita*

I could certainly go on to quote more, but I'm sure you get the picture.

We in modern society seem to believe that if we *are* happy in the moment, we must be doing something wrong—we're lazy; we're not working hard enough; we're letting ourselves off too easily. That's nonsense. It's a myth that doesn't serve us. Earlier, I quoted Henri Bergson, who said, "to exist is to change." At this point, I'd like to add that while change isn't always easy, there's no badge of honor that attaches to the amount or difficulty of our struggle. The degree to which we suffer and the amount of stress and anxiety we endure are not measures of our worth or of our success. In fact, the exact opposite is true. The degree to which we are *happy* in the moment is the degree to which we can say we've been successful. How to manage that is the question we would all do well to consider.

Happiness Comes from Within

It is not easy to find happiness in ourselves,
and it is not possible to find it elsewhere.
—Agnes Reppelier

The eternal quest for happiness and higher truth has been the subject of folklore and fable, fiction and film, and a universal cultural myth throughout recorded history. At the core of every quest story there is a pilgrimage of sorts. A seeker sets out into the unknown to find what's missing in his or her life. One of the most enduringly popular and poignant of these tales is L. Frank Baum's *The Wonderful Wizard of Oz*. The story opens with Dorothy's longing for some intangible something beyond the confines of the Kansas farm where she lives. In the film version, this longing is expressed in the signature Judy Garland song, "Over the Rainbow." Then the tornado arrives, and Dorothy gets her wish. She's transported beyond the rainbow to the Land of Oz, but she doesn't find happiness there. Instead she connects with other seekers, who are also looking for something they feel is missing from their lives. Dorothy, the Tin Man, the Cowardly Lion, and the Scarecrow all believe that if only they can get to see the wizard, he'll have the power to give them what they want. In the end, it turns out the wizard has no power at all, and the source of the pilgrims' happiness lay within them all along.

WALKING BACKWARD
DOWN THE YELLOW BRICK ROAD

When you ask most people if they're happy, they'll say "pretty happy" or "I could be happier." If you ask them why they're not happier, they'll probably say, "Well, given the circumstances . . ." That's like walking backward down the path to happiness, and it's the wrong way to get there.

Our definitions and contexts are the genesis for the behaviors and outcomes of our lives. That's the natural way for our minds to relate to the rest of reality. It is in this sequence that we have great power. Too often, however, we're tempted to deny this natural sequence and convince ourselves that our circumstances determine our behaviors, our contexts, and our thoughts. In this sequence we have no power. We're simply victims of whatever happens. The quality of our lives and our level of happiness are not ours to decide, but rather are determined for us by whatever happens around us and to us. If we use this model as the context within which we process all other information, we've rendered ourselves virtually powerless. And so, it is a context that absolutely doesn't serve us.

If, however, we commit to the context that everything begins with how we define it, we can find great power in our lives, regardless of our circumstances.

Some people take pride in an approach to life that coincides with the old cliché "I calls them as I sees them." I don't. If I had to describe my approach to life in a similar phrase, it would be this: "They ain't nothing until I calls them." While cancer is cancer, it is totally up to me to decide what it means. While past traumas were what they were, I will allow them to be only what I decide they are. Understanding this fundamental aspect of how life works and committing to it is the key to the power of losing control and finding the happiness we seek.

Have you been allowing your outcomes to determine your definitions? Try to commit to the fact that our definitions are the genesis of our outcomes. Experiment, and see if your experience is different the next time. ∎

Another rendition of the pilgrimage theme is the subject of Brazilian writer Paul Coelho's *The Alchemist*, subtitled *A Fable about Following Your Dream*. In Coelho's fable, Santiago, an Andalusian shepherd boy, dreams of a distant treasure in Egypt. And off he goes, literally to follow his dream. Along the way he meets many spiritual guides until, finally, he makes the acquaintance of an alchemist, who tells him that "fear of suffering is worse than the suffering itself. And . . . no heart has ever suffered when it goes in search of its dreams, because every second of the search is a second's encounter with God and with eternity."

In other words, the object of our search lies within us, and the only place to search for God (or happiness or higher truth or whatever you, personally, choose to call your ultimate motivation) is within ourselves.

■ ■ ■

The genesis of many of our problems is that too many of us are peering into the murky future of our secondary world, hoping that there will be something "out there" to finally make us happy. But, in fact, we ought to be looking inward, because the source of true happiness is always available to us. It lies in how we choose to respond to those external circumstances—in our ability to understand, accept, and manage ourselves. This is what will determine how we go about finding our meaning and what kind of higher meaning we can find for ourselves.

HOW DO YOU DEFINE YOURSELF?

Too often, we define ourselves in terms of our achievements, our beliefs, and our relationships. The following test was mentioned by Wayne Dyer as having been posed by one of his college professors. He said it was one of the toughest tests he'd ever taken. If you were to meet a stranger right now and had to identify yourself, what would you tell her? *I'm a banker (lawyer, editor, manufacturer, painter . . .), a father (mother, grandmother . . .), from (name the place). I went to (name the school). . . .* You see how it goes.

Now try to identify yourself without using any of those external markers, such as race, religion, hobbies, job, age, possessions, or family. Can you do that? Try using adjectives instead of the usual nouns. *I'm peaceful, calm, ambitious, driven, artistic, organized, loving, jealous. . . .*

Can you see that this form of identification allows you to examine yourself without reference to anyone or anything in your secondary world? ∎

Happiness and the Five Steps to Wisdom

One of the most useful tools we have for finding the happiness we seek is following the five steps to wisdom.

First of all, we need to raise our awareness of what it is we desire and what it is we run from. And, again, it's important to reiterate that we do this by examining ourselves, not by looking outward to either the past or the future. If you've done the self-definition exercise just above, you'll have a good place to start.

If you're ambitious, to what is your ambition directed? If you're peaceful, what is the source of your inner peace? If you're jealous, what is it you envy, and why? What is it you fear that you lack?

■ ■ ■

Once you've brought that to conscious awareness, you can consider whether the energy that drives those self-imposed truths is really being put to good use and bringing the outcomes you seek. If not, you can consider how shifting your context might help you find other truths about yourself that would change those outcomes. Experiment. If your experience changes, your definitions will change, too. The rule of congruency will ensure that your perception shifts and that you commit to the new reality. You'll have reached a higher level of self-awareness. That was the experience of one woman who came up to me recently after a talk I gave at the company where she worked. "You're right," she said. "I've got to change my story. I didn't realize it, but I've been seeing myself as a 'rescue ranger,' and I don't want to do that anymore." This woman was in her mid-forties, a highly educated and skilled professional who had always sought out relationships with people and jobs with companies who "needed" her. She went in like the rescue ranger she'd defined herself to be, worked her butt off, and saved the day. She realized on the day of our conversation that her jobs and relationships hadn't been the real problem, which was her self-definition. It's pretty hard to find peace and happiness when you're in "rescue mode" all the time. By becoming aware that her self-definition had created her situation, she'd be able to change her circumstances. I asked her if she was ready to let go of her old definition and create a new one that might serve her better. She promised me she would because, as she put it, "my life depends on it." If we deny the fact that we alone are responsible for our own happiness and if we continue to look for it in our secondary world, and hope to experience it at some future date, as a result of something that happens *to* us, we will never be truly happy.

Happiness Can't Be Measured

I remember quite well the day an acquaintance came rushing up to me in the street, bursting to tell me about the "wonderful" motivational speaker she'd just heard. She couldn't wait to share with me how "brilliant" he was, the verve and energy with which he'd conveyed his message, and, above all, the profound breakthrough she'd experienced from the message itself. Needless to say, I couldn't wait to hear that message. What could the man possibly have said to provoke such a dramatic reaction? "Well," she told me, "he said life was all about connections, and that we miss out on making those connections by letting the moment pass us by. For instance, when we meet someone on the street who asks us how we are, we usually just say fine, and that's that. What we should do is to give ourselves a grade and say something like, 'Well, actually I'm about a B-minus today.' That way, the person will have to ask us why, and we'll get to talk about ourselves and make a real connection."

At that point she stopped, smiling broadly and obviously waiting for me to tell her what a great idea that was and how I intended to integrate the concept into my own life immediately. I didn't want to burst her bubble, but if I didn't tell her why that was such a terrible way to make connections, she just might try it the next time she met someone on the street, and I had no doubt what the result of that would be.

"So," I said, "let me just see if I understand what you're saying. If I met you on the street and you asked how I was, I would tell you I was maybe a C-plus."

"That's right," she said enthusiastically, nodding vigorously.

"And then you'd have to ask me why, right?"

Another vigorous nod.

"So, do you think you'd be asking me about all the good things that made me a C-plus, or would you be more likely to want to know what was keeping me from being an A?"

"Well, I guess I'd be asking what was wrong, why you weren't an A," she admitted.

"But if you did that, wouldn't you just be encouraging me to direct my mind to all the bad stuff that was happening, which would certainly make me even more miserable? I'd just be bringing all my psychic energy to the contemplation of bad circumstances and unhappiness rather than to appreciating my good circumstances and the things that make me happy. And what would you do? In an effort to show compassion and understanding, you'd probably feel the need to commiserate and tell me about similar bad experiences in your life. That's just the verbal equivalent of comparing scars. You might have been perfectly happy when you came up to me, but now you'd have to bring your mind to negative circumstances and events in your life, which would only decrease your level of happiness.

"By the end of our conversation, you and I both would be bringing all our psychic energy to whatever was wrong in our lives instead of to what was right. Wouldn't you then begin to associate me with feeling terrible? Would you really want to connect with me again, or would you run for the hills the next time you saw me?

"I'm sorry to say that sounds like just about the worst way to make a genuine connection I've ever heard. Even if we did connect, it would only be because misery loves company, which is certainly neither the healthiest nor the most positive basis on which to build any kind of relationship."

The truth is, happiness can only be experienced; it can't be measured. We can't grade ourselves on how happy we are. Happiness and unhappiness are not mutually exclusive. We can experience them both at the same time to different degrees. And the minute we try to measure how happy we are, the comparative nature of our minds will compel us to consider how much happier we could be. And when we do that, our happiness level will immediately drop.

The only path to happiness is to cultivate our appreciation for those things that give us pleasure. A good example of how this works occurred one day when I was walking with a friend and we both spotted a big old '57 Chevy driving by. It had huge fins and pounds of chrome, and there was no way we couldn't have noticed it. But my friend was much more excited that I was to see it. He literally stopped in his tracks and said, "Wow, would you look at that. Wow, that's amazing!" He was several years older than I, and it turned out he'd actually owned one of those '57 Chevys. I'm not a car guy to begin with, and I didn't have the same nostalgic feeling for this one that he did. He really appreciated that car, and because he appreciated it, it was beautiful to him. Finally, he realized that I couldn't see it the same way he did, and that its beauty was not intrinsic to the car itself but resulted from his view of it. That realization brought a whole new level of understanding to the words, "Beauty is in the eye of the beholder," which have become so much a cliché that we rarely stop to consider their true meaning.

Happiness works the same way. The more we appreciate something—a field of flowers, listening to the ocean, holding a baby—the happier we will feel.

WHAT DO YOU APPRECIATE?

Grab that paper and pencil you must by now be keeping by this book and start to write down everything you enjoy as quickly as possible for one minute. Don't think too much, just put down whatever pops into your head in no particular order. How do you feel now? If you're happier than before, as most people are, it's because you were thinking of things you enjoy to the exclusion of anything else. The more we practice bringing our attention to those things, the more our appreciation and sense of peace will increase. Practice going through your day like that. Cultivate your appreciation. ∎

Take every opportunity that comes along each day to say a silent prayer of thanks, or to state to yourself what it is you appreciate and how happy you are to have whatever that is in your life. You'll be cultivating your appreciation, and happiness will ensue. You won't be chasing happiness, which would be like chasing romance. The best romances just happen; they can't be pursued.

Happiness Can't Be Pursued

Don't aim at success—the more you aim at it and make it your target, the more you're going to miss it. For success, like happiness, can't be pursued; it must ensue— as the unintended side effect of one's personal dedication to a course greater than oneself.
—Viktor Frankl, *Man's Search for Meaning*

If it's the chase and not the prize that we cherish, we *will* find happiness as a side effect or by-product of our enhanced ability to understand, accept, and manage ourselves. It will come through the enrichment of our relationships, the banishment of our fears, our increased faith, and the wisdom that results from raising the level of our awareness about ourselves.

If, on the other hand, we continually keep our eyes on the prize, treasuring the trophy, we run the risk of completing the chase, possibly even achieving great things along the way, yet missing out on the most important element of life—the thing we really want the most—happiness.

It is, perhaps, the central paradox of human existence that we are driven to "becoming" when, at the same time, we're trapped into "being." To discover our higher meaning, to achieve the happiness and fulfillment we all seek, we must find peace in the process, which is the only way we can finally learn how to "be" at the same time we're "becoming."

Chapter 9

Bringing It Home

We shall not cease from exploration
And the end of all our exploring
Will be to arrive where we started
And know the place for the first time.
*—*T. S. Eliot, "Little Gidding"

All along, we've been talking about how the various concepts in this book—the power of driving myths, of contexts and definitions, the power of faith and of letting go, the five steps to wisdom—build upon and enhance one another, how they *connect*. But the greatest and most transforming connection of all is the one you'll make between what you've read and what you do.

Since the Stanford-Binet IQ test was developed in 1910, it has been used as the standard for measuring intelligence across a broad spectrum of the population. Over the years, however, I've developed my own definition of what it means to be smart, and I call that TQ, or Time Quotient. TQ is based on the length of time that passes between when we know we should do something and when we actually do it. Because, as we've already discussed, true wisdom depends on our ability to put knowledge into action.

Until you've gone through the process of becoming aware of new possibilities, considering them, experimenting with them, and experiencing the outcomes—until you put your knowledge into action—you won't really *own* them as your own. But how to begin?

Give Yourself Permission—And Then Work at It

If you don't think you deserve to have what you want, you'll keep on finding ways to be sure you don't get it. You may not even be aware that you think you're unworthy, but if you've constantly fallen short of achieving the happiness, peace, and success that you want, there's probably something about the way you define yourself and the world that is holding you back. You might want to think about some of the concepts discussed in Chapter 2 and consider the myths that are driving your outcomes. Do you think the rich are different or that all men are jerks or that love is only for the very young, or something equally self-defeating? If so, you probably ought to begin by rewriting your story and allowing yourself to start deserving better outcomes.

Certainly, like all serious change, that's going to take a leap of faith, not necessarily in some higher power but in yourself. You simply have to trust yourself (and remember that real trust is freely given, not earned) and know that whatever resources you need will be there when you need them. And then you need to work at it.

As badly as you may want whatever it is you want, you can't ignore the natural order of life. You have to sow before you reap, learn before you teach, and "be" before you "have." Many years ago, I overheard one person describing another as "gracious," and I began to wonder how people might describe me. I thought how nice it would be to hear someone describe *me* as gracious, and decided to try to become more worthy of that description. And eventually I forgot about the end product—to have someone describe me as gracious—and took pleasure simply in the process of becoming more gracious.

Chart Your Own Course, but Know the Waters

We are all explorers, seeking better definitions, contexts, and out-comes. But, unlike those explorers of old who, like Columbus, sailed into completely unknown waters, when it comes to the common human experience, we're sailing on seas and traveling paths where others have gone before.

I happen to live on a river that empties into Lake Erie, and al-though the river is very wide, some parts of it are only three feet deep. From that river, I can travel anywhere I want, but to get there safely, I have to know where the channels are. Luckily, those chan-nels have already been marked by other sailors; I simply need to learn how to read the markers and charts they left behind. By doing that, I can figuratively follow in the wake of someone who's already sailed and mastered the course.

Identify Your Masters

Everyone in life can be our teacher, but not everyone is a master. A master is someone whose life embodies whatever it is you seek. I suspect that you wouldn't consider taking financial advice from someone who seems incapable of handling his or her own money. Similarly, it wouldn't be wise to take advice about relationships from someone who's never been in a successful relationship. So why would you take advice on finding happiness from someone who isn't happy?

There are masters out there, all around you, whether they're members of your own family, in your personal circle of friends, mentors in the workplace, or people you've never met. A friend or family member can certainly be a master—as my father was for me—but keep in mind that sometimes the advice of family and friends is not the best advice, or the advice you need. You don't need to have a personal relationship with your masters. You can study their writings (as I've been doing for many years), listen to their words on tape or DVD, or watch them in action on videos. You can take classes, go to seminars and lectures, and engage the speaker in conversation. Or, you can let that person know that you look upon him or her as a master, and ask the individual to take an active role in helping you.

Our masters aren't always going to be those with whom we feel most comfortable (which is another reason family and friends don't always make the best masters), and sometimes being too comfortable can prevent us from listening to what they have to say. A classic case of this would be to choose a therapist with whom you feel comfortable, and, the moment he starts to help or to advocate change, move on to another one because you no longer feel comfortable. Creating change isn't always comfortable, and sometimes that's the greatest lesson a master can teach us.

What's important is that, once you've found a master, you make yourself his or her apprentice. In times past, that's how everyone learned. People were apprenticed to a master until they learned their craft. Even the greatest masters were once apprentices themselves. Taking lessons from a master is, in itself, a form of apprenticeship. Opera singers study with master teachers; ballet dancers learn from former dancers; musicians learn from those who have mastered their instruments. And you can do the same.

When I was in high school, I used to have role models. But rather than fixing on one person whom I admired in every way, there were several I looked up to for a particular character or personality trait or behavior. And I set out to emulate whatever it was I admired about each one. You don't have to limit yourself to one master. It is quite reasonable to have several people from whom you want to learn a particular form of mastery.

Learn to Emulate Your Masters

There's a movement gaining popularity these days called What Would Jesus Do? (You may have seen people around with bracelets or T-shirts that say WWJD.) These people make decisions and formulate their responses to difficult issues by asking themselves that question and acting accordingly. Christians aspire to being Christ-like, and there's certainly nothing wrong with making Jesus your master, if doing that is in accordance with your beliefs, but the question is also a context that can be given a much more universal application, which may serve non-Christians, as well.

When I was a little kid in third grade or so, I was chubby, with a really geeky brush cut, and definitely not cool. I knew I wasn't cool, but I thought my older brother was, and my mom, and definitely my father. To me, they were the epitome of what I aspired to. And so, whenever I was faced with a problem or a difficult decision, I'd ask myself what one of them would do, and try to respond accordingly.

Today, after I've spent a number of days with the staff of an organization, and they begin to see that the concepts I'm presenting actually work for them, they often ask if they can call or send me an e-mail when they're not quite sure about how to respond in a given situation. Unfortunately, if I took the time to answer every e-mail from every employee of every company I've ever visited, I wouldn't have time to do anything else. So, some time ago, I came up with a plan. I tell these people to write down their questions and then write down the answer as they think I would answer it, and send it to me. I do read those e-mails, and if I think the answer is really off track, I reply. But if the person is thinking in a way that will serve him, I know he's adopted the fundamental concepts I taught him and is using them as a context for approaching the problem at hand.

PRACTICE THINKING LIKE YOUR MASTER

If you've got a problem or a question, write it down. How do you think your master would solve that problem or answer that question? Try to do as you believe he or she would do. Practice thinking like your master. ■

When I began to read the great philosophers, I followed the sequence set forth in Will Durant's *The Story of Philosophy* because I wanted to see how the thinking of each one in turn had built upon and advanced the ideas of those who had gone before him. And by studying the thinking of those masters and how they thought, I, in turn, learned to think better.

Be a Servant to Your Craft

It is a paradox of human growth that all masters are also servants to their craft. It is, in fact, by committing ourselves to serving our craft that we *become* masters. And even in our mastery, we remain servants. Before he began to create his famous cubist paintings, Picasso committed himself to learning the basics of classical perspective and composition; without mastering the basics, he couldn't ever have become the innovative genius that he was. And that's true of any true innovator. A jazz pianist can't riff on the melody until he's learned it. A choreographer needs to learn the elements of classical dance. A highly successful entrepreneur needs to have a good understanding of the basics of business.

On a shelf in my living room I have a tattered, faded copy of a book called *Arban's Celebrated Method for the Trumpet*. Trumpet players for decades have come to know it as "the trumpet player's bible." It belonged to my dad when he was a kid, and now it's well over fifty years old. In that book there is everything from information on how to clean the trumpet's valves to scales and exercises to difficult études. I keep it to remind myself that although, as a musician, Mick developed his own style and went his own way, he remained a servant to the trumpet. He studied the basics; he committed himself to his craft.

If we are good and faithful servants, if we continue to recommit ourselves to studying the basics, we will, as a by-product of that commitment, become masters. And to serve our mastery, we will commit to serving others by becoming their teachers.

Learn to Practice and to Play

We learn to speak by speaking; we learn to run by running; and we learn to love by loving; there is no other way.
—Saint Francis de Sales

Just because you're no longer a child, there's no reason to stop playing, and you can never be master enough to stop practicing. Remember that musicians and athletes are constantly "playing," and doctors and lawyers "practice" every day.

There are two areas that it would serve you to begin to practice and play with: awareness and sincerity.

Awareness

This is where it all begins. It's the first step to wisdom. And since our happiness and success are determined by how well we understand, accept, and manage ourselves, we can benefit most by raising our level of awareness about ourselves.

- Count the negative statements you hear coming out of your mouth. Give a close friend permission to bring it to your attention, if necessary. Become aware of your *buts*. It's hard for anyone to feel that you're honoring his or her perception when the first word out of *your* mouth after he or she speaks is *but*.

- Practice seeing that other people need to be right, and practice letting them be right.

- Practice becoming more aware of when *you* need to be right and to have your "rightness" validated.

- Instead of allowing your desire to be right to justify the thoughts and emotions that make you and those around you feel bad, practice letting go of them by changing your context.

A powerful example of how self-imposed contexts and definitions can fail to serve us was brought home to me when a corporate CEO asked me to work with one of his managers. This woman, whom I'll call Marjorie, was a high-level manager who was clearly extremely bright and capable but also so passionate about her work and the company she worked for that any small mistake or inadequacy on the part of a member of her staff would make her furious and send her off into an angry tirade. Needless to say, her staff members learned to do everything in their power to escape her wrath, which sometimes made them too cautious and unwilling to venture an opinion, and had begun to create missed opportunities for the organization as a whole.

At the point I was called in, the CEO had realized that Marjorie was becoming a very expensive employee, but he also knew how bright she was and how deeply she cared about the company. He wanted to save her for the good of the organization, which would also mean saving her from herself.

At our first meeting, Marjorie was perfectly polite and cooperative, but the first two things she told me were, first of all, that I didn't know anything about the company's business or about how infuriating it was to see "these young kids screwing up." And, secondly, that I needed to understand that she was a "passionate person" because, after all, she was Italian and it was in her blood.

What she'd done, without realizing it, I'm sure, was to try to neutralize any suggestion I might make by telling me, in effect, that I didn't know what I was talking about (before she'd even heard what I might have to say), and to validate the power of her myth by attaching it to something greater than herself and out of her control, her genetic makeup.

We talked about the fact that passion, like any emotion, can be something very good; it can drive one to achieve excellence. But passion can also be a negative if we use it in a context that doesn't serve us. I validated her truth by agreeing that the company needed her passion and her experience, but also suggested that what the company didn't need were the problems her passion was causing. I told her that I didn't want her to try to be less passionate, I simply wanted her to consider shifting what she was passionate about. I suggested that she practice being more passionate about the solutions and less passionate about the problems.

That context hit a chord with Marjorie, and, to this day, she keeps a note card with those words written on it on the bulletin board above her desk.

You, too, can do that. Practice shifting your context by bringing your passion to the solutions rather than to the problems in your life.

- Practice choosing your battles and becoming aware of those that don't serve you or that you can't possibly win. No warrior is strong enough or powerful enough to fight on all fronts at all times and win. The smartest generals have learned to strategize, and pick the battles they want to fight. You can do the same.

- Practice becoming acutely aware that the "happily ever after" that you seek will come to you one day at a time, one thought at a time, one feeling at a time. Most of us continue to long for some time in the future that we've decided will be "our time," but our time—yours and mine—is always right now. In order to bring the concepts in this book home, you don't need to get it right all the time. You just have to get it right now.

Sincerity

It's true that some people are blessed with more opportunities and talents in certain areas than others, but even the most talented must practice to hone their skills and nurture their gifts. There's an apocryphal story about a woman who, upon staring in awe at the beauty of Michelangelo's statue of David, approached the sculptor and said, "Your mastery is quite impressive." Whereupon the master replied, "Woman, if you knew how hard I worked for my mastery, you wouldn't be so impressed."

- Practice being sincere in your efforts to master "the art of living," even—or especially—when it seems that you're stuck or that you're focusing on situations you know you can't control.

Sincerity adds value to whatever we do, and if we make our sincerest effort, more often than not it will do the job.

- Practice hardest in the areas where you think you have the least talent. In fact, our most sincere efforts ought to be devoted to those areas where we might not be so naturally talented. Perhaps, for example, you don't see yourself as someone who's good at remembering names, or perhaps you forget to ask people how they are (and genuinely listen to their response) before you tell them what you want. When those efforts are turned toward self-awareness and growth, it's called building character. While we live alone in our primary world, our words, our actions, and even our dreams impact the lives of others, and for that reason, we have a duty to work hard to develop our mastery.

In the "art of life" our success won't be determined by how much natural talent we have when we begin the process but by how committed we are to mastering the art.

- Practice sincerely and openly complimenting that which you admire and respect. There's an old adage that says a man should never stop complimenting his wife, because soon after he stops complimenting her, he's likely to stop noticing that which he admired. Understand that not everyone you compliment will respond positively. Some people find it difficult to accept a compliment, and they'll let you know that by the way they respond. Don't stop complimenting, though, as long as you're sincere. Simply tone it down for those who might be made uncomfortable by too much effusiveness.

Be Sure You've Got Enough Provisions

Whenever you start on a journey, you have to plan ahead, and assume there will be some bumps in the road or an unexpected detour. You wouldn't hit the trail for a long hike in the woods without a compass in case you got lost or enough food and water to see you through. Creating change in and for yourself is like embarking on a journey. You can count on the fact that there *will* be difficulties down the road, and the better prepared you are to deal with them, the greater will be your chances for success.

I'm sure many of us have been on a diet at some point in our life. Isn't there usually some particular time of day when you find it most difficult not to "cheat"? Maybe it's around three o'clock in the afternoon, when your energy level drops and you really want a chocolate bar from the candy machine in the lobby. If you've thought ahead and brought a sweet piece of fruit to work that morning, you'll be able to satisfy your sugar craving without compromising your diet. Or maybe it's in the evening, when you've already had dinner and are watching television before going to bed. You know there's ice cream in the freezer, but if you also have some air-popped popcorn on hand, you can eat your snack and diet, too.

No matter what it is we're trying to accomplish, it's at those difficult junctures that we want to be armed with whatever we'll need to keep us from going off course. In the journey of life, it helps to have your bag packed with contexts and definitions that will serve you well and to have been fortified by your commitment to them. If you *know* you've packed the right stuff, you can have faith that there won't be anything down the road you can't handle.

When the road is roughest, we're most likely to fall back on our worst contexts. If you're a James Bond fan, you might remember the 1997 movie version of *Tomorrow Never Dies*. At a certain point, Bond and Colonel Wai-Lin, a beautiful female agent of the Chinese People's External Security Force, are captured by the goons working for the evil telecommunications genius. They're handcuffed together and taken to the evil genius's office to be tortured and killed. Their only possible avenue of escape is out a window that's forty-five stories above the ground. Needless to say, they manage to get away and steal a motorcycle. But as they're speeding toward safety, they're pursued by a helicopter that finally traps them in a dead-end street blocked by an iron gate. "Trapped," says Wai-Lin. "Never," says Bond. Although they're sharing an identical experience, their very different responses reveal not only their own self-image but also their definition of the experience itself. Bond's context was that there was an answer to every problem, a way out of every situation, and that it was just up to him to figure it out. And he had more trust in that context than he did in his fears, because he knew that context had always served him well while his fears very often had not.

I still can't help smiling when I remember the way my youngest brother Rob used to lose things all the time when we were kids. Invariably, one of us older boys would be relaxing in front of the television or doing our homework when Rob would appear, looking both exasperated and resigned. "What's the problem?" we'd ask.

"I lost my pen" (or my sneakers, or my math workbook—it didn't matter, at one time or another Rob lost all of them).

"Well, where's it gone? Where'd you have it last?"

"I dunno," he'd say, raising his shoulders in disbelief. To Rob, things just disappeared into some kind of parallel universe, leaving him completely helpless. He didn't even try to find them, because his context was that they were lost and gone forever. Without knowing what a context was, we used to tease him about it and call his approach. "The Rob Caruso School of Search." We older guys knew, however, that things didn't just disappear. They had to be somewhere, and with enough patience and searching, we generally found them. Rob thought this was some kind of magic, but it was really his negative context driving his helpless behavior.

If we're prepared with enough positive definitions and contexts, it's like having money in the bank, a deposit we can draw on when the chips are down and we need to make an emergency withdrawal.

Practice Letting Go

Sometimes your bags can get too heavy. Usually that means you're still carrying around stuff you should have left behind. If you feel yourself being held back or dragged down instead of moving forward, it can help to change your physical surroundings.

I remember a young woman who came to me because she didn't think she was "maturing" and becoming independent as quickly or successfully as she would have wanted. She had just graduated from college, was looking for a job, and was still living at home at the time. She *wanted* to become the young working professional she knew she could and should be, but she was having a difficult time with the transition. And she also believed that her seeming inability to present a more mature image was preventing her from getting the kind of job she wanted and was certainly capable of doing.

In the course of our conversation, I asked her to describe her bedroom. It turned out, as I had suspected, that she was surrounded by mementos of her childhood, from her dolls to her children's books and school pennants. I suggested that she put those things away for six months or so. I didn't tell her to *throw* them away, just to get them out of sight so that she didn't wake up and go to bed every day in the physical context of childhood. I also suggested that she try changing her wardrobe. Since she still wore the same size as in her senior year of high school, she was still wearing those clothes—and looking more like a high school senior than a college graduate.

I'm certainly not suggesting that creating change in oneself is as simple as changing one's surroundings or one's wardrobe, but in this young lady's case, those things were triggers that reminded her of happy times gone by—times that were past. And those triggers were—unconsciously, to be sure—encouraging her to repeat old scripts instead of writing new ones that would serve her better in her new situation. She lovingly boxed up all those childhood things and put them away in the closet. Six months later, she'd lost all interest in them, and after a year they were just happy memories that no longer had the power to shape her behavior. When it comes to our personal growth, it's sometimes safer and more enjoyable to reminisce from a distance.

If you really want to shift your context, you might want to let go of some of the anchors that are keeping you from moving. Even rearranging the furniture can serve as a trigger to remind you to stay vigilant in your commitment to your new way of thinking.

Until you change your way of thinking, using whatever tools you have at your disposal, you won't be able to let go of who you've been, and you won't experience new and better outcomes. I still have a friend whom I met during my "musician" days and who, these many years later, seems unable to let go of his old self-definition. He's actually a real technology wiz and could easily use his talent and expertise in that area to earn a very good salary and live a comfortable life. But he hasn't done that. Instead he's still playing piano a few evenings a week at a local nightspot. He's perpetually in debt and chronically depressed about his financial situation, to the point where his debt is actually driving his life. But whenever we sit down to talk about how he can improve his financial situation and finally get out of debt, his first and only suggestion is that he could play a couple more nights a week, or get another gig at a better-paying spot. I can tell him a thousand times that there aren't enough nights in the year or any gigs that pay enough to make that plan viable, but he doesn't hear me. He still defines himself as a musician, and he's using that definition as a context that isn't going to serve him any better in the future than it has in the past. Until he can let go of that context, and stop equating playing the piano with anything other than side money, he won't be able to create a different outcome for himself.

You Are Your Greatest Masterpiece

After one of my presentations, during which I'd discussed driving myths and self-definitions, a woman came up and reminded me of an old story. Three men are moving rocks from one side of a field to the other. A passerby comes up to them and asks what they're doing. "Moving rocks," say the first guy. "Building a building," says the second. "Building a cathedral," says the third.

"I know I'm moving rocks," the woman at the presentation said, "and I know I'm doing it for the greater good of the company, but where is the cathedral? I just can't see what I do as being as noble as that."

It was a good question. "*You* are the cathedral," I told her. "In the *way* you do your work, and in what you bring to the people you work with, you're creating yourself in the process. And that's the greatest piece of art there could be."

Accept, Adjust, Advance

When a painter sets out to create a work of art, he or she begins with a blank canvas. She may have an image in her mind of what she's trying to achieve, but once she's committed paint to canvas, there's no going back. A splotch of green in not quite the right spot can't be erased, and may require an adjustment in another area. By accepting what's on the canvas, continuing to adjust, and adding a stroke here or more color there, the painting advances and eventually is completed.

About fifteen years ago, I was with my friend Greg at the Freedom Festival, which is held along the riverfront in Detroit each July. Because Detroit shares a border with Canada, we don't call our shared celebration Fourth of July, but we do have all the fireworks, bands, and other festivities that are traditional for the Fourth of July. On this day, Greg and I had been taking in the festivities all morning, and we were getting hungry. As we started to cross the jam-packed plaza to get to the garage where we'd parked our car, I was, in effect, walking blind. As a short guy (I'm only five feet five inches tall) in the midst of a crowd, all I could see were the backs of the people in front of me (sort of like being a kid in the back of a crowded elevator.) As we were shuffling along, we were suddenly pushed violently backward by the crowd in front of us. I, of course, couldn't see what was going on, but I did notice that everyone around me seemed to be looking up.

When I looked to see what they were all staring at, I saw first a pair of feet, followed by a pair of legs, which turned into a man dropping from the sky. It was a military paratrooper. He gently landed in the space the crowd had cleared for him only seconds earlier (by stepping backward into Greg and me), gathered up his parachute as quickly as possible, moved to the side, and then looked up. So we all looked up. And in came a second paratrooper, who landed in precisely the same spot, and just as quickly moved aside. They looked up, so again we looked up. One more guy dropped out of the sky into the exact same spot. Three guys, same spot. When I looked up to see if there were any more (there weren't), I also noticed that there wasn't a cloud in the sky. The reason I took note of that seemingly unimportant fact was that I was looking for the airplane they must have jumped from, but it was nowhere in sight.

As we headed into the garage toward the car so we could finally get some food, Greg and I commented on how impressed we were by the paratroopers. Approaching the car, I couldn't help but notice Greg's pace slowing almost to a dead stop. His hands were in his pockets, and his head was slowly moving back and forth while he kept repeating the same words over and over. "Unbelievable." "Awesome." By this time I was really hungry, and I just wanted to get out of there. When I finally couldn't stand it anymore, I said, "Greg, come on. I'm hungry."

"Joe," he said, squaring his shoulders to me and using his most serious voice. "Don't you realize what you just saw?"

"Yes," I said, "I told you, it was very impressive. Now let's go eat."

But Greg wouldn't quit. "No, really. I want you to take a minute, and consider something. When those guys jumped out of that plane, they were *miles* high and probably miles from that plaza. As they stood in the doorway of that plane and strained to see the spot where they wanted to land, it must have looked almost impossible to get there. Imagine what it must have taken for them to jump from that plane, open their chutes, and know they could stay on course for all that time over all that distance and hit their mark. Unbelievable! Awesome."

"Greg," I said, "you're right, it was pretty amazing. And I didn't really picture it from their vantage point the way you described it but there's something wrong with your version."

"What are you talking about?" he shot back.

"Well, I agree that they jumped out of their plane and pulled their ripcords, and I can't deny that they hit their mark. What I don't agree with is that they were on course the entire way down. In fact, I contend that they were never on course from the moment they opened their chutes."

Greg just shook his head. "That isn't logical. There's no way they could have been off course the entire time and still hit their mark."

"While it might not sound logical, I'll suggest that it is a fact. And further, I'll suggest that they never expected to be on course."

"Now, this I gotta hear," invited Greg.

"The minute they opened their chutes, they began to drift—either to the left or the right, forward or back. They simply continuously adjusted all the time they were falling toward their mark, until finally they landed."

"You're right," said Greg. "It makes total sense once you put it that way."

Most of us can relate to those paratroopers as they stood in the doorway of that plane. Sometimes it feels as if the distance between where we are and what we want is so great that no matter what course we set, it will be nearly impossible to get there. But we can take two lessons from the paratroopers.

1. Make a leap of commitment with our first step.

2. When forces beyond our control take us off course, all we need to do is . . . accept, adjust, and advance.

We need to remember that we can get off course and still hit our mark if we'll just accept what is happening, adjust to the new conditions, and keep going toward what we want.

The search that we're on is never direct, but if we keep accepting, adjusting, and advancing, we'll eventually arrive where we want to be, which is home! Again, the game of baseball provides the perfect metaphor. When we hit a home run, what do we do? We circle the bases until we return to the place we began, but at a higher level—we bring it home.

BRING IT HOME

Now might be the time to go back through this book and choose an exercise you'd like or think you need to practice. See if by going back to the basics you can make that concept your own and really bring it home. ∎

I don't expect that you'll agree with every concept in this book, and, as an author, I don't think that would be the worst outcome. To me, the worst outcome would be if you agreed with what I have to say and didn't use those ideas to improve the quality of your life—if you didn't claim them as your own and bring them home. Home is where we live and where we keep our special things—the things that are nearest and dearest to us. If the concepts I discuss work for you, and if you commit to them, they will become special. You *will* have brought them home.

Chapter 10

Your Legacy Is None of Your Business

That life is worth living is the most necessary of assumptions, and were it not assumed, the most miserable of conclusions.

—George Santayana

We are the only species capable of contemplating our own mortality. Our death frightens us, and yet we are compelled to consider it, which, at the same time, compels us to contemplate the meaning of our life. I suspect that every one of us has, at some point, thought about how we'll be remembered after we're gone. It's a central fact of human nature that we all want to believe our living has had some purpose, and that we will in some way leave our mark on the world for having been here. That's the ultimate expression of the second rule of engagement: Everyone's greatest desire is to be right. The greatest validation of our "rightness" would be to have lived a life that in some way denies our mortality, a life that is bigger than ourselves.

Building a Monument One Stone at a Time

When I was on the island of Maui—on that same occasion when I "discovered" Orion for the first time—we were in a valley, completely surrounded by lush vegetation, majestic mountains, and unbelievably blue skies. Everything as far as the eye could see was vast and apparently untouched by time.

During the course of our stay, I became fascinated by the apparent compulsion tourists had to make little piles of the small, flat rocks that lie all over the island. I asked several people why they were doing that and received several different answers. One person told me he thought it was an ancient Hawaiian tradition having something to do with the gods and spirituality. But even if that meant something to the Hawaiians, it didn't account for why so many tourists were involved in a ritual that had to be meaningless to them. Other people said they'd read about the practice in a tour guide, but there wasn't anything about it in my tour guide. Were all these other people reading the same guide? And why was this rather meaningless activity so compelling to them? When I asked the people in my own group, they said they weren't really sure why they were doing it, but they did feel better afterward.

I finally concluded that the reason so many people were piling those rocks had nothing to do with the rocks or with any ancient Hawaiian ritual. Rather, it had to do with them. For whatever reason, they piled the rocks because they all felt compelled in some way to leave their mark on that island.

Maui's magnificence is so vast and timeless that encountering it for the first time can easily make one feel comparatively small and insignificant. Encountering nature on that scale makes us suddenly aware of our own brief moment in time. Without realizing it, some of us feel the need to respond in some way to whatever has created that feeling. In this case, to think that we can, even in so small a way, affect that awesome landscape, that our little pile of stones will remain even after we've left the island, allows us to feel that we have somehow cheated or denied our mortality and become a part of its eternity.

■ ■ ■

Civilizations going back to ancient times have left their mark in the form of excavated ruins and monuments that have survived for centuries—the pyramids of ancient Egypt, Stonehenge, and the Parthenon, to name just a few of the most instantly recognizable. A couple of years ago when I was visiting Egypt with my wife, Carol, we found ourselves standing in front of the Sphinx with hundreds of other tourists from all over the world. We began to talk about how many millions of people over so many centuries had come to marvel at its creation. Even the ancient Romans had hired tour guides to take them sightseeing in Egypt to view what *they* called "the ancient ruins." But of all the millions of those who have come to stare upon it, there are few who know who built it, or for what purpose. And so, what kind of a legacy is it, after all? An ancient pharaoh needed to leave his mark, just as those tourists on Maui needed to leave their mark, and in the end, we're left with a magnificent pile of stones in Cairo called the Sphinx and small piles of stones on Maui, and the meaning of both is lost to all of us.

■ ■ ■

A few individuals, it is true, have left their mark in this world through participation in some world-changing event; by inventing something that changes the lives of future generations; even by being infamous. And yet, most us won't leave those kinds of monuments or marks. Few of us will successfully sacrifice our lives for the sake of something greater than ourselves, and if we set out with that as our purpose, we run the risk of losing out on the life we are living. For most of us, our legacy, like our happiness and success, will be a by-product of all we have done, from day to day, and how we did it. Our legacy will result from the *process* of living our life.

The Buddha Was Right

One of the primary tenets of Buddhism is that we shouldn't spend too much time thinking about the future, because the future hasn't happened yet and whatever we're thinking about it might, in fact, never happen. Understanding and accepting that concept in our everyday lives is also fundamental to the power of losing control, and it's basic to ensuring that we *will* leave our mark, at least upon those with whom we interact on a daily basis.

We don't do that by thinking about our future. We don't do it by focusing on our achievements, on how much wealth we can accumulate or how much power we can amass. We do that by living, as much as possible, in the moment and by trying to bring all that we are to everything we do every day.

Not too long ago, I was asked by the new director of our local YMCA if I would speak to his staff, whose members were mainly volunteers. He'd previously been the director of the YMCA in Chicago, one of the largest and most active Y's in the country, and was dismayed by the lack of what he called "customer service" in our comparatively small, community organization. I was to be the one who would open the minds and raise the awareness of his staff in preparation for his announcing his new plan. Given that many of these people were volunteers, I didn't think there would be much chance of their "volunteering" to come to hear a speech on their own time, so I suggested that he put my appearance in the context of a potluck dinner, which would make the event seem more like a party than a lecture.

That evening I was hanging around as part of the crowd, which is what I usually do before I speak. No one knows who I am, and so I'm free to disappear, so to speak, while keeping my eyes and ears open. As the volunteers (mostly women) entered the hall that had been hired for the evening, they all immediately gravitated to the kitchen, where they began putting the food on plates and into bowls, getting out silverware and utensils, and setting up the buffet. Then I saw a man of indeterminate age entering the room carrying a pie. He was wearing thick glasses and walked with a limp, and it was clear from his expression and manner that he was learning disabled but obviously functioning. I later learned that he was a fixture at the Y, performing whatever small tasks he was assigned. But it's what he did as I watched that made him unforgettable. He took that pie into the kitchen and proudly "presented" it to one of the women, saying, "I just made this pie today, especially for this evening." He then spoke to each of the older women individually, honoring them by asking this one about her sore knee, that one about her grandchild, another about her knitting. Having said a few words to each one, he then approached the rest of his colleagues and worked that same magic on them. To a guy wearing a football jersey he said, "Hey, how about those Lions!" To another he mentioned a favorite television program. And, finally, he came back into the main room and began crossing the floor toward me, holding his hand out. I started to move toward him, and when we met, he shook my hand and said, "Hi, you must be the speaker because you're the only person here I don't know. Thank you for coming." I was immediately touched by his kind words and consideration. Disabled or not, he was obviously a master of getting people to like themselves when they were with him.

When I got up to start my talk, I could see that people were nervous. In an effort to help break the ice, I began by saying, "I don't know what all of you do, so why don't we go around the room and you can tell me your name and your job." So, they started introducing themselves in turn: "I'm Suzy, and I'm the receptionist." "I'm Joan and I'm the administrative assistant." And so on until we got to the man who had shaken my hand. "Hi," he said without hesitation. "I'm Bob, and my job is . . ." And with that he simply froze, and a blank look came over his face. He just "went away." I didn't know what to do at that point, but after a minute or two he came out of it and, as if nothing had happened, started again. "Hi, I'm Bob, and my job is . . ." And it started again. Everyone in the room was visibly uncomfortable, and I was feeling anxious myself. I felt horribly guilty for having put him on the spot and creating the whole situation, but I didn't really know what to do. Finally, after what seemed like an hour, he snapped out of it again, and this time he said, "My job is to make people happy."

Once again, I was impressed by Bob's words. He was the only one in that room who got it right. While we can't truly *make* people happy, we're sometimes so busy doing what we think is our job that we forget we're responsible for helping them to like themselves while they're with us. Bob came the closest that evening to defining what it means to bring all we have to everything we do—whatever that may be. He came the closest to indicating not only that he understood the elements of how one creates a personal legacy but also the point the new director was hoping to make to his volunteer staff—that customer service, making people happy, was their real job, and everything else was just the specific functions they performed while they did that.

■ ■ ■

I had a friend who, while certainly not impaired in any way, reminded me of Bob. His name was Howie. He was much older than I and, sadly, is no longer with us, but we used to meet for lunch on a regular basis at one or another of his favorite local diners. The waitresses in these places were all pretty world-weary. They'd seen it all more than once and were not about to waste much time chatting up the customers. But by the end of our lunch, Howie had always made a new best friend. Our previously crabby waitress would be smiling and telling Howie to come back soon. One day, as we were walking out after yet another one of Howie's conquests, I couldn't help commenting, "Boy, you really know how to make people feel good!"

"That's my job," he replied matter-of-factly. He really believed that, and it was a definition that served him—and those around him—very well.

I thought of Howie just recently, when I was dining in a very "smart" French restaurant with one of my clients. As the captain was leading us to our table, a waiter bumped into me and pushed right on without even stopping for an instant to say, "Excuse me." The collision was so obvious that my client just looked at me, speechless. "Some of us are working so hard to do our job that we forget what our job is," I said.

ARE YOU DOING YOUR JOB?

At some point, most of us have been in a "couples" relationship where each person has certain responsibilities that become part of the expectations of the relationship on a practical level—one person doing the dishes while the other puts out the garbage, one doing the laundry while the other mows the lawn, for example. Living up to those responsibilities is one of the ways you express your love. So, what's more important in determining the success and quality of the relationship, that you love your partner or that your partner *knows* you love him or her? It has to be the latter, because if you do love your partner and your partner doesn't know it, you've both got a problem. While you're doing your job, you can't forget to let your partner know you love her or him, or else you'll soon be out of a job. ■

Be Undeniable

As with many of the fundamental truths I've come to accept and to live by, it was my father—my best friend, my hero, my wisest teacher—who first showed me how important it is to always give everything we have to everything we do.

I'm sure we all have our own memories of adolescent angst, but when I was in seventh grade, I was in developmental hell. I was short, chubby, and worst of all for a boy, I was terrible at sports. Nevertheless, I *loved* baseball. Since I couldn't throw, catch, or hit, there was no way I could even hope to make the school team. But I learned about something called intramural baseball—a group of teams composed of anyone who simply *wanted* to play. All I had to do was sign up. Game days, however, were bittersweet for me. On the one hand, I was excited to be able to play; on the other, I was always anxious about being teased by the other boys.

One beautiful day in May I was playing right field, as usual—a lonely but appropriate position for the worst player on the team, since no one in seventh grade was capable of hitting the ball to right field—and thinking about my upcoming turn at bat. I was sure that my moment at the plate wouldn't last very long since I invariably struck out. I was so scared of getting hit by the ball that I tended to pull away rather than stepping into every pitch.

That day, however, when my turn came, by some quirk of fate (ironically, I think I was actually hit by a pitch) I found myself on first base. There was only one out, and the next kid up was a pretty good hitter. There was actually a chance I'd get to run some bases. Maybe I'd even get all the way home! I was definitely on cloud nine because I *knew* this would no doubt be the only chance I'd have to run the bases the whole year.

And then I heard a voice from the bleachers yelling, "Attaboy, Joe, way to go!" It was my father. I couldn't believe it. In those days Mick worked six days a week and was *never* able to attend my games. But there he was, on the one day I'd actually gotten on base. I was practically delirious with joy.

"Okay, no pitcher up there. Wait for your pitch," I yelled to the kid at the plate in my best team-player voice. My teammate responded to this encouragement by hitting a little ground-ball dribbler directly at the shortstop. For a moment I was stunned motionless. I couldn't believe my luck would be so bad that he was going to ruin my one chance of running the bases. Then I took off for second. When I got close, I looked up for the very first time. I knew I'd see the second baseman there with the ball in his hand just waiting to tag me out. But what I saw was a completely different picture. I don't know what happened with the shortstop, but he must have bobbled the catch in the worst way. The ball was just now getting to the second baseman, and the ump was hovering over the bag as I started my slide. It was going to be close, but a tie, I knew, would go to the runner. I slid into base just as I was tagged, and the second baseman and I both looked at the umpire. Everything I wanted was now up to him.

"You're OUT!" he shouted.

I was devastated. How could he have called me out? Didn't he know how badly I wanted to get there in time, how much I wanted to run the bases, just once, and especially on the day that my dad was there to watch? I got up slowly, dusted myself off, and, head down, made my way back to the bench, fully prepared to be greeted by the taunts of my teammates. I sat down, studying my feet, and waited for the teasing to begin. As if I didn't feel bad enough already.

There was only one seat open on the bench, and as fate would have it, it was right between one of the best players on the team and Bruce, who just happened to be the kid who made fun of me the most. *Perfect*, I thought sarcastically. And, just as I thought, it didn't take more than a few seconds for the kid on my left to hit me on the leg and comment on the play. I braced myself emotionally for the onslaught.

"Don't worry about it," he said. "You were there."

I couldn't believe my ears. He wasn't picking on me. As I was still trying to understand what was happening, Bruce backhanded me on the right thigh and said eight words that would ring triumphantly in my little seventh-grade brain. "Yeah, man, you were there. Ump was blind."

I was back on cloud nine. *I was there. Ump was blind.* I spent the remainder of the game running in and out of right field repeating to myself, *I was there! Ump was blind!* For me, that game had all the makings of a heroic journey—the highs and lows, the high hopes and dashed dreams—but by the time it was over, those words had turned defeat into victory. It was the best game of my life.

"Good game," my father said as I climbed into the station wagon next to him.

"Yep," I agreed in my jockiest voice. I figured he must have been talking about the only play in the game that mattered—my run for second base. And of course I couldn't wait to say the words. "I was there. Ump was blind."

My dad was an insightful man who knew immediately what I was talking about. His response was calm and matter-of-fact, and it knocked me off my cloud, nearly breaking my fragile seventh-grade heart.

"You didn't deserve it," he said matter-of-factly.

My father, being a sensitive man, could see his words had upset me. "You really wanted second base, didn't you?" he asked, sounding oddly surprised.

Of course I wanted second base. More than anything in the world I wanted to be able to keep running the bases and playing baseball. What could he possibly mean by telling me I didn't deserve it? I felt my eyes beginning to well up with tears. "Yes," I blurted around the lump that was forming in my throat. "Of course I wanted second base." I couldn't believe how fast I could go from feeling so good to feeling so terrible again.

"Don't get me wrong, Joe," he continued. "I really wanted you to have it, too. But you didn't deserve it."

Didn't deserve it? What is he talking about?

"You see, Joe, baseball is a great game, and like all great games, it's a lot like life. In life, if we want something and other people get to decide whether or not we deserve it, we can't make it so close that they have a problem deciding. Next time, when someone hits the ball, no matter how well he hits it, you've got to start running sooner so that when you get to the next base there won't be any doubt that you deserve it. Whether it's in baseball or in life, if you really want something, you've got to be *undeniable.*"

My father obviously knew how much I'd wanted to be safe on second. He knew what it meant to me, but he didn't like the way I'd chosen to respond, by assuming the role of defiant victim. He saw that I was viewing what had happened within a context that wasn't going to serve me, and through his words, he was able to help me shift that context. He wasn't trying to *control* my behavior as a child, much less to control who I'd be when I grew up. But he was concerned about me in that moment, and found the power to express that concern in a way that would serve us both. To me, that was a really powerful lesson, one I've remembered and tried to live up to all my life. I've used that story in seminars, management retreats, and leadership meetings as a clear illustration of the need to bring all you have to all you do, and its message has resonated in the hearts and minds of many people and many organizations. Several years ago I decided to make it the subject of one of my newspaper columns.

Another Lesson—Learning the Meaning of Legacy

At the time I wrote my column about "being undeniable," my father wasn't well, and I was living at home to be more available to him. I knew he'd be reading the column in our local paper, and I was sure he'd have something to say about the writing, as he did about almost every one of my columns. Nevertheless, I relished the thought of his knowing that, after thirty years, I was using the lesson he'd taught me as a kid in order to help others.

On the evening of the day it appeared, he called down the stairs, as he did every night, "Hey, Joe, I'm going to bed."

"Okay, Mick," I yelled back. "Sleep well." I couldn't believe it. I knew he'd read the paper. I'd seen him reading it. But he wasn't going to say anything about the column! This had been my public love letter to my father, my thank you for the lesson he'd taught not only me but all those who had heard it and had come to use that phrase as a context for their own lives, as well. How could he not say something about it?

I was just on my way back to my office when he called out again, "Hey, Joe . . ."

"Yeah, Mick, what is it?"

"Good column!"

"Thanks, Mick." I think I was just as happy in that moment as I'd been the day I made it to first base. He'd liked the column! I hoped it had made him proud. And then, after another moment he called out again.

"Joe?"

"Yeah, Mick?"

"Was that story true?"

I was dumbstruck. How could he not remember such an important and meaningful moment—a life lesson that guided and still guides me, a magical father-son moment in time? Somehow I managed to respond, "Yeah, Mick—every word."

"Hmmm . . . Well, anyway, good column. Good night, Joe."

"Good night, Mick."

I stumbled back into my office struggling with trying to make sense of what had just happened. I couldn't understand how what had been for me a life-shaping experience had been just another day for him. And then, a new depth of understanding started to become clear in my mind, and as it did, I felt an unusual sensation sweep over me. It's that feeling you get when you truly learn something new. I can only describe it as a sense of peace, exhilaration, humility, and pride, all mixed together. The true and higher meaning of something I thought I had understood for decades finally became clear to me.

I'd been thinking for thirty years that the meaning of my father's lesson had been that by bringing our best to everything we do, we'll enhance our chances of being undeniable and of getting what we need or want. And it was. But now, with those four simple words, "was that story true?" he'd made me see it on an entirely different level.

The reason my father didn't remember that lesson was that he hadn't been trying to teach me a lesson in the first place. He didn't look on those words as his legacy to me. He wasn't trying to leave his mark on my life. He was simply bringing all he had to that moment—just another of millions of moments he'd have over the course of his life with one of his four sons. It's what he did every day because he understood, probably without ever consciously thinking about it, that it was all he *could* do, and he had faith that it would be enough. His legacy lay in the undeniable power of his example.

The Power of Baseball as a Metaphor for Life

To me, the power of those two stories is that together they form the central lesson by which I've tried to live my life, and they illustrate as clearly as anything I can think of the importance of living in the present and enhancing our awareness by bringing all our focus to our gig of the moment. My father would never have thought to compare himself to Mahatma Gandhi, but Mick, too, could easily have said, "My life is my message." And for me, my brothers, and all who knew Mickey Caruso, his legacy has been as powerful as his example.

The Power of Mick's Legacy

We all have a purpose, but we can't skip through our moments saving our best for some time in the future when every circumstance is just right. We can't diminish the importance of our "now" for some more important "later." Life is difficult because true growth requires the focus of all our attention, the power of our will, and a higher understanding of the seemingly paradoxical notion that we serve ourselves by serving others. Fear tries to manipulate us into attempting to control what we can't while in our hearts and minds we know that those efforts will only perpetuate our unhappiness.

Legacies aren't left in stone or even in books stored in musty libraries. More often than not, we won't know our legacy within our own lifetime, and that's how it should be. But if we bring all our heart and our entire mind to our particular moment in time, we might just have the honor and privilege of touching the hearts and minds of other lives in a time other than our own. Our purpose is entirely our own responsibility and our business, if you will; our legacy is for others to decide and is none of our business.

The Legacy of Love

Love is an emotion that transcends our life on earth, and, therefore, it can be the ultimate legacy. In December 1997 my lifelong best friend, my teacher, my father passed on. He'd rarely been sick for most of his life, almost never even had a headache that I can remember, but during the last six months of his life Mick was in and out of the hospital as his tired body began to quit on him.

The holiday season that year was particularly difficult for my brothers and me. For the first time in our lives, Mickey wasn't there to celebrate with us. My youngest brother, Rob, called one evening just before Christmas. His job had recently transferred him to another state, and he was feeling a bit homesick. We talked about his daughters and his work for a few minutes, but all the while we both knew that what we really needed to talk about was Mick.

"I really miss Dad," he finally said quietly.

"I know. Me, too."

"Sometimes it can get real bad, you know. I mean sometimes, every once in a while, for no particular reason, it can overwhelm me."

I could hear that he was starting to cry quietly. "Yeah, me, too, Gooch." Rob's nickname as a kid had been Gooch because when he was a baby, Mick used to call him Goochy, and the name had just clung.

"What do you do when it happens to you?" he asked.

"Well, Rob, this may sound stupid, but I talk to him. I don't mean that I carry on a long conversation in my mind. I just say, 'I miss you, Mick.' I actually say the words quietly to myself wherever I am, and somehow, it seems to help." I wished there were something else I could say that might help my brother feel better, but that was all I could think of.

Rob thanked me and said he needed to go. I could tell he was having one of his "Mick moments." After I hung up, I sat there alone in my study. Our conversation had saddened me, and I began thinking about Mick, too. I thought about how much I missed talking to him and laughing with him. I wondered what we might be talking about if he were with me—what advice he'd have for me and what he might say that would make me smile.

I realized that in many ways he had been my master and I his apprentice. And that even though he was gone, his legacy of love and wisdom had never been more alive in my heart. With that realization, I decided to take my own advice. I'd write down what I might have said to him if he were with me and see if I could imagine how my master would respond. Maybe it would be silly; maybe it would help me. I didn't know. But it was all I had.

■ ■ ■

"Dad? Can you hear me?"
    "Yes, son, I hear you."
"I miss you, Dad."
    "I'm right here."
"But I miss our closeness."
    "I'm closer now."
"I miss your love."
    "I can love you even more now."
"I miss learning from you."
    "I can teach you better now."
"I miss laughing with you."
    "I get all your jokes now."
"I miss sharing things with you."
    "Now we share everything."
"I miss talking to you."

"We're talking now."

"But I miss the sound of your voice."

"My voice was always less important than my words."

"I feel like I should say I'm sorry."

"I feel like I should say thank you."

"I guess I should be the one saying thank you."

"And I would like to say I'm sorry."

"What could you possibly regret? What is it you feel sorry about?"

"Sorrow and regret are two different things."

"Okay, then, what do you regret?"

"Nothing. There is no use for such a concept here."

"Where is here?"

"You wouldn't understand."

"Then what are you sorry for?"

"For seeing the illusions of my weaknesses and fears as real, and for letting them negatively affect you."

"You mean they're not real?"

"They're like a mirror. They only reflect what is shown to them. Smile into a mirror, and it will smile back. Snarl into a mirror, and it will snarl back."

"What does that mean?"

"When you're looking into a mirror, always remember that you're only seeing an image."

"That seems obvious."

"If it were obvious to more people, you would think they'd be less true to their illusions and more true to themselves."

"You said you can teach me better now. So, what should I know about life that I don't?"

"You know everything you should—that's the best part."

"Then why don't I feel smart?"

"Because you want to know everything. It's impossible to know everything. One knows what one should know. What's more important is how and what we're doing with what we know."

"How am I doing?"

"You know."

In Conclusion

I don't ask that you make me your master, any more than Mick would have thought to ask that I make him mine. I do hope, however, that having gone through this process with me—the process of coming to understand the power of losing control—you'll allow me to become a teacher and will use the tools in this book to help you see yourself and your world a bit differently, from a perspective that provides you with greater peace and more happiness than you may have enjoyed until now.

Attaining wisdom is, as I hope I've made clear, an ongoing process, one that will never be concluded so long as we live and grow. I know that I'm a lot wiser now than I was when I first promised myself I would try to learn all that I could from the great thinkers of the world past and present. But if I thought I'd achieved some kind of ultimate or perfect wisdom, I'd only be revealing the fact that I'd achieved nothing of the kind. Instead, I continue to practice the five steps to wisdom, constantly recommitting myself to experimenting with myself, experiencing new truths, and becoming more aware of how I can enhance the meaning of my own life by helping others to elevate theirs.

I know that the work I do works. I've seen it work in corporate settings as well as in the lives of individuals, and I can't deny the evidence of my experience. If I've truly known my gig in the writing of this book, if I've been able to explain how our self-definitions, driving myths, and contexts can work either for us or against us and how we can redefine, rewrite, and shift those that don't serve us, I'll have made the same meaningful connection with you, the reader, that I do when I work face-to-face with my clients.

I know that I've brought all I have to doing that, and, up until now, it's always been all that I needed. As I've said, the rules of engagement have never failed to help me make the connections I've needed to make. I believe they're transferable to the printed page, but, unlike when I'm sitting across from someone at a table or addressing a group from a podium, I can't look into your eyes and see whether or not my words have provided the validation you need to accept what I'm saying as a potentially new and better truth.

So I am, in effect, taking the leap of faith that you'll be willing at least to consider what I'm saying and experiment with applying it to your own life. I'm not expecting you to let go all at once of everything you've so far known to be true about yourself and your world, but I'm urging you to take the first baby steps that might, with practice, allow you to burn the path behind you and find an easier road ahead.

Both you and I will always live in a world that's beyond our control. That's the way things are—and the way they're supposed to be. Our power lies in recognizing how much of life is constructed of the choices we make one moment, one thought, and one response at a time. My desire is to help you better understand, accept, and manage yourself so that you'll be able to make the choices that serve you better and enrich your life. That's all the power any of us has. It's all the power we need.

Suggested Reading

But how does one acquire wisdom? By practicing it daily, in however modest a degree; by examining our conduct of each day at its close; by being harsh to your own faults and lenient of those of others; by associating with those who exceed you in wisdom and virtue; by taking some acknowledged sage as your invisible counselor and judge. You will be helped by the original works; give over hoping that you can skim, by means of epigrams, the wisdom of distinguished men. Every one of these men will send you away happier and more devoted, no one of them will allow you to depart empty handed.

—Epicurus

Allen, James. *As a Man Thinketh*. Marina del Rey: Devorss & Co., 1983.

Aristotle. *Basic Works of Aristotle*. New York: Random House, 1941.

Armstrong, Karen. *A History of God: The 4,000-Year Quest of Judaism, Christianity and Islam*. New York: Ballantine Books, 1994.

Auden, Wystan Hugh. *Collected Poems*. New York: Vintage, 1991.

Benson, Herbert. *The Relaxation Response*. New York: Avon, 1990.

Campbell, Joseph. *The Inner Reaches of Outer Space: Metaphor as Myth and as Religion*. New York: Harper Perennial, 1995.

Cleary, Thomas (translator). *Essential Confucius*. Edison, NJ: Castle, 2000.

Coelho, Paulo. *The Alchemist: A Fable about Following Your Dream*. San Francisco: Harper San Francisco, 1995.

Collins, Jim. *Good to Great: Why Some Companies Make the Leap . . . and Others Don't*. New York: HarperCollins, 2001.

Cousins, Norman. *Anatomy of an Illness as Perceived by the Patient*. New York: Bantam Doubleday Dell, 1991.

Csikszentmihalyi, Mihaly. *Flow: The Psychology of Optimal Experience*. New York: HarperCollins, 1991.

Descartes, René. *Discourse on Methods and Meditations on First Philosophy*. Indianapolis: Hackett Publishing Company, 1999.

Donne, John. *The Complete Poetry & Selected Prose of John Donne*. New York: Modern Library, 1994.

Durant, Will. *Caesar and Christ*. New York: Simon & Schuster, 1983.

———. *The Story of Philosophy*. New York: Pocket Books, 1991.

Easwaran, Eknath. *Climbing the Blue Mountain: A Guide for the Spiritual Journey*. Tomales, Calif.: Nilgiri Press, 1992.

———. *Gandhi, the Man*. Tomales, Calif.: Nilgiri Press, 1997.

Emerson, Ralph Waldo. *Essential Writing*. Princeton: Princeton Review, 2000.

Frankl, Viktor. *Man's Search for Meaning*. New York: Washington Square Press, 1997.

Franklin, Benjamin. *Benjamin Franklin's The Art of Virtue: His Formula for Successful Living*. South Waverly, NY: Acorn, 1996.

Gracian, Balthazar. *The Art of Worldly Wisdom*. New York: Doubleday/ Currency, 1992.

Hawking, Stephen. *A Brief History of Time*. New York: Bantam Doubleday Dell, 1998.

Haynes, Renee. *Seeing Eye Seeing I*. New York: St. Martin's Press, 1976.

Hegel, Georg Wilhelm Friedrich. *Phenomenology of Spirit*. New York: Oxford University Press, 1979.

Hoffer, Eric. *The True Believer: Thoughts on the Nature of Mass Movements*. New York: HarperCollins, 1989.

Huxley, Aldous. *The Perennial Philosophy*. New York: HarperCollins, 1990.

Jager, Willigis. *Search for the Meaning of Life*. Chicago: Triumph Books, 1995.

Jampolsky, Gerald et al. *Love Is Letting Go of Fear*. Berkeley: Celestial Arts, 1988.

Jung, Carl Gustave. *Modern Man in Search of a Soul*. Eugene, Ore.: Harvest Books, 1955.

Kennedy, John Fitzgerald. *Profiles in Courage*. New York: Harper Perennial, 2000.

Lao-tzu. *The Way of Life according to Lao-tzu*. (Witter Brynner, translator). New York: Perigee, 1995.

Liebman, Joshua Loth. *Peace of Mind: Insights on Human Nature that Can Change Your Life*. New York: Simon & Schuster, 1946.

McGreal, Ian P., editor. *Great Thinkers of the Western World*. New York: HarperCollins, 1992.

Marinoff, Lou. *Plato, Not Prozac!: Applying Philosophy to Everyday Problems*. New York: Harper Perennial, 2000.

Merton, Thomas, *No Man Is an Island*. Eugene, Ore.: Harvest, 1978.

Miller, Timothy. *How to Want What You Have*. New York: Henry Holt & Co., 1995.

Peck, M. Scott. *The Road Less Traveled*. New York: Touchstone Books, 1998.

Perls, Fritz. *The Gestalt Approach and Eye Witness to Therapy*. Palo Alto, Calif.: Science & Behavior Books, 1973.

Plato. *Complete Works* (John M. Cooper and D.S Hutchinson, editors). Indianapolis: Hackett Publishing Co., Inc. 1997.

Schopenhauer, Arthur. *The World as Will and Idea: Abridged in One Volume*. Boston: Charles E. Tuttle Co., 1995.

Schwartz, Jeffrey M. *Brain Lock*. New York: HarperCollins, 1997.

Seldes, George, compiler. *Great Thoughts*. New York: Ballantine, 1996.

Thoreau, Henry David. *Walden*. Boston: Beacon Press, 1998.

Tolle, Eckhart. *The Power of Now: A Guide to Spiritual Enlightenment*. Novato, Calif.: New World Library, 1999.

Trott, Susan. *The Holy Man*. New York: Riverhead Books, 1995.

Twain, Mark. *The Autobiography of Mark Twain*. New York: Harper Perennial, 2000.

Voltaire, François. *Philosophical Dictionary*. New York: Viking Press, 1984.

Watts, Alan. *The Way of Zen*. New York: Vintage Books, 1993.

Wilber, Ken. *The Spectrum of Consciousness*. Wheaton, Ill.: Quest Books, 1993.

About the Author

Joe Caruso is an author, columnist, entrepreneur, international speaker, consultant, and founder of Caruso Leadership Institute, which specializes in helping individuals and organizations use transformational thinking and congruency training in order to create better outcomes in their lives and their work.

He specializes in training and advising CEOs and senior-level managers, and also brings his proven approaches to the business of communication, service, team-building, management, leadership, and sales. He travels up to 159 days per year, speaking and consulting, and is often a featured keynote speaker at national association meetings.

He's been featured in major newspapers, magazines, and television specials. For a list of additional learning tools, booking information, and more about Joe Caruso and Caruso Leadership Institute, visit Joe's website at www.carusoleadership.com.

Joe Caruso lives with his wife, Carol, on the lovely island of Grosse Ile, located between Michigan and Canada, where, when he's not traveling, he video-conferences with many of his clients directly from his study.